A Killing Art

A Killing Art

THE UNTOLD HISTORY OF TAE KWON DO

ALEX GILLIS

ECW Press

Published by ECW Press
2120 Queen Street East, Suite 200, Toronto, Ontario, Canada M4E 1E2
info@ecwpress.com / 416.694.3348

LIBRARY AND ARCHIVES CANADA CATALOGUING IN PUBLICATION

Gillis, Alex
A killing art : the untold history of tae kwon do / Alex Gillis.

ISBN 978-1-55022-825-0

ALSO ISSUED AS:
978-1-55490-674-1 (EPUB); 978-1-55490-825-7 (PDF)

1. Tae kwon do—History. 2. Choi, Hong Hi. 3. Kim, Un-yong, 1931-.
4. Gillis, Alex. 5. Tae kwon do—Biography. I. Title.

GV1114.9.G55 2008   796.815'3   C2007-907099-X

Editor: Michael Holmes
Text Design: Tania Craan
Korean Tenets: John Koh
Author Photo: Michael Phang
Back Cover Photo: courtesy of the author and Rhee Ki Ha
Production & Typesetting: Gail Nina
Printing: Thomson-Shore   3 4 5

This book is set in Sabon and Choc and was printed on 30% post consumer recycled paper.

The publication of *A Killing Art* has been generously supported by the Canada Council for the Arts,
which last year invested $20.1 million in writing and publishing throughout Canada, by the Ontario
Arts Council, by the Government of Ontario through Ontario Book Publishing Tax Credit, by the
OMDC Book Fund, an initiative of the Ontario Media Development Corporation, and by the
Government of Canada through the Book Publishing Industry Development Program (BPIDP).

PRINTED AND BOUND IN THE UNITED STATES

ECW PRESS
ecwpress.com

For Mr. Lenny Di Vecchia,
and instructors like him around the world.

Contents

INTRODUCTION

The farther away you are from the truth, the more the hateful and pleasurable states will arise. There is also self-deception.

— Bodhidharma, as quoted in *The Bodhisattva Warriors*[1]

Tae Kwon Do leads to enlightenment along one of five paths, some people believe, but I have my doubts. I am stuck on the path of Courtesy, which instructors in small gyms around the world know well but which is largely ignored by Tae Kwon Do's leaders. This book is about Courtesy, Integrity, Perseverance, Self-Control, and Indomitable Spirit — the tenets of Tae Kwon Do — a true story about a martial art that I love in spite of its bizarre and wondrous history. Most of us have heard about Tae Kwon Do through children, whose laughter dominates evening and weekend classes in North America, but the art hides a history of secret-service agents, gangsterism, and "fearsome weaponry," as one of its founders, Choi Hong-Hi, once described it. He wrote that Tae Kwon Do is "able to take lives easily, when needed, by defending and attacking 72 vital spots using 16 well-trained parts of the body." Choi had a fondness for numbers. He liked their devastating precision.

Few young people in Olympic Tae Kwon Do know about Choi, who more than anyone deserves the label "founder" in this martial art. Other "founders" — and there are many — erased him from the popular record long ago. *A Killing Art* restores h im and his pioneers to their place in Tae Kwon Do history. This book is based on Choi's memoirs, the memoirs of Kim Un-yong (a founder of Olympic Tae Kwon Do), and on the hundreds of interviews and documents that I list in the footnotes and bibliography.

I would like to thank many people, especially Choi Hong-Hi, Jung-Hwa Choi, and a handful of martial arts masters and grandmasters, such as Joe Cariati, Joon-Pyo Choi, and Jhoon Rhee, for sharing their astonishing stories. Rhee, in particular, set me straight on much of Kim Un-yong's and Tae Kwon Do's history in the 1960s and 1970s — a story of sports mixed with politics, espionage, and myth. Jung-Hwa Choi was open about the art's history from the 1980s to the present, and I want to thank him for his frankness. Sun-Ha Lim told me about the lives of Koreans during the Second World War and the Korean War. The work of historian Bruce Cumings provided a context for Tae Kwon Do's role within modern Korea, both North and South.

Some grandmasters bravely recounted what others were reluctant to share: Nam Tae-hi, C. K. Choi, Kong Young-il, and Jong-Soo Park (my former instructor), for instance. Some interviews were off the record — and I thank those men, too. My other instructors, the WTF's Yoon Yeo-bong and the ITF's Park Jung-Taek, Phap Lu, Alfonso Gabbidon, and especially Lenny Di Vecchia, inspired me in the martial art and in my research and interviews.

Mr. Di Vecchia, in particular, inspired me to write the book; he peppered his intense martial arts instruction with history, moral training, and a sense of humour that prevented his students from taking themselves too seriously — even though the training itself was deadly serious. I liked his after-class aphorisms. One of them was two words long: "Keep moving." He said that a doctor had told him that once and that it referred to more than your body and thoughts.

I would never have finished this book without my black belt friends — Floyd Belle, Martin Crawford, Marc Thériault, and many others — who meet every Saturday to practise Tae Kwon Do without politics or talk, an increasingly rare situation in the world of black belts. A journalist once telephoned a famous grandmaster, Duk-Sung Son, for an interview, but Son said, "No, no more talking. I'm going to train now," and he hung up. My training with Mr. Di Vecchia, Floyd, Martin, and Marc countered the darker parts of this book. Many times, I'd finish a difficult interview or chapter and trudge to the gym, hoping to find them there — for more training and less talk — hoping for a reprieve.

For editing, research, and support, thank you to Loren Lind, Mark Dixie, Susan Folkins, Jane Ngan, Katie Gare, Diane Gillis, Renée Sapp, Laurie Gillis, and Hana Kim, who is the Korea Studies Librarian at the East Asian Library at the University of Toronto. John Koh was an excellent translator and interpreter who offered insights along the way. Thank you also to the Ontario Arts Council for grants, and to Michael Holmes and Jack David at ECW Press — and to my agent, Hilary McMahon, who warmly encouraged me even on her days off.

And a special thanks to Deborah Adelman, who made more sacrifices for this book than perhaps she should have.

About Korean names

"Tae Kwon Do" is usually spelled "Taekwondo" for the Olympic sport (run by the World Taekwondo Federation) but "Taekwon-Do" for the traditional style (the International Taekwon-Do Federation). Instructors from both styles sometimes use "Tae Kwon Do," and there has been so much overlap between the WTF, ITF, and their offshoots that I have stuck with "Tae Kwon Do" throughout the book, except in titles and quotations from documents.

Most Koreans have three names and write their family names first, but some switch the order. So "Kim Un-yong," for example, can be written "Un-yong Kim." A hyphen connects the first names, with the second word of the first name beginning with a lower case letter ("Un-yong"), but many Koreans begin both with an upper case letter, with or without a hyphen ("Un Yong" and "Un-Yong"). The whole thing can be confusing. I settled on using either what the person in question uses or on the Korean standard, which is last name first ("Kim Un-yong").

To make things more confusing, Korean names can be spelled in different ways. "Un-yong," for example, can be spelled "Un-young" or "Woon-yong" — and those are all correct spellings! On top of this, many otherwise good sources spell names wrongly. I have provided the various spellings in the index but have used only one consistently throughout the book.

Whenever possible, I used McCune-Reischauer spelling for Korean words.

Alex Gillis
Akillingart.com

Part 1

INDOMITABLE SPIRIT

Were I to die a hundred times,
Then die and die again,
With all my bones no more than dust,
My soul gone far from men,
Yet still my red blood, shed for you,
Shall witness that my heart was true.

— Po-Eun, poet, 1392[2]

백

절

불

굴

Chapter 1

MEN OF THE SACRED BONE

When I need a break from my life, when I need to confront stress, fear, and madness, I flee to a place of power, to a room where meditation meets brute force. I climb to a third-floor studio or descend to a basement gym, and as I feel a hardwood floor or a padded cement slab under my bare feet, I smell the sweat and effort of those who came before me, and I hear their laughter and yells, and, occasionally, I remember the blood that fell. I find reprieve in sweat and struggle.

This is not a hobby for everyone, and it is perhaps odd to call it a "break," especially because the Korean martial art that I practise, Tae Kwon Do, is extremely difficult to master and can lead to real breaks — bone breaks. Its creators embedded innumerable tests within its techniques, but the training is usually safe, and I always look forward to going. I walk into my *dojang*, the Korean name for a martial arts gym, hoping that my instructor, Mr. Di Vecchia, will be there with his old stories and wisdom, that Floyd will be stretching and preparing for one of his spectacular jumping front kicks, that Marc will show us the mid-air split kick once again, and that Martin will push us with his spirited sparring at the end of class. Anyone can begin the fundamentals of the art, but few can stick with it as these men have. I began Tae Kwon Do when I was a teenager, twenty-five years ago — when the art peaked in many ways — and I met these martial artists over the decades, as the physical moves hardened my muscles and strengthened my heart and mind.

The Koreans who created the martial art consciously set out to strengthen individuals and, eventually, entire nations. Tae Kwon Do is an art of self-defence, but if you enter the closed rooms of its history, you realize that it is the art of killing and if practised with care and intent, an art of empowerment. It can empower more than the body. The best martial artists apply physical techniques to mental states; they can erode or raise emotional substrata; they can build or destroy reputations, careers, friends, families, and countries. The complex paths they take — for better or worse — often depend on age-old loyalties and new-found betrayals.

I discovered this the hard way many years ago. On April 20, 2001, in the year of the Snake, I walked into the Novotel Hotel in Toronto, Canada, to wait for the "Father of Tae Kwon Do," General Choi Hong-Hi, who would lead a three-day seminar for black belts. I was naive then, and revered the eighty-two-year-old Choi and the other founding members of Tae Kwon Do, including a man named Kim Un-yong, and I felt intimidated walking into the seminar room, partly because Choi was a hard taskmaster. He had become a major-general in the South Korean army at the age of thirty-three, and even though he had retired from the military in 1962, he was still known as "the General." He and his men had sacrificed their bodies, careers, and families to perfect a martial art now practised by an estimated 70 million people in nearly 180 countries.

I can picture the first day of his 2001 seminar as if it were today: I wait in the Amsterdam Room of the Novotel with 100 black belts from the United States, Canada, Chile, Peru, Paraguay, Uruguay, Argentina, and Honduras. Standing among the bowing, whispering martial artists, I feel as though I could be waiting within a palace of the Chosŏn dynasty in 1394 — I imagine the ancient warriors waiting for dynastic rulers, the floors heated in the old style (invisible and underground), and the Korean geisha girls ready to sing the *p'ansori* verses that praise Confucian values and sagacious leaders.

The General and his men are extremely late, however. He is upstairs, talking and arguing with his son and the masters and grandmasters who will help during the seminar. These men once fought, parted, and threatened to kill one another over politics and, in some cases, over personal matters, but the masters and grandmasters know they owe their fortunes and reputations to the General, and everyone is trying to reconcile past threats with present ambitions.

The General takes lineage and loyalty as seriously as others view love. He has charted his family tree back eighteen generations to the Chosŏn dynasty, when, in the mid-fifteenth century, a king ordered a military noble, Choi's ancestor, to move to a northern part of the peninsula to protect several towns. The Chosŏn aristocrats, who reigned for 500 years, structured society around the "three relationships" and the "five injunctions."[3] The General and his men seem plucked from that era, and are working on the fifth injunction — let faithfulness unite friends — abandoning the other injunctions for now (honour your ruler, honour your father, honour your elder brother, and assign man and wife different duties).

For an outsider, especially a non-Korean, it is difficult to understand the culture of these men and the conflicts among them — conflicts that have lasted decades, which is much the same as saying centuries. "Loyalty and filial piety form the deepest wellspring of Korean virtue, nurtured over thousands of years," writes scholar Bruce Cumings. Stories from the Chosŏn era are full of dynastic leaders with "rare powers, magnificent ethics and bottomless omniscience." For fifty years, the General has reigned like a dynastic leader and has quoted the poet Po-Eun's call to loyalty: "I would not serve a second master though I might be crucified a hundred times."[4]

We are expecting a good seminar and no crucifixions, but the General is still late, and the floor is cold, and the women have mastered head kicks rather than geisha songs. Waiting here with my black belt classmates, I wonder why the art I love is so often practised in cold basements of suburban deserts (like this one), or in dark gyms in alleyways, or at the back of concrete malls. For years, I trained in a Tae Kwon Do gym where asbestos crumbled through the ceiling and rats hid in the cracks of the shower stalls; the gym was run by a world-renowned grandmaster who did not have enough money to fix the plumbing.

In the Amsterdam Room, an eight-metre banner hangs on a wall above the head table:

Welcome to the General Choi Seminar
Founder of Taekwon-Do

Many people question the word *founder*, including me, but I am in a minority in this room. The seminar will be the General's last in

Canada; he is getting old and must travel to other places. He is also rounding up his old warriors for a new mission that I find difficult to believe: helping to reunify North and South Korea by merging his Tae Kwon Do, which is based in North Korea, with Olympic Tae Kwon Do, based in South Korea. I wonder if the General is a megalomaniac. He does want to take over all of Tae Kwon Do, and there are rumours that he will meet Kim Un-yong, the president of the World Taekwondo Federation (WTF), the South Korean organization that runs Olympic Tae Kwon Do.[5] Kim is the General's enemy, but an enemy worth negotiating with, because one of Kim's coughs is worth more than a thousand of our yells.

Choi is the General, but Kim is the President. He is not in the room, but he is here in spirit. Kim began a patriotic career in the Korean CIA in a South Korean dictatorship in the 1960s. He borrowed the General's "Tae Kwon Do" name in the 1970s, inserted it into the Olympics in the 1980s and became one of the most powerful people in international sports in the 1990s. The only goal Kim has not yet achieved is immortality, and we have heard that he is working on that: North and South Korea are in the middle of negotiations and part of the plan is to hold joint Tae Kwon Do events in the autumn.[6]

The merger talk is unnerving many black belts, because Tae Kwon Do is supposed to be apolitical and instructors are weary of the espionage, gangsterism, and politics, but the goal is admirable — and attainable, if you consider the history and culture of these men and their art. They are modern *yangban* — men of the sacred bone. Tae Kwon Do supposedly flourished 1,300 years ago under a general who held an extremely high rank in the Silla dynasty, perhaps even the rank of "sacred bone," which meant that he was near-immortal. Choi acted as if he were that rank. He is also known for being generous, funny, and approachable. Most of us in the room have read "the bible of Tae Kwon Do," as Choi dubbed his training manual,[7] and most of us have trained until we bled. But most of us are naive, believing that the General is like a god — in the same group as the other men who developed a martial art in the twentieth century: Gichin Funakoshi (Karate), Kano Jigoro (Judo), and Morihei Ueshiba (Aikido), all of whom were Japanese. Legions of Olympic Tae Kwon Do students place Kim Un-yong in the same pantheon.

"Attention!" someone calls. All chatting stops. General Choi enters, and we bow. Seeing him in person is my first shock: he is puny — only five feet tall and about a hundred pounds. Men always pushed him around, no matter how politically cunning he was, no matter how many barroom tables he split with his bare hands. He often faced bigger opponents — generals more powerful and presidents more ruthless.

I sit on the carpet with the other black belts as one of the grandmasters attaches a microphone to the General's shirt. Before starting the action, the General introduces the men at the head table, including Grandmaster Jong-Soo Park, who owns the gym I attend but who has not worked with the General in more than two decades.

"Most of you do not know him," the General says. "He is one of my most beloved students. Give him a big hand."

We applaud, not seeing the trap. It has taken me years to learn the Rule of Opposites, a rule I discovered as I studied my martial art. It goes like this: when a martial artist says something dramatic of another who is or was a known opponent, such as "He is a beloved student," listeners should automatically assume the opposite, or close to it. According to this rule, Park is not the General's "most beloved," but they are now attempting to reconcile. Both men stopped speaking to each other in the late 1970s, after the General accused Park of co-operating with the Korean CIA in a plot to kidnap him. Park denied the charge. He is a renowned martial artist who introduced the art to the Netherlands and Canada in the 1960s.[8] In his prime, he was a powerful heavyweight with fast reflexes — a devastating combination — and I could see why people had called him "the tiger." During sparring, he could be as immobile as a big cat, then leap in an instant — and seem to float at head level, remaining there far too long, kicking and punching all the while. During a 1976 demonstration, I saw him take a few steps, jump, and, with one kick, break two boards held nine feet above the floor. In those days, he overwhelmed opponents, but even Park is in awe of the General, who once considered Park a disciple and surrogate son. It seems odd that the General once accused him of a plot.

It is difficult to understand the gap between feelings and words in these men, between truths and half-truths in their world; ambivalence and shame creep through the seminar like an unseen fog.

Team demonstrations are routine events at seminars, but when someone announces that Park's demo team can begin, no one stands

and Park is not in the room. Black belt instructors hear the announcement again. There are at least twenty of Park's black belts here, a couple of them former world champions, but none rise. Some of us, the young ones, are bewildered and embarrassed; Park organized this seminar in honour of the General, but he did not prepare a team? We soon find out why.

It is the manner and the tone with which the General offers advice

Jong-Soo Park springs into a jumping kick.

Photo courtesy of Park.

— his no-holds-barred method of teaching — that leaves students stunned. You could call it the "old way," a way that once involved sticks on the shins, training until you vomited, and sparring after you bled. He beckons one of Park's sixth-degree black belts, an American, to the head table at the front of the room. The General asks him to explain how one would teach a new student. The black belt begins talking, but the General immediately says, "No, stop!" and points out that the first thing to teach students is how to bow. Evidently, the black belt himself did not bow properly. "That's why your school never grows," the General scolds. "The students never listen." The implication is that if students are lazy about bowing correctly, how can they obey during strenuous classes.

The General then motions with his hand for another of Park's former students to stand near the head table: Richard Parris is a sixth-degree black belt and former world sparring champion who runs his own *dojang* in Toronto. Once, during a world championship, I saw him fake two kicks, then, with the leg that faked still in the air, jump, spin, and execute a reverse hooking kick with the other leg, aiming his heel at his opponent's jaw. The combination jump-spin-kick with the same leg is difficult to perfect, and the combination was so unexpected at the championship that the crowd and television commentators spontaneously yelled in amazement. Even his opponent, a Karate champion, smiled in admiration after the kick beaned the top of his head.

"How do you teach a side piercing kick?" the General asks Parris, who says only three words when the General interrupts. "You know this much," the General says, putting a thumb on a forefinger. I notice that the General's thumb is on his forefinger; there is no space between. The cutting comment erupts faster than a punch, but the interpreter translates it into Spanish for the South and Central Americans. I have seen Parris easily break seven wooden boards with this side piercing kick, but the former champion does not move. There are many ex-champions in the room, but no one says a word. Parris sits down.

"Beware phony instructors!" the General suddenly warns.

This is how the seminar goes while Park prowls the restaurant and hallways of the hotel. Most of Tae Kwon Do's techniques have changed during the lost years in which he and the General did not speak. The General seems so frustrated by our techniques, which in his view need updating, that he sometimes can only yell "Whaaa!"

in frustration. He is punishing us for the lost years and for the betrayals — unproven — of Park, his beloved student who refused to accompany him to North Korea on what seemed to be a suicide mission in 1980. And perhaps he is punishing Park for reasons I do not know.

Richard Parris breaks seven boards with a lead-leg side kick.

Photo courtesy of Parris.

In any case, Tae Kwon Do has evolved but we have not, and the General and his men are still deciding how Park and his schools will join the General's International Taekwon-Do Federation — and how much the whole thing will cost. Much of the General's criticism centres on a movement called sine wave that he developed in the early 1980s long after Park had left him to run sixteen *dojangs* and star in martial arts movies. The best practitioners in any martial art know how to throw their body weight into a technique, but the General dubbed this process sine wave and added his own signature to it when he ordered that Tae Kwon Do students should raise the body at the beginning of a technique and lower it at the end.[9] Sine wave applies to almost every technique in traditional Tae Kwon Do and clearly distinguishes it from Olympic Tae Kwon Do and Karate, but Park is not in the room to hear any of this.

Those of us not being verbally attacked laugh uncomfortably. The General is a wicked, witty genius, and we are here to learn.

A young woman rises to demonstrate another technique and does it wrongly.

"You're a lady?" the General asks.

"Yes, I am," she replies.

He motions for her to sit down, waves for a man to stand, and asks him to do a low block. The man's fist is off by a quarter-inch.

"Who taught you that?" the General asks.

The black belt names the master.

"Don't know him," the General says. "You should get your money back." I feel sorry for the black belt. Tae Kwon Do has always had a dysfunctional relationship with profit; the two are fire and water. For this seminar alone, black belts paid U.S.$250 to $410 each. Park organized the event, and I volunteered to help, so I saw what happened on the first day: most black belts were well behaved but a few barged through the door without paying, and sixteen members of a South American team were either tricked into thinking that the seminar would be free or else they lied. Sometime during the three-day seminar at least $1,000 will disappear. This is what sometimes occurs when money meets the martial arts — a mix of warrior and clown, tradition and farce — and why Tae Kwon Do is sometimes pronounced "Take My Dough," as my friend Martin pointed out.

Money is the least of our worries, however. What many of us do not know is that Tae Kwon Do has been connected with espionage, terrorism, and gangsterism since its birth — and many of these masters and grandmasters lived through that time. Some were ensnared in brutal campaigns. The General has bragged about sacrificing students and even his own children[10] to promote the art, a brag that, in some ways, has its roots in his personality — "a tornado," as he once put it.

You can tell much about a man who has chosen to study a martial art developed by a tornado. Bruce Lee, Bill Clinton, Steven Seagal, and King Juan Carlos of Spain have all studied Tae Kwon Do.[11] Traditional Tae Kwon Do includes bone-on-bone blocks, strikes that can break ribs and rupture organs, and techniques that are supposed to end a conflict with one blow. In short, when cornered, men such as the General and Park do not roll in the dirt trying to flip or lock an opponent; they try to maim or kill you as fast as possible.

But Park is not having a good day here. The General says the word *phony* so many times during the seminar that, years later, when I tell Park in a relaxed moment that he is "funny," he stops and asks, "What did you say?"

"I said you're 'funny' — your comment is funny."

He stares at me like a tiger, the cold stare of a cat measuring its prey.

"Funny sounds like phony," he says calmly. Funny. Phony. I never realized how similar they sound. Park is not phony — in a martial art filled with overnight grandmasters, he is a genuine pioneer — but I will never again tell a grandmaster that he is funny.

✘ ✘ ✘

At the front of the seminar room, the General teaches a black belt from South America how to block.

"Always look your opponent in the black ball," the General tells him.

"Eyeball!" whispers his son, who is standing a couple of feet behind.

"Always look in the eyeball," the General corrects. He smiles and taps his forehead with a thick, callused finger. "I am getting old. Lucky I have a good son."

Master Jung-Hwa Choi lowers his head, which is when I realize that he is probably indispensable. He is forty-six years old and taller and stockier than his father and is another "beloved" master, if you know the history between the two men. He will be the General's heir, if all goes well. Jung-Hwa began his martial arts training when he was a child and is an eighth-degree black belt, one degree away from the last rank of grandmaster. He is Secretary General of the International Taekwon-Do Federation, which means he is the second most powerful person in the room, after his father. He says very little during the seminar. He is one of the few people who is not standing like a Chosŏn servant or a killer from

The Sopranos.

Jung-Hwa and his father have not been getting along for years, but they are trying now. Their lives are filled with Tae Kwon Do, and Jung-Hwa addresses his father as "General" or "Sir" in public. They have had few good personal memories together. One that Jung-Hwa later describes is from his childhood in South Korea. He spent many nights lying on the floor behind his father as the elder Choi played poker with the other generals. Jung-Hwa would inhale the smell of the appetizers brought out one by one, the aroma floating through the comforting smell of cigarettes, sake, and Johnnie Walker. All the generals drank Scotch then. Jung-Hwa would hear his father's voice, the men's voices, strong, as they laughed. "Father, don't lose," Jung-Hwa would whisper as he tried not to fall asleep on the floor. "I never lose," the General would reply. It is Jung-Hwa's misfortune that his father never loses, that his father knows the outcome before a gamble begins.[12]

"Tae Kwon Do is easy to learn," the General says into the microphone. "That is why it has spread like wildfire all over the world. Someday, it will be on the moon and the stars." Day one of the seminar and he is already dreaming about a world beyond time and space.

He falls to the ground and does push-ups on his knuckles. We cheer; he is eighty-two after all.

He tells us to read the books, his books, especially the *Moral Guide Book*, in which he encourages us to live justly and honestly. "Tae Kwon Do is not only about punching and kicking," he reminds us. It is about doing the right thing, which he has tried to do all his life, even when he seemed not to.

That day, the General insults the co-organizer of the seminar, Son Myung-Soo, and Son's black belts from the Royal TKD Academy all drop out.

✗ ✗ ✗

On the second day, one of the first black belts to demonstrate is a woman from eastern Canada. The General asks her to perform Tae Kwon Do's pattern for beginners, *Chon-Ji,* which means "heaven and earth" — a series of punches and blocks that can immediately indicate the proficiency of a martial artist, no matter what the belt level.

"Very good," he says when she finishes. "What school are you from?"

"Downey's Tae Kwon Do, in Newfoundland," she says.

The General is impressed. She demonstrated excellent poise and power. Unbeknownst to us, someone spoke to the General about his sexist comment yesterday. The General believes that men should have more power than women, and misogyny is everywhere in this martial art, but some are trying to stop it.

Today's demonstrations are much better than yesterday's. A fifth-degree black belt jumps into the air, spins 180 degrees, and breaks four boards with a side kick while in mid-air. Later, after someone explains that Tae Kwon Do is the only martial art with a "twisting kick," someone else demonstrates by running, jumping, and breaking a board held six or seven feet above the ground. I have been in awe of this kick ever since my instructor, Mr. Di Vecchia, showed it to me. It requires an odd contortion at the hips: the upper body goes one way and the kicking leg, the opposite way. Before even attempting it, you need to be able to do the splits, or close to it, and your toes have to bend back at a ninety-degree angle. When executed properly, you can kick someone directly behind you while you continue to face forward. The twisting kick is one of the General's favourites.

But the General seems to be in a bad mood. Besides "phony," his refrain throughout the seminar is, "He'd be killed in combat," as if combat were at the next café. And he uses *suicide* as a verb. "The WTF," he grandly announces, "they don't know what they're doing. They all suicide."

The General loathes the style of the World Taekwondo Federation — the only style allowed in the Olympics and the style run by the General's nemesis, Kim Un-yong. The Olympic martial art is easily the most popular Tae Kwon Do on the planet. Perhaps the General is jealous? He has always wanted his traditional Tae Kwon Do in the games. Throughout the seminar, he makes fun of the WTF, which he argues is as bad as Karate. He asks a black belt to begin a pattern called *Toi-Gye* (which the General created and named after a sixteenth-century scholar of neo-Confucianism), and he instructs the man to redo a strike to the pubis, a technique called an "upset fingertip strike."[13]

"Why do you withdraw your hand after the strike?" the General asks him.

The black belt explains that he is ripping off the opponent's scrotum.

"No," General says. "That's Karate and WTF style."

That reminds the General of a joke: "A woman told another, 'Don't marry a guy who studied WTF.' 'Why?' asks the second woman. 'Because he has no weapon,' said the first."

We laugh, because there is evidently too much scrotum ripping in the WTF, but more than that, we laugh because he is not castrating *us* for these few minutes.

"I want you to laugh, because you're so serious," he says.

Another one of his refrains is "This is a bad habit from Karate," as if bad habits pass through dynasties, handed from instructor to instructor. But what the General is not telling us is that he developed Tae Kwon Do from Shotokan Karate and has been trying to cover his Karate roots for fifty years.[14]

I wonder what Kim Un-yong would think about all the bragging, because he does not suffer egos gladly. Besides running Olympic Tae Kwon Do, he is a vice-president on the International Olympic Committee and a member of South Korea's National Assembly. I cringe when the General announces, "Tae Kwon Do in the Olympics can't stay longer. In a couple of years, it will be kaput, because it has no technique." Judging by the way he brags, he will likely be no match for Kim, who has assimilated bigger egos.

✘ ✘ ✘

On the last day of the seminar, Bob Wall, the legendary martial artist who won many Karate championship between 1965 and 1972 and who starred in three Bruce Lee movies, materializes to sell services for martial artists: phone cards; credit cards; online martial-arts courses; cable and internet services; and "collectible items," such as postcards and key chains. "You can imagine what these will be worth, because they're limited," Wall says. "The value goes up when the person is deceased." He adds that the General gave an eighth-degree black belt to Chuck Norris, who has 182 schools. Norris considers himself a student of the General's, as do Jackie Chan and Wesley Snipes. These superstars own the card apparently, and we can collect points for airplane mileage just as they do. "You could have flown here free," Wall says.

As if on cue, the General stands and says, "Everyone should participate in this plan. You should tell your students. We'll make it the best martial-arts-run company in the world."

One of the grandmasters from Montreal is asleep at the head table. Perhaps he does not need phone cards. Perhaps he is applying the Rule of Opposites. Perhaps he is tired.

General Choi blocks kicks from his son Choi Jung-Hwa (on the right) and Park Jung-Taek, my first instructor.

Photo courtesy of General Choi.

Chapter 2

Though Ten Million Opponents Might Rise Against Him

Building a skyscaper begins with a shovel of dirt.

– Choi, translating philosopher Lao-Tzu[15]

I warily step into the lives of General Choi and Kim Un-yong beginning in Korea in 1938, the year of the Tiger, when longing and violence stalked the world. The essence of Tae Kwon Do began during a poker game in that year, on the most reckless day of Choi's life. He lived in a small house in the village of Yongwon, in northern Korea, when Japan crushed the nation like a rabbit in a trap. The sun had set on the Chosŏn dynasty — Japan now ruled Korea — but Choi was twenty years old, full of rebellion and, like most Koreans, refused to forget his past. He had inherited his father's small, sharp eyes and a chin usually tilted upwards or cocked to the side, making him look, as was often necessary, far taller than his five feet.

On that day in 1938, he faced his mother under the dim light of a lamp.[16] He was preparing to travel to Japan in two days to complete his education, a common dream for Koreans. After filial virtues, the second most important set of values in Korea revolved around education, the ideal student mastering both heart and mind.[17] In those days, children studied diligently because the ideal was as alive in Choi's youth as it had been centuries before.

Choi's mother took a thick wad of money from her pocket. "Be careful not to lose this," she said. She had worked hard, from dawn to midnight on many days, selling tofu and sewing clothes to save the money. She folded the bills twice, tucked them inside his belt, and sewed the seam of the belt shut. Given how important filial duties were in his family, I can only speculate as to why Choi did not obey her, why he lost the money; in their part of the world, the "four books" and "five classics" ensured that nothing surpassed his duties as a son. Studies were intense and focused on Confucian learning, which was a fundamental part of Choi's life and, later, of my martial art. The main section of *Great Learning*, the seven-hundred-year-old first volume of the four books, explained it this way:

> Wishing to order well their States, they first regulated their families.
> Wishing to regulate their families, they first cultivated their persons.
> Wishing to cultivate their persons, they first rectified their hearts [*sim*].
> Wishing to rectify their hearts, they first sought to be sincere in their thoughts.
> Wishing to be sincere in their thoughts, they first extended to the utmost their knowledge.[18]

Regulate. Cultivate. Rectify. These ideals were distinctly Korean and lived in Choi, and they would later surge like blood through Tae Kwon Do. If you replace "States" with "martial art" in the passage, you can see how intense the early days were.

After his mother went to sleep, however, Choi planned to regulate and cultivate poker. Perhaps his rebellion was due to his lifestyle: he had been gambling, drinking, and smoking since the age of seven. Perhaps he was simply stubborn: if he wanted to join his friends in a game of *Hwatu*, a popular Korean card game, then he would! The stubbornness permeated deep in his body, but he saw it as a sign of confidence: when he set his mind on a goal, he would stick to it. "A man of confidence fearlessly pursues what he thinks is right, though 10 million opponents might rise against him," he once wrote, quoting a disciple of Confucius.[19]

Perhaps, also, he was too much like his father — poker plagued them like the sake both men loved. For many years, Choi's father had owned a successful brewery, allowing the older man to descend into levels of debauchery usually associated with kings and dreams. Choi's father eventually deserted his wife, taking Hong-Hi Choi and the two other children to live with a beautiful *kisaeng* woman, a

Korean geisha. Living with *kisaengs* had been an old practice from the Chosŏn dynasty, but one that should not have involved abandoning the first wife, according to Confucian thought.

The *kisaeng* had ruined several men's lives already, but she had left an impression on Choi, whom he thought was worldly and sophisticated compared to his mother. Choi had been six years old when the *kisaeng* had become his stepmother; that such a thing happened showed how deeply his father had become a slave to lust.[20] Those were the years when the boy learned how to gamble, smoke, and drink. His stepmother had been an opium addict, running a tavern, cooking her excellent food, and singing her perfect *p'ansori* songs, the classical vocal music favoured by *kisaengs*. Choi saw how his father was naive, obstinate, and deeply indulgent, giving her everything he had. Finally, his father lost so much money gambling that he sold the brewery. In those early days, the young Choi rarely visited his real mother, who was soon living in poverty.

Perhaps Choi's streak for insubordination began when he tried to deliver soup to his mother in another part of the village, and his *kisaeng* stepmother found out and sent a thug to knock the bowl out of his hands. Choi was devastated as he watched dogs lap the food from the dirt. He would never forget that day, not even after his stepmother died at the age of thirty-eight, and his father, as Confucian custom dictated, returned to the first wife. Choi had been ten years old then. His parents rarely spoke to each other afterwards and dark clouds settled over their lives.

To support the family, Choi helped his mother on their small plot of land, tending the garden, feeding the animals, growing vegetables, and making tofu. The process of soaking, grinding, cooking, straining, and pounding the tofu was such hard work that for the rest of his life he would be addicted to eating it, because it reminded him of his mother. As was the custom during meals, Choi's father ate first. Choi's mother would place rice and side dishes on a table while the rest of the family waited. Choi and his brother would peek through a little hole in a door to see if their father would leave some of the rice uneaten, the delicious smell floating into their noses.

But Choi soon fled all that. In 1938, after his mother sewed the money into his belt and went to sleep, Choi snuck out of the house and met his friends, including a local wrestling champion, Haak-Soon Huh, at a place near a hospital. Choi loved the parties that went with poker, and he was very good at strategic games with *Hwatu* cards, which depicted trees and flowers: *Maple, Peony, Cherry blossoms, Chrysanthemum*. He played so well that he could spot cheaters, which meant that he could probably cheat with the best of them, but at this table the gamblers were professionals, so cheating would be impossible.

In rapid succession, he and the others laid down the colourful cards and staked their money, but as the game progressed, Choi fared badly. "That is strange," he thought. "I am losing." He continued gambling, hoping to win back his losses.

Some of the *Hwatu* cards have more poetic names, such as *Crane and Sun*, but the poetry may have been lost on Choi when he detached the education money from his belt and gambled more. Soon, he lost all the money that his mother had given him, but he convinced the wrestler and the others to continue playing. Dawn was still far away, Choi said, and they should give him a chance to win back his losses.

Did he throw *Man Strolling with Umbrella?* The gamblers played for another hour. *Warbler in a Tree?* They knew Choi was finished and that he could not borrow from anyone in the village. *Boar?*

Finally, the wrestler stood up. "The purpose of gambling is to win money," he said. "I've waited long enough."

Choi wanted to attack him, but knew that would be like a fox jumping a tiger; Choi knew some kicks and dodges, but the wrestler was bigger and a prizefighter. As he sat there, Choi remembered a thick bottle of ink on a desk nearby. I wonder if he pictured the next few seconds in advance: the way the room blackened before his eyes; the way the wrestler, only a country boy, put his money in a pocket; the way Choi's hand suddenly found the bottle of ink; and the way it sailed at the wrestler. The bottle smashed on his forehead — a lucky hit. The wrestler fell on his back, blood and ink trickling down his face. While the other gamblers watched, Choi walked to the body, pulled the money from the man's pocket, counted what he had lost, and fled. No one stopped him, perhaps because they knew the wrestler would soon hunt him down.

Choi rushed home, cold and sweaty, and wondered if he had murdered the man — all that blood! What would his parents do when they found out? He and his brother and sister obeyed their father, who had studied the works of Confucius, read the classics, and become a doctor of Chinese medicine before opening the brewery. Their minds were laden with obligations and traditions, a Confucian legacy so advanced that Choi's grandmother kept her nail clippings, because respect for parents meant respecting every part of one's body.

But non-Confucian values — those of the heart — thrived in Choi and his time: values related to superstition and intuition, to shamans and sorcerers; values attuned to the nature of things, and to insight and freedom; values felt during passion and drunkenness.[21] In Choi's household, obedience lived alongside rice wine and geisha girls, and attacking a man after losing a poker game would perhaps fit into the non-Confucian category. In any case, Choi had created intolerable trouble for his parents once again.

As he walked home, did he remember the first time he had created trouble for them, which was when he was born, in 1918? That was the year of the Horse — a year in which the Japanese government arrested, tortured, or killed 140,000 Koreans who were suspected of resisting the Japanese empire.[22] It was a year when cunning and independence were at the centre of the world. Choi was born a runt and looked destined to die young. His mother came from a wealthy family, but hated her husband, and each time she had given birth, she had left him to bring up the newborns in her father's Confucian but comfortable home. Her father treated her like a servant, because daughters, after marriage, were not to return to their parents unless they were visiting, but she bore the humiliation for the sake of all eight of her babies, only three of whom lived past the age of two.

Choi had sometimes heard her grumble, "After the greater ones are all gone, the worst weakling survived to give me a headache." Choi, the youngest, was sickly for the first four years of his life. In desperation, his mother tugged at his legs night after night as he slept, trying to make him taller.

Did he wonder if his father would kill him when he found out about the poker game? Although the boy had vowed he would never be like him and had been always on the lookout for his blows that struck like lightening, Choi respected his father's attempts to educate him, one of the few caring things that his father had done for him. Choi's father was a miser, but he astonished the fifteen-year-old Choi when he paid a calligraphy instructor, Han Il-Dong, a fee equivalent to that of ten students to instruct Choi in calligraphy and, for thirteen months, T'aekkyŏn, a martial arts game that had nearly died out when Japan outlawed it from 1910 to 1945.[23] His father had wanted to strengthen Choi's skinny body.

Still, did he wonder if his father would kill him?

When Choi's father had arranged for him to marry a girl who was older and much taller, Choi married her in his early teens.[24] They had a daughter, Song-Jook Choi.[25] In those days, child marriages meant that the young wife became a servant in her husband's household.

Did Choi wonder if his father would kill him in front of her?

When his father announced that Choi would study in Japan, where the Japanese routinely abused Koreans but where Choi would receive an excellent education, he agreed to go. He would be the first in the family to complete middle school, and it would be a great honour, even though he would be forced to adopt a Japanese name, Yuseki Nishiyama, which means Brave Stone of the West Mountain.[26] The Japanese government not only banned people from speaking Korean, but forced them to change their identities, too.

Choi Hong-Hi stands on the left.

Photo courtesy of Choi.

As Choi left the poker game, he wondered if the wrestler was dead. Had he killed the prizefighter? Not likely, but, afraid of his own parents, Choi avoided going home, avoided the wrestler, the police, and the town, and fled one day early. He walked sixteen kilometres past cow-driven carts to a train station, travelled twenty hours on a train to a Pusan port, and caught a ship to Kyoto, Japan. This experience marked him; for the rest of his life, he would embroil himself in conflict, then flee, seemingly on the run forever.

Months after arriving in Kyoto, Choi met a man from his village who told him that the wrestler had recovered and was counting the days to Choi's return. Choi felt doomed and began training in

Shotokan Karate, a Japanese martial art that Gichin Funakoshi had transferred from Okinawa to Japan in 1922.[27] Choi had observed a Karate class and concluded that it was devastatingly powerful; it aimed punches right to the heart, solar plexus, or whatever vital spot could lead to death with one blow, the approach that Funakoshi promoted. Beginning in 1938, Karate strengthened a trait in Choi that Westerners associate with Japanese *kamikaze* pilots during the Second World War or with samurai warriors one thousand years ago.[28] Choi called it Indomitable Spirit: "A serious student of Tae Kwon Do will at all times be modest and honest. If confronted with injustice, he will deal with the belligerent without any fear or hesitation at all, with indomitable spirit, regardless of whosoever and however many the number may be."[29]

Choi practised diligently in Japan, keeping the wrestler in mind, and within two years obtained a first-degree black belt. Today, a black belt can mean very little, but in those days it was difficult to attain, and, most likely, Choi could kill with his bare hands. He kicked wooden street poles, punched sand to toughen his fists, and trained so much that he failed his first academic year in middle school, which he thought was yet another reason to avoid going home.

The Karate also proved useful in Japan, where people insulted him and his Korean friends, told them they smelled like garlic, physically attacked them, and treated them like servants. Choi was constantly getting into fights. He was not special in this regard; Japanese bullies had been abusing Koreans for decades, and Japan had been trampling on Korea since 1894. One of Choi's fights began after he warned two boys to stop bullying a friend. The boys took the warning as a challenge and followed him after school, but as they approached him he hit one in the face. The boy fell and Choi immediately pinned him to the ground with a foot on the neck as the boy's wooden sandals flailed in the air. The second boy ran away and Choi released the first, marvelling at his new-found power.

He stayed in Japan for four years, never once visiting his village, telling his parents that he was too sick to travel. He saved money and sent it to his mother. At the age of twenty-four, however, after finishing middle school and gaining a second-degree black belt in Karate, he finally felt powerful enough to fight the wrestler, Haak-Soon Huh. He returned to his village, proudly carrying a new sewing machine for his mother. It was 1942, the middle of the Second World War, and Japan was brutalizing Asia-Pacific, but Choi was concerned with Huh and the many villagers who were ganging up against Choi.

Shortly after his arrival, the wrestler saw him in a pine grove near the village kicking small trees and smashing clay roof tiles. He thought Choi was mad and having seizures, because from a distance Choi's fast movements did not look like any martial art that Huh had seen.

No, Choi was not mad, a friend explained to the wrestler. He was practicing Karate, a Japanese martial art that could kill with one blow. The wrestler chose not to challenge the wild claim and instead avoided Choi. In the end, the runt defeated his opponent without a fight — and that is when Choi's real problems began.

Chapter 3

A SUPERPOWER
ON EVERY BORDER

This is very hard; I'm neither a writer nor a historian, but I'm going to write this. Mizahara, one of my friends in the Japanese army, said, "I'm going to pretend to become crazy." So I said, "What are you talking about? How can you become crazy?" . . . His Korean name was Yum . . . The very next day, during the Japanese army roll call, he wasn't there. All of a sudden, behind us, he was balancing on a board above us, naked, peeing and saying, "You, Japanese, go drink my pee!" They grabbed him and took him away. Three days later, he came out, beaten, and I went to his bed. His room was right next to mine. At first, I said I was sorry, for I had taken him lightly, then I said, "Don't do this again, you won't be able to, you will be killed." He didn't say anything . . . But he again went out . . . After the war, I found him, and he was crazy. He had become crazy.

– General Sun-Ha Lim talking about the Korean soldiers who rebelled against
Japan during the Second World War[30]

How does one survive an indomitable force? I ask myself that as I review the difficult history of Korea during the Second World War and the powers that helped form Tae Kwon Do soon after. In 1943, Japan forced Choi and 4,300 Korean students to join the Japanese Imperial Army.[31] Choi tried to escape the draft by starving himself and, when that failed, by beating up a Japanese police officer, but he was stationed with the 30th Division in P'yŏngyang, Korea.[32] Unconquerable Japan, along with Nazi Germany and Italy, was taking over the world: Japan had massacred 300,000 civilians during six weeks in Nanking, China, and had conducted medical experiments on prisoners in Manchuria. It had worked prisoners to death in Burma and Thailand, and, in Korea, was forcing 100,000 girls and young women to become sex slaves, so-called comfort women for Japanese soldiers.[33] Many Koreans liked fighting alongside the Japanese, but Choi was a rebel, and in P'yŏngyang, he joined a mutinous plot to escape his Japanese unit, a plot that would become known as the P'yŏngyang Incident.[34]

In those days, Choi was so hungry that he sometimes stole food from the horses in the unit, but there was hope that he and his Korean companions would escape. Another man in his division had succeeded, a soldier who had hidden in an air duct under loose floorboards for five days, then run to a military ground, where he had lain in a straw-covered storage bin for forty days. Japanese soldiers practised their drills around the bin and had no idea that he was hiding inside. The Korean civilian who owned the bin and worked for the soldiers fed him during the day, but the panic-soaked soldier inside lost his mind, died from typhoid, saw hell and heaven, and rose from the dead, as he later recounted.[35] Choi and the twenty-nine other soldier rebels would perhaps accomplish a similar miracle: a gunfight against the Japanese and an escape to join rebel leader Kim Il Sung. This was, of course, the same Kim who would one day rule North Korea; at the time, Japan considered Kim one of the most dangerous guerrillas in the country.

But Japan was unbeatable. A spy, a fellow Korean soldier, betrayed Choi and the leaders of the plot, and in November 1944, the military arrested them. After several days of interrogation, Japanese soldiers took Choi to a detention house, where he turned to look at one of his friends. "Bastard!" yelled a guard in Japanese, and he slapped Choi on the face. That was how Choi learned that he was to look straight ahead at all times — until his probable execution.

Indoors, he and the other rebels sat like stones in their cells. Outside, they stood motionless in the sub-zero cold with only one layer of clothing. Choi pretended to completely repent and, over time, his Japanese jailers allowed him to practise Karate in the detention house, which kept him sane. The martial art's punches and kicks — spear hand, sword foot, front kick, side kick — impressed some of the Japanese guards, especially after Choi broke eight roof tiles with one strike, but Choi expected to be sentenced to death during his upcoming trial. Still, the guards asked him to teach them Karate, and they transformed part of the detention centre into a gym. Choi relished the sound of martial arts cries echoing through the room. As before, he gained more than physical power from the techniques.

Seven months later, the Japanese military charged Choi with breaking a military-service law.[36] He was sentenced to seven years in jail and transferred to P'yŏngyang Prison, but Choi was happy, because he had avoided execution. He assumed that life would improve; the new prison was bigger and contained Korean guards.

On Choi's first day in the new jail, one of the guards, a Korean, led him to a prison cell. Choi stopped in the doorway. Inside, he saw three prisoners; one was leaning on a blanket that was black with dirt, pus oozing from wounds on his side. The two other men looked deformed, their hip bones and shoulders protruding like pots, their skin covered in scabs. They are lepers, thought Choi. The cell walls were covered with bloody marks from smeared bed bugs. The toilet crate smelled worse than the sour sake it had once held, and the beds were slick with pus from the prisoners' skin. Choi was so revolted and horrified that he could only stand there.

"They should have killed this kind of bum," the Korean jailer said of Choi. "What is the use of feeding him bloody beans and rice for seven more years?" He cursed Choi and the other Korean prisoners even more than the Japanese guards had, then kicked him into the cell.

Choi cried, and he had good reason to; if he did not die from disease, he would die from shame for his fellow soldiers who were now Japanese collaborators. He asked himself how a Korean jailer could become as sadistic as a Japanese one. This was not Korea's war after all. When Japan took over in 1910, most Koreans — certainly anyone who was not part of the aristocracy — did not want to co-operate with the invaders. By the 1930s, however, Japanese oppression had a Korean face: Korean men had rounded up many of the Korean comfort women and nearly half of the Japanese-run National Police was Korean.[37] Choi was now seeing the horror of this oppression in his tiny prison cell in 1945, and, even as he vowed to fight it and to make his woebegone nation stronger, his body became infected with his cellmates' diseases.

✗ ✗ ✗

One summer day, a Korean guard, Mr. Kim, walked by with a huge bucket of cold water, splashing it and taunting the thirsty prisoners. The guards never gave them enough to drink and the splashes from

Choi Hong-Hi (fifth from the left, in the third row from the front) studied in Japan just before the Second World War. As with many other Koreans, he had to use a Japanese name, Yuseki Nishiyama.

Photo courtesy of Choi.

Kim's bucket were a fresh torment. Choi now suffered from the oozing skin infection that everyone in prison endured, and each day corpses on stretchers floated past his cell.

"Here, I have water!" Kim announced. "I am going to give a dipper of it as a prize for the cell that has a good singer. How about that?"

He stood outside Choi's cell. None of Choi's cellmates wanted to sing — they had no energy, no talent, and it was yet another humiliation — but in spite of his desperate state, Choi stood up and sang a popular folk tune.

Kim gave him and the others a cup of precious water. "Sing another song," he ordered. "I'll give you another dipper." Choi began a folk song.

Suddenly, from the backyard, a second Korean guard screamed, "Who was it?" in Japanese. He rushed to Choi's cell like a tiger and flung open the door. "Who was singing just now?" he yelled.

"It was me," Choi said and raised his hand.

The guard slapped him and every man in the cell, and he handcuffed Choi's arms behind his back. Choi seethed but was immobilized by pain in his arms. Why would one guard ask him to sing and a second tell him to stop? The two guards disliked each other, even though they were both Korean, but they hated the Korean prisoners more.

Later, alone in his cell, Choi felt the pain in his body devour his anger. He had lost the feeling in his handcuffed arms; they were pinned behind his back in a classic torture position. He could not lie on his back, so he tried to lie on his side, but his upper arm felt dislocated. He lay on his front, but his chin mashed into the ground. I'll have to eat like a pig, he thought. He was too weak to stand, so he sat all night.

In the morning, breakfast arrived; he was dizzy with hunger, but he pretended otherwise. His cellmates ate his food. Lunch arrived and he ignored it. The men in his cell begged him to eat, but Choi had chosen suicide. Many men had suffered from torture, malnutrition, and insanity in Japanese prisons during the Second World War; they had simply lain down and given up the will to live.[38] Choi fainted.

He woke up around five in the afternoon and the second Korean guard, the one who had slapped and handcuffed him, led him to the office of the chief of guards. "This guy is a good singer," the guard joked to the chief.

Choi could not believe it.

"Sing," the guard demanded. He removed Choi's handcuffs.

Choi looked at the two men, his arms dangling at his sides. "I cannot sing," he said. Choi did not mention Kim, the first guard, who had wanted songs for water. The chief did not force Choi to entertain them, and the guard returned Choi to his cell.

The first guard soon visited Choi and apologized for the singing game, but the apology and jail politics did little to help Choi, who was so malnourished and diseased that he felt he would die. Because he had not mentioned the water torment to Kim's superiors, Choi was spared more turmoil, and Kim visited him often and secretly gave him medicine for the skin disease. The men eventually became friends, which perhaps showed the jailer's foresight; Japan was losing the war by this time, and jailers would soon become prisoners.

Two months later, Choi heard speakers crackle in his cell. They had been off for the entire nine months he had been in prison, but they now bristled with static and what sounded like the impossible: the Japanese Emperor, whom Choi had never heard before, was crying and reading his nation's surrender. Japan had lost the war.

Long live Korea! Choi screamed to himself. He wanted to dance for joy, but Mr. Kim warned him to remain quiet, because there was a chance that retreating Japanese and Korean jailers would kill the prisoners. The next day, however, the jailers left and Choi stepped outside the iron gates. Wearing a loose shirt, black baggy pants, and straw slippers, he followed Mr. Kim through jubilant crowds, past the Korean flag at P'yŏngyang's city hall and into Mr. Kim's house. Both men were alive, Korea was free, and miracles did occur — which, of course, was a temporary delusion.

Much of Choi's life had been one long battle raged against his father, the wrestler, and Japan, and he now had a chance to make something of himself, to make good all the promises and prayers he had whispered in prison. After four decades of oppression, all Koreans had a second chance, and the country blew up into a storm of new-found hope and revenge killings.

Choi's P'yŏngyang Incident was one of the few Korean revolts against the Japanese during the Second World War, but there was nothing special about Choi's torments and tortures. Most prisoners, especially foreign prisoners of war, had survived worse. However, Choi's experiences resembled those of other Koreans who bent or broke under Japan's rule. Two generations of Koreans had survived Japanese bullying and colonialism (and the attendant poverty, war, and humiliation), and the martial artists among the Koreans would go on to create Tae Kwon Do, Tang Soo Do, Hapkido, and other martial arts that would empower them.

A week after his liberation, an emaciated Choi trudged through the chaos and jubilation back to his family in Yongwon, which had transformed in the two years he had been away. To his surprise, communism hovered like a dark cloud over the village and much of northern Korea. He was devastated.[39] Korea was free of Japan but now had to contend with communists from the USSR, who had staked their Korean territory. Worse, two American colonels had taken only thirty minutes to decide arbitrarily that the thirty-eighth parallel would divide Korea into north and south, and the USSR had agreed to oversee the north.[40] Even in the south, Koreans now added the insult "pro-American" to the popular "pro-Japanese" and "national traitor."[41] Overnight, Choi's birthplace became a den of communists.

A couple of months later, in 1945, he wandered back to Seoul, where no one seemed to be in charge.[42] People sometimes fought on the streets and a knowledge of martial arts came in handy. The nation fell into another state of war, this time between communists backed by the USSR and nationalists backed by the United States. It was here that those two superpowers began the Cold War — when Korea was a police state spiked with terror.

No one could control men like Choi, who jumped from one Korean youth group to another. The youth groups were often violent gangs organized around a tough tyrant.[43] Even after he killed his Japanese name, Yuseki Nishiyama, his Korean nickname stuck: *chadol*, a small stone difficult to break. He sided against the communists and, as with many young ex-soldiers, channelled his strength and anger into a new military school in Seoul. The Americans had helped Korea to establish a Korean Military Academy, the start of a future army, and Choi, the tornado, was one of the first to enroll.[44]

Within a year, he led the local constabulary and taught them Karate, which was as effective as it was popular. In Japanese, people called it Karate-Do and, in Korean, either Tang Soo Do (Way of the Chinese Hand) or Kong Soo Do (Way of the Empty Hand). Karate's founder, Gichin Funakoshi, had changed "Chinese" to "Empty," which some viewed as insolence, since "Chinese Hand" had been around for centuries.[45] Many Koreans, such as Choi, remained loyal to China and stuck with the old name, Tang Soo Do. Choi knew the history and controversy, and he had once visited Funakoshi's gym while studying in Japan. After the war, Koreans practised these two types of Karate, and nine main gyms (or *kwans*) contained the instructors and students who would go on to become the pioneers of all future styles of Tae Kwon Do.[46]

Choi and other martial artists used their fists as much as their brains to get what they wanted. Choi's signature move before a fight was to burn his knuckles with a lit cigarette — but only the knuckles on his right hand, because his left was to remain unscarred in respect of his parents and Confucian values. He had toughened his right fist into a callused hammer. He often challenged racist or arrogant, American superiors, even though they were helping Korea's generals to build an army. Once, he clenched his fist in front of his commander's nose; the man was an American lieutenant and reached for a gun. "Your reach for shooting is not closer than the reach of my fist," Choi growled. "It is a pity if you have to die." The lieutenant backed down, and Choi would later brag: "There is a Korean proverb, saying 'A crazy guy can defeat a tiger.' That was how a fist made in Korea, the small and little-known country, repelled a gun made in America, the so-called strongest country in the world."[47]

In spite of chaos on Seoul's streets and a South Korean strongman installed by the Americans, Choi felt he could lead an army. At that time, he met Sun-Ha Lim, who had been a student soldier and admired Choi because of the P'yŏngyang Incident. Lim would soon become a general, helping to set up Korea's military. He noticed that Choi liked to lead his friends as much as entertain them. During parties, Choi liked to have a good time and loved to see people laugh, so he would jump on a table and dance and sing folk songs.⁴⁸ He had to be the centre of attention, and his friends laughed their heads off. On the streets, Choi would walk in front of his friends, not beside or behind, kicking street poles and punching anything he could, until his embarrassed friends would yell at him to stop making a spectacle.⁴⁹ Lim wondered what would become of this brash, young soldier, whose superiors wanted more military art and less martial art from him.

In 1946, when Choi was a second lieutenant, he became ashamed of teaching Karate to his soldiers. During a time when Koreans were rediscovering their culture after decades of war and oppression, he asked himself, Why on earth am I teaching a Japanese martial art to our Korean soldiers after I was almost killed by the Japanese?⁵⁰

That year, he created his first technique — a "low block" that was a variation of a Karate block.⁵¹ His technique protected the front of the belly with a forearm, while the Karate version had the forearm hovering over the knee. To anyone who did not know the martial arts, the two blocks looked identical and protected the same area. Choi had simply moved the arm a couple of inches to the right, so that it stopped in front of the belly instead of to the side of the belly. For Choi, though, this was a start. He began thinking about a new martial art, one that would be better than Karate and would strengthen him, his soldiers, and his country, because, in his world, a wrestler lurked around every corner and superpowers gathered at every border.

That did not stop him, however, from pursuing a beautiful woman who he saw at army headquarters. It was a day in 1948. She was visiting a friend, a typist, in the office, and after she left, Choi discovered that she lived with her father. He carried a huge bouquet of flowers to her home every evening, calling her name as he stood at the door, announcing that she should be his future wife. Sometimes, she would open the door for him and he would be standing there, so short that all she could see was a bouquet with legs.⁵²

Chapter 4

SuperNam

There must be a single courage . . .

– The Art of War, by Sun-Tzu, sixth century BC[53]

Within a couple of years, the Cold War blew up into the Korean War, which North Korea called the "Fatherland Liberation War" and which China called the "War of Resistance Against the Americans and in Support of the Koreans."[54] More than two million Koreans died, the majority of them civilians killed by napalm that the Americans dropped on 1,000 square miles of North Korea.[55]

After the war, people wandered around traumatized. Orphans walked through the streets, and maimed or starved adults begged for food, but Koreans were thankful that American President Harry Truman had not dropped the atomic bombs that he had prepared for North Korea, which would have contaminated the entire peninsula. Most houses and buildings in both Koreas were destroyed. Translator John Koh, who helped me with this book, was ten years old when the war ended and his family returned from refuge to Seoul. He found his house in ashes and, in its place, two bound, dead men. As Koh looked at one of the dead bodies, the face seemed to be moving. Strange. Koh moved closer and saw maggots crawling under the skin, the face tortured even after death.

It was a time of rot and chaos, and the military and martial arts provided ready masters. In 1952, Choi was thirty-three years old and already a two-star general.[56] He had survived a decisive battle that his unit had lost, but his commanding officer, father and calligraphy teacher (a surrogate father) had died in the same year. He married his second wife — the beautiful woman who had stared at the bouquet with legs — and they had a daughter, Meeyun. He had left his first wife and first daughter, Song-Jook Choi, and for the rest of his life would rarely talk about them.[57] In this regard, he seemed much like his father.

While leading his men in the Korean War, he had made sure that they had learned martial arts to keep them strong, but as he became busier he realized that he needed a martial arts instructor for his soldiers — someone who could teach hundreds of war-toughened men, an athlete who could perform the most difficult techniques. In short, he needed a superman, and, in 1952, he found him: Nam Tae-hi, proficient in Tang Soo Do and known for using martial arts in a desperate Korean War battle that many people remembered with awe.

Second Lieutenant Nam's story began — or, rather, ended — on a cold morning on May 22, 1951, when he woke up on top of a dead body.[58] Lying there, did he wonder if he were dead, if he had a body, a mind? Yes, he had both, but he had become mindless at some point during the battle last night. He sat up and, in terror, thought that he was in enemy territory. He was near the top of Yongmun Mountain, near Seoul. It was spring and a light snow lay on the ground. Korean poetry and folklore are full of tales of legendary events near impressive mountains, usually involving Korea's great men, the *yangban*.[59] Nam and General Choi had much in common: they had trained in Shotokan Karate, shot at North Korean communists, and survived horrific battles. Now, here was Nam facing death after nearly three days of continuous fighting, much of it hand-to-hand combat. He was not in enemy territory, but the situation of his Third Battalion looked bleak.

Earlier in the week, Chinese and North Korean communists had completely surrounded Nam's battalion[60] in a nearby township, and the division commander blamed Nam's regiment for the crisis, even though the communists had outnumbered the South Koreans three to one.[61] As punishment, the commander sent Nam's regiment to a no-man's land on Yongmun Mountain, a dangerous outpost ten kilometres south of the division's main defensive line, which meant ten kilometres closer to the enemy, China's 187th, 188th, and 189th divisions. Usually only a squadron or platoon was sent to such an outpost, not an entire regiment, and Nam feared a bloodbath. His unit, the Third Battalion, set up machine guns on a plateau.

On the first night, May 18, Nam heard the communists attack his compatriots, the Second Battalion, on the next plateau. Chinese soldiers often attacked in waves during the Korean War, usually at night, overwhelming American and South Korean forces; they had overrun most of the Korean peninsula with this strategy. Nam heard the communists retreat at daybreak after the battle with the Second Battalion, which is what they usually did after a night raid in order to avoid American bombers.

On the second night, the Chinese army flowed uphill to Nam's plateau, destroyed the machine-gun emplacements with cannon fire, demolished Nam's base, and infiltrated his unit, which retreated. Nam was responsible for thirty-one soldiers in the battalion, and all of them moved into the trenches they had dug. The communists attacked, tentatively at first, sneaking into the trenches. It was so dark that Nam and his soldiers could not use guns, for fear they would kill each other. The Chinese soldiers seemed to have the same terrors. Who was friend and who foe? They had no idea.

In the dark, Nam heard a noise, ran into somebody, and tried to grab the man's hair during the scuffle. The Chinese soldier was trying to do the same. With no light, the only way to distinguish friend from foe was by grabbing at a head, because communists had crew cuts and South Koreans had slightly longer hair. In that trench, Nam felt short hair — almost bald — and he struck. His enemy fell.

He heard another soldier. He punched, flailed. Ran on. As the two armies fought in the dark trenches, Nam tapped men's heads when he could. Crew cut meant attack; long hair, pull back. He could not use a bayonet and fought with his hands all night, thinking of nothing — no mind — stumbling through the dark, striking, kneeing, moving. When he fell, he would stand again.

The next day, the communists retreated from the trenches and the fighting continued with guns. The enemy still had Nam's unit surrounded; he saw many of his men shot.

Night fell again, and the communists attacked again. Nam kept moving along the dark trenches. He collided into a body and struck. He fell, stood, broke noses and jaws. How many did he hit? He did not count. He had no idea if those he hit lived or died. Cracked bones. Split stomachs.

The next day's battle ended as night fell, but Nam kept fighting. Most of his thirty-one men were dead, and he had not slept for

three nights. He had not eaten in how many days? He worked out that he had missed nine meals.[62] He collapsed from exhaustion.

Nam Tae-hi is in the bottom row, fourth from the left. Choi Hong-Hi sits beside him, fifth from the left.

Photo courtesy of Choi.

The next morning, he awoke to see that he was using a dead soldier, a communist, for a pillow. The body had been more comfortable than a rock. Nam's own body was intact and he was not stuck in enemy territory, but the battle was still on. However, as the sun rose, the enemy retreated and Nam's regimental commander ordered a retreat when the American 24th Armoured Division came to their rescue. Nam and the Americans were still hopelessly outnumbered, but, miraculously, the South Korean and American divisions seemed to be holding their own against the communists; innumerable Chinese bodies lay in a nearby river.

That day, during the retreat, Nam wandered to a spot where he had fought during the night before. He found many dead bodies and counted more than two dozen with no bullet or knife wounds. They were the ones he had hit during the night, the ones with broken faces and bones, but there was no time to dwell on these things. Seeing the Chinese divisions weakened, all the South Koreans, including the main line ten kilometres away, counter-attacked and chased the communists over Yongmun Mountain. Thanks to Nam and his battalion, one

Korean division backed by an American division defeated three communist divisions. The battle would soon be in Korea's military records: a famous, horrific lesson in how to defend a mountain top against a 360-degree attack.

General Choi Hong-Hi was impressed. Word had spread that Nam was a Korean Karate expert who had killed communists with his bare hands, and Choi wanted him in his division. With men like Nam, they believed that tiny Korea would banish Chinese communists just as it had Japanese fascists.

✗ ✗ ✗

I ask myself how someone can kill two dozen men in hand-to-hand combat. Years later, long after Nam and Choi had become a formidable duo in Tae Kwon Do, I met Nam in Chicago in 2001 and asked about the battle. What techniques had he used on Yongmun? He said he did not remember, and, in any case, what a question! It was like asking which way the wind had blown after falling into a pit. It was clear that he had expected to die during the night fighting. Nam had been an expert in Korean Karate, or Tang Soo Do, as the Koreans called it, but what he unleashed during the battle was not a formal martial art. He said that he had punched and kicked, applying his Tang Soo Do, which he and Choi would later rename Tae Kwon Do.

Years before the battle, Nam had started studying Karate for the same reason that other children and teenagers had: Japanese bullying. He was born in Seoul on March 22, 1929, and, like Choi, needed a martial art to defend himself. "When I was in elementary school, I had lots of conflicts with the Japanese boys in the playground," Nam told me. "No matter where I used to go, the boys gave me a hard time, so I always beat them up. Eventually, they told me, 'We can't beat you, but we have a Karate black belt who will.' I didn't know what Karate was. Someone explained that Karate was a martial art, and with one *kihup!* they break everything — and, even, when you do Karate, those who are twenty metres away, their arms break! I wanted to learn."

Nam's bullies perhaps knew about the books that were popular in Asia then, such as *The Complete Illustrated Book of the Secret Lessons of Soft and Hard Gong*, by the Master of Wu Tai Mountain, who wrote about climbing walls, striking your knees with a metal hammer to make them stronger, and throwing your fist to hit a target several metres away.[63] Martial arts have always been surrounded by such fantasies, but Nam did not need them.

At eighteen years old, Nam had begun training after school five days a week at Won-kuk Lee's Chung Do Kwan ("Gym of the Blue Way"), the first Karate gym in Korea and the source of many future Tae Kwon Do pioneers.[64] Won-kuk Lee was a pioneer of Korean Karate and was a famous martial arts leader.[65] Born in 1907 (older than both Choi and Nam), Lee had studied Karate with Gichin Funakoshi in the 1920s, long before Choi began.[66] In 1944, after four decades of Japanese suppression of Korean martial arts, a Japanese governor allowed Lee to open the Chung Do Kwan during the Second World War. Because of this relationship, the Korean government after the Second World War charged Lee with being pro-Japanese. But he and his students were using their martial art to help police fight gangs on the chaotic streets of Seoul, and the Chung Do Kwan became known as the gym of the National Police Headquarters. Unlike Choi, Nam, and most others, Lee refused to support South Korea's new strongman, who accused Lee of leading a group of assassins. The Karate master and his wife fled to Japan in 1950, but, before that, Nam perfected his techniques with him, hardening his hands and feet by breaking wooden boards and roof tiles. Nam never saw Lee kill anyone, but he said that one kick from him would have been fatal.

The martial art in those days was extremely basic by today's standards. "In the early days, *Chung Do* [Tae Kwon Do] consisted of ten hand and eight kicking techniques all aimed at the vital points of the body," Lee once told a journalist. "The hand techniques were punch, spear-hand, palm, knife-hand, inner ridge-hand (between thumb and forefinger), twin fingers, single finger, back fist and tiger fist. The kicking techniques consisted of front, side, round and back kick and these were aimed at various levels of the body."[67]

A couple of years ago, I asked Nam about one of those hand techniques, a specialized movement called a "straight-fingertip strike," sometimes called a "spear-hand." It is similar to a punch but uses one's fingertips, instead of a fist, to thrust into an opponent's abdomen or solar plexus. It is an attacking tool that is found supposedly only in Tae Kwon Do.[68] To my utter amazement, my instructor, Mr. Di Vecchia, once informed me that the strike, with proper and diligent training and properly generated power, was intended to puncture an opponent's skin — the fingertips into the body. General Choi elaborated during the 2001 black belt seminar in Toronto when he advised that, in the instant before striking, you should half-twist the technique, so that the fingertips corkscrew through the skin. In addition, Mr. Di Vecchia added that your hand might become embedded in the person's organs after the strike, so a second technique — immediately withdrawing your hand — was essential.

I told Nam all this when I met him and asked if it was possible to perform such a technique. I will never forget his reply, because he looked at me calmly, slightly perplexed, and said, "You cannot stay in the opponent's stomach. You have another opponent, maybe. And though you made a hole in the first man's body, it does not mean your opponent will stay still; he will still punch and kick. Pull back and prepare the next action." It was then that I realized the difference between training now and fifty years ago, between my part-time hobby of learning a martial art and his full-time job of teaching a killing art.

There are good reasons for the yells in Tae Kwon Do.

Nam and I also talked about the lead-leg side kick, a simple technique in which a fighter, from a basic stance, lifts the front leg and kicks with the heel or the outside edge of the sole of the foot. Because there is very little space to build momentum (compared to kicking with the rear leg), the kick is difficult to do with power and speed, and, during intense sparring, most defenders simply absorb a weak side kick or grab the attacking leg. One of my instructors, Jong-Soo Park, who had been a student of Nam's, told me that the best fighters mastered the kick so that the edge of the foot became a sword — a "foot sword," as Choi put it — breaking an arm, thigh, foot, rib, anything in the way. "The purpose of the attack is to immobilize the opponent," Nam explained. "One punch, one kick, can do a lot of damage: broken bones, skin problems . . . Traditionally speaking, one strike, one kick, can kill. We trained hard to develop more power, more energy. Instead of punching two or three times, we punched once — for a knock down." Many great fighters who studied Tang Soo Do (which relies mainly on arm techniques) improved their sparring with the lead-leg side kick, becoming as agile with their legs as they were with their arms: Bruce Lee, Joe Lewis, and Bill "Superfoot" Wallace, for example.[69]

"Tae Kwon Do is different now," Nam told me. "Some people aren't capable, but they're still black belts. Some take it as a recreational activity. I understand . . . But I'm sorry for such a change. I wish that there were a mainstream . . . I want Tae Kwon Do to go back to the traditional way: hard-working — physically and mentally — with total concentration . . . I'm sorry. I wish I could train instructors as before." Nam was a humble man for a former soldier, and it was surreal to hear him apologize for no longer teaching men how to maim or kill with one blow. Perhaps he had mellowed with age; he was seventy-one when I first spoke to him in 2001. Choi liked to take most of the credit for founding Tae Kwon Do, but, in reality, Nam Tae-hi played a large part and was also a founder.

✗ ✗ ✗

On Cheju Island in 1953, General Choi summoned Nam to teach Tang Soo Do in a new division, the 29th Infantry Division, which would become the incubator for Tae Kwon Do. Choi now led 100,000 men on Cheju, and he told regimental commanders to send athletes or martial artists to train eight hours a day under Captain Nam. Fifty soldiers arrived, some from Won-kuk Lee's Chung Do Kwan. Today, Nam still remembers a few of the first men: Kim Suk-kyu; Woo Jong-Lim (who would train many great instructors); and Han Cha-gyo (who could jump over a standing opponent).[70] Also from the Chung Do Kwan, in the near future, were Chang Keun (C. K.) Choi and Jhoon Goo Rhee, who would later befriend Bruce Lee and rule a Tae Kwon Do empire in the United States.[71] Many famous athletes from the Chung Do Kwan soon taught or trained with Nam, including Uhm Woon-kyu and Lee Chong-woo (both leaders of Olympic Tae Kwon Do today) and Hyun Jong-myung (who helped to develop the Olympic style).[72] These pioneers were part of the first wave of Tae Kwon Do.

The 29th Division would go on to train thousands of martial arts soldiers, including the Black Tigers, an elite unit assigned to espionage and assassination missions in North Korea.[73] Tigers continually leap into Korean stories and minds, and Choi took pride in the Black Tigers, whose name echoed the famed Korean "tiger fighters" of 1861, when an American squadron of ships attempted to take over Korean ports at Kanghwa. For hundreds of years, Korea had been known for repelling foreigners. The United States had decided to open the ports by force in 1861, but 650 Koreans repelled them until their weapons were empty, after which they fought to the last man, desperately throwing sand in the Americans' eyes and attacking them with their bare hands.[74] The Americans killed every Korean fighter, whose bodies lay in bloodied white garments on the beach around a citadel. In the end, after fruitless negotiations with local leaders, the Americans retreated.

Approximately ninety years later, in 1953, the Americans were using more subtle tactics. They supported men such as Choi and Nam, who were part of the Korean military's efforts to rebuild the nation, and the two martial artists made it their mission to empower soldiers, because the streets were dangerous, everyone was traumatized, and the Korean War had metastasized into a covert war between North and South Korea and a global Cold War between the United States and the USSR.

Choi ensured that the training was strict in the 29th Division. Some of Nam's students had trudged for days from North to South Korea, leaving behind their homes in their attempts to escape a communist state set up by Kim Il Sung. They had few belongings and practised on drill grounds of the 29th Division, which had no indoor gym.[75] They trained barefoot in the snow not because they were trying to be tough, but because they did not want to wear out the one pair of shoes that each owned.

Hee-Il Cho, who later became a well known Tae Kwon Do expert in the United States, began martial arts training in those days, when the martial arts were not for exercise but for survival and military training. "Although they were not really gang members, young people used to roam from town to town and beat up kids," Cho told a journalist. "The martial arts facilities were very basic then," he said. "The buildings had a roof, but sometimes they didn't have walls. The floor was dirt. Many children didn't have shoes, so we all walked around barefoot." Hunger was the norm; they ate once a day. "Training is like driving a car — you have to put gas in your tank," he said. "In those days, because of malnutrition, many things were not so effective. After training we would get dizzy . . ."[76]

In the early years of Tae Kwon Do, when it was still called Tang Soo Do, Choi dreamed and Nam made the dreams physical. Very few of Choi's men saw Choi do much martial arts during the fifty years in which they worked with him. He did not have to; he was a two-star general. He gave the orders to lower-ranking athletes, such as Nam, who brought the art to life.[77] Choi ran the show, but Nam *was* the show.

By 1954, they were confident enough in their fifty martial artists from the 29th Division that they organized a demonstration for South Korea's president, Syngman Rhee. Choi wanted to show Rhee that the 29th Division contained great soldiers.

Nam would never forget the day of the demonstration, which took place on the grass of an outdoor stadium, part of an anniversary celebration for the First Army Corps. President Rhee watched from an elevated platform, along with anyone else who mattered in Korea's military. Thousands of soldiers watched Nam and his soldiers complete patterns, self-defence, bayonet-defence, and sparring. When Nam's team finished, President Rhee remained standing, wishing them to continue. He must have known about Nam's hand-to-hand battle on Yongmun Mountain in the Korean War, because he had awarded special honours to Nam's division.[78] Nam and his assistant, Han Cha-gyo, had been given only fifteen minutes for a demonstration, so they improvised from what they knew during the extra time, exploding in a series of knife-hands and other techniques in a pattern called *Hwa-Rang* that Nam had created from a Korean Karate pattern. Nam also defended against an attack by two men, then three.

At one point, he walked up to a pile of thirteen clay roof tiles, each of which was three-quarters of an inch thick. Someone with no martial arts training would have found it difficult to break two tiles, and these thirteen protruded from the ground more than a foot. Nam exuded power, but he was not a tall man, so as he stood over the tiles and raised his hand, the soldiers must have wondered if breaking them would be possible.

Nam smashed the curved tiles with a single downward punch.

The president was amazed. "What was on his hand?" he asked General Choi.

"Nothing," Choi replied. "He broke them with his fist, his bare hand."

"Is this the part he used?" the president asked, pointing to his first two knuckles.

"Yes, sir," Choi replied.

The president asked for the martial art's name. Choi had anticipated this and had told Nam to prepare a summary of the demonstration. However, after Choi had read Nam's draft, he struck out the parts about Tang Soo Do, or Korean Karate, because the president, who was a hardcore nationalist, loathed the Japanese and would have a fit if he knew South Korean soldiers were practising

In 1954, Choi, President Rhee and South Korean generals share a laugh. Nam Tae-hi had just broken thirteen roof tiles with a punch. *Photo courtesy of Choi.*

Choi explains to Rhee how Nam broke the tiles with the first two knuckles. *Photo courtesy of Choi.*

a Japanese martial art. After all, Rhee had accused Korea's first Karate master, Nam's teacher, Won-kuk Lee, of being an assassin — and Lee had fled for his life.

Before Choi could reply to the president, someone blurted the truth: "It is Tang Soo Do."

"No, it's T'aekkyŏn," the president countered, averting a fit but creating a problem for Choi and Nam. The two arts were completely different; T'aekkyŏn was a traditional Korean game that required mainly leg techniques, while Tang Soo Do was Karate and relied on hand techniques.[79] Rhee probably remembered T'aekkyŏn from childhood. Impressed by Nam's demonstration, he ordered Choi to teach this art to more of Korea's soldiers. The military was now the strongest institution in Korea; it had grown from 100,000 to 600,000 personnel in three years, and every male had to go through military duty: boot camps, disciplinary training, anticommunist speeches, and "an authoritarian practice that chilled even the most hard-bitten American officers."[80] Martial arts would now be added to the training.

The 1954 demo — the story of it — grew into one of the most memorable moments in the lives of Choi and Nam, and the events that followed were extraordinary for them. They had gained the admiration of their president but faced a dilemma: they could not teach Karate and call it T'aekkyŏn.[81] Although T'aekkyŏn used the hands for various blocks, it had few hand or elbow strikes, few attacks to vital areas, and nearly no full-powered kicks, all of which were fundamental moves in Karate. For hundreds of years, in the area of Seoul, T'aekkyŏn had been synonymous with a rhythmic foot-fighting game based on leg sweeps, jumps, pushes, and stamps.[82] In short, T'aekkyŏn was not Karate, and Choi was no fool.

While he and Nam meditated on the problem, the 29th Division became known in the Korean army because of Nam's demo, and Choi became closer to the president of South Korea and, therefore, gained more power.[83] In 1954, Choi ordered the military to construct a new martial arts gym inside a military base in Kangwon Province.[84] He called it the Oh Do Kwan ("Gym of My Way" or "Gym of Our Way"). Also that year, he became honorary director of Won-kuk Lee's renowned Chung Do Kwan, the civilian gym where Nam had learned Karate at age eighteen.[85] The leader there, Duk-Sung Son, gave Choi an honorary fourth-degree black belt, because he wanted to use Choi's military influence to spread the martial art.[86] Choi transferred martial arts training from the 29th Division to these two gyms, and Nam needed a microphone to train 300 men in the Oh Do Kwan alone.[87]

Choi's military and civilian gyms were two of the nine pioneering gyms (called *kwans*) that later merged into Tae Kwon Do. Choi was the administrator at both gyms, but others taught. Nam would request something for the Oh Do Kwan and Choi would order soldiers to jump to it. Together, their vision expanded until it was larger than the South Korean president's ego: every soldier would learn a new martial art — one that would take the best of Tang Soo Do, add some T'aekkyŏn, and grow from there. The spectacular techniques would strengthen their soldiers, bring glory to Korean athletes, and empower a ravaged South Korea.

More, the martial art would make Choi immortal, or so he dreamed. First, he had to rename it, because he could not call it Tang Soo Do, Kong Soo Do, or any of the other names for Korean Karate.

Many martial arts leaders agreed that a new name was urgently need-ed, but the South Korean president liked the name T'aekkyŏn. How could Choi and Nam convince the dictator and martial arts leaders to change the name — and what should the new name be?

There was only one thing to do: arrange a dinner party at Choi's favourite *kisaeng* restaurant, the high-class, Korean geisha house where men could buy power along with the best sake, women, and dreams.

Part 11

PERSEVERANCE

I will tell you how to eat bark.
It has to be from young pine trees.
You peel off the bark . . .
You scrape it with a knife. It is sweet.
Of course I did not eat it as a meal, but it helped to allay the
hunger.
In the mountains there are many things to eat.
Korea is famous for spring flowers. We plucked them and
ate. In spring, I ate the flower petals of azalea. In summer-
time, I ate acacia.
When American soldiers threw away food garbage, Koreans
bought the garbage and boiled and sold it as food. We called
it pig soup.
I ate frog, ate the skin of rice . . .

— John Koh, translator, sent me this e-mail about life for
many Koreans in the 1950s

인

너

Chapter 5

Tae Kwon Do Is Named in a Korean Geisha House

It was fitting that on an evening in 1955, General Choi hosted a martial arts meeting in a *kisaeng* house, a place of desire and myth.[88] The Kugilgwan was one of Seoul's most distinguished Korean geisha houses, built in the nineteenth century during the Chosŏn dynasty. Lounging near a royal shrine and an ancient belfry that gave the street its name, Bell Street, the Kugilgwan was one of the most famous three in Korea, a *kisaeng* where the newly rich opened their hearts and wallets, where stories and fantasies spread like liquor through their minds. The manager of the Kugilgwan was the South Korean president's secretary, Yi Ki-bung, an immeasurably useful connection for General Choi; after the president, Yi was the second most powerful politician in the country.[89]

Traditional Koreans with new money and power liked the old rituals of the Kugilgwan. After the Second World War, a provincial police chief had ordered the *kisaeng* house to westernize within three days (to add tables and chairs and to switch to western dishes, such as steak and chicken soup), but the *kisaeng* house gently refused. Venerable families, old money from the Chosŏn era, preferred the two other *kisaeng* houses, but the Kugilgwan maintained the Chosŏn food and décor. Many people were starving at the time, and, occasionally, angry students would break up the parties, asking how government officials who conducted secret meetings in *kisaeng* houses could represent the people. Political and military leaders conducted most of the nation's business in *kisaeng* houses — what we in the West would call "backroom politics." *Kisaeng* politics was the only one that mattered in this war-devastated country.[90]

In 1955, on the day of General Choi's martial arts meeting in the Kugilgwan, five candles rested on a low table that overflowed with drinks and appetizers. The room's heat spread beneath them as Choi and his companions sat on the floor. Women whispered into their ears and served rice wine. One could order the *kisaeng* women from a special book and ask for them by flower names — Peoni, Laurel, Chrysanthemum. Men visited *kisaeng* houses not only to drink and deal, but to talk to the *kisaengs*. For the women, becoming a *kisaeng* was progress during the Chosŏn era, when women ranked low, and their behaviour was governed by a thousand rituals. Confucianism relegated most women indoors and out of sight, but the *kisaeng* women lived in an elevated class, both revered and reviled. Some became *kisaengs* to escape Confucian society, but most in Choi's time were sold as young girls to *kisaeng* houses to be brought up as entertainers and mistresses. They lived like the geisha women in Japan and their careers were finished by their late twenties.

Occasionally, a wicked truth would emerge from a *kisaeng* house and shatter society's myths about the lifestyle. Once, a tragic figure from the Kugilgwan became the subject of a 1973 Korean movie: a *kisaeng* woman, Kim So-San, was accused of being a North Korean spy. Rather than arrest her, South Korea forced her to become a counter-spy, but the North Koreans suddenly ordered her to kill an anti-communist prosecutor. Caught between the two Koreas, the Kugilgwan geisha attempted suicide, but the pistol did not go off.

Usually, such high drama was left to the men as they drank excellent *Ch'ŏngju,* the strained rice wine that flowed during these meetings. Choi liked to drink, but he was not an alcoholic. He believed that when a man wanted to be recognized as great, he had to be good at drinking, gambling, and fighting, and he had to be a playboy with at least one concubine. In that sense, Choi understood his father's way of living of thirty years earlier. He now had two wives and four children: a daughter with the first wife and a son and two daughters with the second. The three daughters sometimes played together, but everyone behaved as if the first wife did not exist. This was a world where teenage boys married once in a village, a second time in a city (when their social status rose), and a third time in their dreams, with *kisaengs*. Choi's second wife felt

A newspaper article about the 1955 meeting in a *kisaeng* house. Choi Hong-Hi is third from the left and Duk-Sung Son is second from left.

Photo courtesy of Choi Hong-Hi and Jeong-Soon Cheon.

uncomfortable with his visits to the *kisaeng* houses, but she had no say in the matter, because, as Choi put it, a man had to show off his wealth and power.

Gathering in a *kisaeng* house to discuss a new name for a martial art was only natural. This was not the first time that a Karate leader had tried to organize the nine dominant gyms in the country; the first serious meetings between the *kwans* began during the Korean War in 1951.[91] Now, however, Choi was possibly powerful enough to succeed at what everyone else had failed to do: he and the South Korean president got along, Choi ran two of the nine gyms, and he had decided to treat his illustrious guests to a good dinner for the first time in his army life.

That night, trench coats hung like bodyguards on the flowered dividers that surrounded their table. Near Choi sat Nam Tae-hi, head instructor of Choi's military gym (the Oh Do Kwan). To Choi's right sat Duk-Sung Son, the powerful leader of Choi's civilian gym (the Chung Do Kwan). Choi and Son got along like fox and wolf, but they co-operated. Son had brought his head instructor to the *kisaeng* house.[92] Eight other men sat at the table, men who perhaps got along, perhaps loathed each other: Korea's most powerful general, two influential politicians, two businessmen, and three journalists. They were known as the "First Advisory Committee for Duk-Sung Son's Chung Do Kwan." Only later would the meeting become momentous enough for Choi to call it "Tae Kwon Do's Naming Committee," deleting Son in the process.

"We have come here to create a new name unifying the confused and varied terms applied to one martial art," Choi said. The names had developed from Korean Karate: "Way of the Chinese Hand" and "Way of the Empty Hand" — Tang Soo Do and Kong Soo Do. Choi suggested that they vote anonymously to pick one name.

Each man scribbled his choice on a piece of paper, and when the ballots were opened, Choi saw that everyone had chosen the venerable name Tang Soo Do. Only he and Nam had suggested a new one, Tae Kwon Do. Someone wondered where the odd-sounding *Tae Kwon* had come from. The character *Kwon* was well known, but *Tae* was unusual, and no one had ever seen the two joined into *Tae Kwon*.

"Could whoever suggested this name explain the meaning please?" the chairman asked.

"*Tae* means jumping, kicking, or stamping," Choi said. "*Kwon* is, as you all know, a fist. Yet, here, the fist is not only the clenched palm, but also the various movements of a martial art, such as thrusting, punching, and striking." *Do* meant "art" or "way," as in Karate-Do. He and Nam had made up *Tae Kwon* using Chinese and Korean dictionaries.[93]

Then Choi took a gamble; he claimed that *Tae Kwon* could be related to the name T'aekkyŏn, Korea's old art that South Korea's president wanted to promote.[94] In Confucian society, legitimacy means ancient history, and connecting *Tae Kwon* to the centuries-old T'aekkyŏn was useful — but Choi's connection between the two was a fiction. In Korean and Chinese, the words *Tae* and *Kwon* were not the same as the words *T'aek* and *kyŏn*.[95] In fact, the term T'aekkyŏn probably did not exist in Chinese and is similar to *Tae Kwon* only when translated into English. More to the point, the physical moves of the two were completely different.

One of the businessmen had immediate reservations about Tae Kwon Do: "Re-naming is very important, but, rather than deciding in this place, further historical research is necessary." Korea's deputy Parliamentary speaker, who was also present, suggested that three of them form a subcommittee to find historical proof linking

Tae Kwon Do to T'aekkyŏn. A deadline of December 31, 1955, was set. The meeting ended and the men departed in their dark trench coats.

The "historical research" later offered by the brash Choi was rooted in three ancient dynasties.[96]

1) Paintings of warriors in the labyrinthine caves of the Koguryŏ tombs that were near P'yŏngyang, North Korea, proved, according to Choi, that Tae Kwon Do's techniques had started in the Koguryŏ dynasty (37 BCE to 668 CE).
2) A statue of a Buddhist guardian (Kumkang Yuksa) depicted martial arts moves from the Silla dynasty (5 BCE to 668 CE).
3) A martial arts manual from 1759, called the *Muyechebo*, showed T'aekkyŏn practitioners during the Yi dynasty.

Martial arts historians have debunked this bogus research (which made little mention of Japanese Karate), but people have since devoted rivers of ink to the myths, which still thrive in mainstream martial arts today.

The most popular anecdotes swirl around the Buddhist statue from the Silla dynasty, especially around myths about the *hwarang*, an elite corps of martial-arts warriors who were possibly immortal. In 1952, Choi had named Tae Kwon Do's first pattern after the *hwarang*, and, today, sounding highly Confucian, Tae Kwon Do's leaders force black belts to memorize the *hwarang's* five venerable rules:

Loyalty to the king
Filial love toward one's parents
Fidelity in friendship
Bravery in battle
No wanton killing or unnecessary violence

I like to imagine that the *hwarang* still stride the earth somewhere, teaching ancient secrets to martial artists in hidden basements and shopping malls. In the *kisaeng* houses of the 1950s, the *hwarang* stories must have been as intoxicating as the sake and women; better to have thousand-year-old warriors on your side than face the truth that Tae Kwon Do is basically a martial art of Japan, your long-time enemy.

Soon after the *kisaeng* party, Choi stopped claiming that Tae Kwon Do *could be* T'aekkyŏn and stated that it *was*. He added that it had prospered since the early Silla dynasty, through the Koguryŏ dynasty, and into the early part of the Yi dynasty. Who could argue with three empires? Who could argue with Choi, one of Korea's powerful generals?

Even though no one voted for the name Tae Kwon Do, Choi and Nam boldly ordered their soldiers to use it in their military gym, the Oh Do Kwan, and to yell "Tae Kwon!" when they bowed, but Duk-Sung Son at the Chung Do Kwan and the rest of Korea's martial artists stuck with the name Tang Soo Do.

South Korea's leader did not agree to call it Tae Kwon Do however. "The president would like to write the name as T'aekkyŏn," the chief of the presidential guard told Choi a couple of days after the *kisaeng* party. Choi almost fainted. How could he convince the president that the martial art was not their childhood game, T'aekkyŏn?[97]

It was time for another party at the luxurious *kisaeng* house, and this time he invited the most influential members of the president's entourage, including the president's right-hand man. Choi's superiors might later attack him for handing out favours and bribes, but that was worth the risk, he thought. During the party, the *kisaeng* women served Chosŏn food and Choi served strategic threats. Eventually, after the party, someone on behalf of Choi and Nam convinced South Korea's president to accept the name "Tae Kwon Do" — a memorable occasion, because Choi and Nam could invoke the president to force martial arts leaders to call their art Tae Kwon Do.

Even fifty years later, Nam would cry when telling the story about how he and Choi had convinced the president to accept the name, insisting also, that he, Nam, disliked *kisaengs* and liquor, because Nam Tae-hi had become a devotedly religious man, unlike Choi.

✘ ✘ ✘

In 1956, South Korea's president ordered the high-flying Choi to quit the military because of corruption charges, which devastated Choi. He began drinking heavily, telling people that he could not support his family — could not even afford a pack of cigarettes on some days.[98] To pass the time, he played Korean poker, *Hwatu*, with Korea's richest men and women, always reserving "some muscle power," as he put it, in case of threats and fist fights. His wife ignored his gambling but abhorred his trips out for other fun. Korea was still in a shambles, as was Choi's life. Despite his best efforts and threats, only two gyms used the name Tae Kwon Do.

Never one to give up, he began writing a Tae Kwon Do book, and after 1957, when Shotokan Karate's founder, Gichin Funakoshi, died, Choi borrowed many of his ideas and words. Choi felt that he was improving Karate. He wanted Korea to have its own art, one that would be superior to anything from Japan, but his lies were outrageous now: he accused Japan of taking Korea's T'aekkyŏn and renaming it Karate during Japan's occupation of Korea before the Second World War.[99] Choi loathed the Japanese, whose armies and governments had bullied Korea. He thought nothing of stealing Funakoshi's "elbow," "ball of the foot," "back of the heel," and "sword foot."[100] It was only fair, perhaps, because Funakoshi had originally borrowed them from Chinese martial arts. Choi also took the "sword hand," "four-finger spear hand," and "two-finger spear hand," all of which appeared in Funakoshi's 1943 Japanese-language book, *Karate-Do Nyumon*. Funakoshi wrote that to strengthen a fist, one should punch a tapered wooden post.[101] Choi described exactly the same post for Tae Kwon Do, and included Funakoshi's advice to bury it one-third in the ground and wrap it in rice straw at the top. These all went into Choi's book.

His five-year-old creation myth became beautifully simple: "Tae Kwon Do is an ancient, Korean martial art," a claim that would be emblazoned on gym walls and people's minds for the next fifty years. Always the dramatic storyteller, he added wondrous 1,300-year-old anecdotes about the *hwarang* warriors: "T'aekkyŏn was so advanced that the history books of that period describe martial artists jumping over the high walls and attacking the enemy on the other side." Another, wrote Choi, described martial artists, "kicking a ceiling after jumping from a sitting position."[102] The jumps were possibly the only true part of the myth, but the *hwarang* could not leap through time.

Plagiarism aside, Choi's book contained an important innovation: the "Theory of Power," which applied physics to martial arts techniques and explained how a human body could generate tremendous power — a priority for someone who weighed only 100 pounds. Funakoshi had taught that power comes from three things during a technique: rotating the hips to put all one's weight into a punch for instance; pulling the non-punching hand to the waist; and, at the moment of impact, screwing the punch into the target. Choi said the same thing in a 1960 book but added scientific formulas, such as Newton's Third Law of Motion, which states that every action has an equal and opposite reaction — a theory that explains why one must pull the non-punching hand backwards with a force equal to that of the punching hand.

In later years, Choi summarized his Theory of Power into six parts:

1) Reaction Force (based on Newton's Third Law)
2) Concentration (based on pressure being equal to force multiplied by area)
3) Equilibrium (maintaining one's centre of gravity)
4) Breath Control
5) Mass
6) Speed (the most essential factor, because it united the five others).

He used a classical mechanics equation to summarize the relationship between mass, speed, and power. Martial artists knew that strengthening one's muscles and throwing all one's weight into a technique were crucial, but Choi applied the formula $E = \frac{1}{2} m \times s^2$ to show why a fast lightweight could generate more power than a relatively slower heavyweight. The physics formula states that the energy of a moving object (E) equals its mass (m) multiplied by its squared speed (s) divided by two. So, if you somehow doubled the mass behind your punch, then your resulting energy, or power, would increase by two units (half the mass), but if you doubled the speed of your punch, then your power would increase four times (speed squared). In short, a speedy lightweight could create more power than a relatively slower but muscular heavyweight.

The physics had implications for training — and for people's egos. Martial artists knew about mass and speed instinctively, but Choi was brilliant at explaining how to increase power. He maximized power in every way he could, which is one reason that board-breaking later became an impressive aspect of Tae Kwon Do — with Choi adding board after board. Alongside his obsession with

Leaders of the 1959 Korean Tae Kwon Do Association. Bottom row, from left to right: Hwang Kee (from the Moo Duk Kwan); Yoon Tae-yong (probably the Jidokwan); Choi Hong-Hi (wearing uniform); Ro Byung-jik (Song Moo Kwan); an unknown Korean Athletic Association representative; Lee Nam-suk (Chang Moo Kwan); Uhm Woon-kyu (Chung Do Kwan); and Hyun Jong-myung (Chung and Oh Do kwans). Top row, from left: Kim Soon-bae (Chang Moo Kwan); Ko Jae-hwa (Chung and Oh Do kwans); Nam Tae-hi (Chung Do Kwan); unknown; unknown.

Photo courtesy Choi Hong-Hi.

martial arts power was his ambition for military and political power, which was one reason that he was soon back in the military.

In 1959, after beginning a job as acting commander of an army corps, Choi moved quickly to promote Tae Kwon Do. He published the book that he had worked on during his low period, and in 1960, after the now-unpopular South Korean president fled to exile in Hawaii, Choi issued a second edition, *Introductory Tutorial to Tae Kwon Do.* And the two gyms that he oversaw, the Oh Do Kwan and Chung Do Kwan, were running satellite schools and doing well, sending their fourth-dan black belts to a special academy for instructors that provided training, which included preparing them for culture shock when they were posted overseas.

Also in 1959, Choi and other martial arts leaders finally unified some of the styles and organizations, placing them within the Korean Tae Kwon Do Association (KTA).[103] Choi elbowed his way to the position of president, past Uhm Woon-kyu, Hyun Jong-myung, and other martial arts leaders. This was a crucial event, because Choi would later claim to be Tae Kwon Do's sole founder when, in fact, he was one of the founding members at the time. The KTA would later be implicated in espionage missions in the United States, but in 1959, it was an empowering force for the military and for civilians. Still, many big men challenged the puny Choi in those years, and few people called the martial art Tae Kwon Do.

In 1961, as Choi and a couple of generals sat drinking in a high-class *kisaeng* house in Taegu, which was about 250 kilometres south of Seoul, they complained about the state of the country now that President Rhee had fled. Recent elections had resulted in a weak government, student protests, and more chaos. The transition from dictatorship to the nation's first democracy was a messy affair, and, in their view, the country needed drastic change. They decided to take matters into their own hands.

Chapter 6

One Coup, Two Presidents, and the Three Spheres of Power

I came across a maxim, which Lao-Tzu wrote, "Even after death, those who are remembered will remain." While I was writing the Taekwon-Do manual in English, I realized that through Taekwon-Do, I wanted to dwell in the world existing beyond the limits of time and space.

– Choi Hong-Hi, 1965[104]

Choi did not lead the coup d'état on May 16, 1961, but he followed the colonels and generals who planned to paralyze South Korea,[105] install a new government, eradicate corruption, and revive everyone with a "Revolution," as they called it. The coup began in Seoul at 3 a.m. — an easy, bloodless revolution that was backed by the Americans. Twelve hours later, while Choi and his soldiers were celebrating in Taegu, Major Nam Tae-hi called from Seoul.

"How is it?" Choi asked.

"Not good, sir," Nam replied in a shaky voice.

"What on earth is happening?" Choi asked.

"Right now, fully armoured troops have gathered in the square of Army Headquarters," Nam explained.

Choi was shocked. Their general ran that headquarters. Their superior, who was supposedly leading the coup, was completely surrounded by troops. That could mean only one thing: the Revolution had failed.

Nam called back to announce that, no, the coup had not failed. The military had taken over Seoul, but their general was not leading the coup. A little known general named Park Chung-hee was. Choi was astonished. Park? The former Japanese collaborator

56

during the Second World War? Park? The man who Choi had once voted to execute for communist activities?

Yes, that Park.

Choi was in deep trouble — and he was angry and perhaps jealous: angry because Park had tricked him into supporting the May Revolution; jealous because Park had been cunning enough to seize power. Now Choi would be forced to obey Park, whom Choi considered a subordinate. Many Koreans, Choi included, graded people by rank or status, using elaborate honorifics that were built into the language. In a past dynasty, the high-born — men of the sacred bone — not only lived the high life on earth, but after death were believed to rise to the top of the hierarchy in paradise as well.[106] Choi and Park were both sons of rural folk, and through war, hardship, and the Korean Military Academy, had jumped to the top of Korean society. But Choi was superior to Park, in Choi's view, because he had joined the Military Academy before Park. It was a minor but crucial difference in a society obsessed with status. Choi would now have to address the new leader as "President Park" and "Honourable President Park" — and this was a man who might or might not include Choi in a military government, and might or might not forgive him for helping to issue a death sentence thirteen years ago.

Reading about Choi's role, I wondered if he hid a desire to rule the nation. This feeling would have conflicted with what he had promised himself during his Second World War imprisonment. He had been near death and had dreamt of a nation backed by a powerful military and individuals strengthened by a powerful martial art. He knew that Koreans had long prided themselves on their civilian leaders, "had long held the Man on Horseback in supercilious contempt," as historian Bruce Cumings put it. Yet here was Choi doing the opposite of what he had promised himself. The coup looked like one of the most reckless moves of his life, one that would lead, suddenly and ironically, to Tae Kwon Do's expansion.

The Man on Horseback, General Park Chung-hee, would lead the Supreme Council for National Reconstruction, an ominous campaign to eliminate corruption and purify Korea. The "purification" began immediately after the coup: more than 15,000 people arrested or purged within two months, 4,300 politicians banned from politics, and 14,000 "hooligans" arrested within a year.[107] Choi began sounding like a rebel; he refused to say "Honourable

President Park," and he did worse: he criticized the military leader behind his back, which meant that the newly created Korean Central Intelligence Agency added his name to a list somewhere.

Three military men had helped Park to lead the coup, three who would build and transform parts of Tae Kwon Do over the next twenty-five years.[108] The brains behind the coup, Kim Chŏng-p'il, was one of them. Soon after the coup, he created the KCIA with the help of the American CIA, institutionalizing the purifications and purges.[109] How the Americans helped still remains classified information, but the United States was tactfully appalled when the KCIA exploded out of control. This was no surprise to anyone who knew Generalissimo Park; he had specialized in political assassinations and repression for the Japanese during the Second World War. The KCIA became a terrifying force in Korea; its mandate included everything that the CIA and FBI did in the United States, plus much more.

Martial artists worked in the dictator's Presidential Security Force and the KCIA's sixth branch, which was in charge of assassinations, abductions, and sabotage. They were probably in the fifth branch as well, a unit that oversaw internal security. Koreans feared the fifth branch, which seemed to have spies everywhere.[110] A KCIA director would later admit to American government leaders, "I had extensive powers at my disposal — more power than you can imagine — covering every aspect of my country."[111] For most of the 1960s, the KCIA's power extended deep into political, economic, cultural, religious, and sports activities, including Tae Kwon Do.

Despite standing on the wrong side of the South Korean dictator, Choi was still powerful, because he had supported the coup. He had connections in the new KCIA, commanded 100,000 soldiers in five divisions, and partied at influential *kisaeng* houses. President Park did not frequent the same *kisaeng* establishments as his generals — and certainly not the Kugilgwan in Seoul. He opened his own *kisaeng* house, called *An-ga*, operated by the KCIA, which organized the parties.

That autumn, in 1961, martial arts leaders asked the new dictator to help reunify the martial arts in South Korea, and Park authorized a name change for the Korean Tae Kwon Do Association — to the Korean Tae Soo Do Association, effectively killing the name Tae Kwon Do after its two short years in an association.[112] The group was still the "KTA," and its dozen leaders were a who's who of martial arts leaders in the country, but they

erased Choi and Nam's Tae Kwon Do with a made-up name, Tae Soo Do.[113]

In 1961, Choi (in uniform on the far left) partied with Park Chung-hee (standing in the middle of the shot, wearing civilian clothes).

Photo courtesy of Choi.

Choi grew annoyed as they marginalized him and Tae Kwon Do. Soon after, in 1962, one of Choi and Nam's gyms, the Oh Do Kwan, hosted the first Tae Kwon Do tournament in Korea, and Choi began a mission to force martial arts leaders to revert to the name Tae Kwon Do.[114] The personal vendetta worsened between him and the South Korean president, who eventually banished Choi to an ambassadorship in Malaysia. The posting seemed cozy, but for the blunt-talking, scrappy Choi it would be excruciating; forcing him to become a diplomat was like putting a fox in a chicken coop. What would become of him?

To celebrate Choi's posting, the president hosted a farewell party at the nation's best restaurant. At one point, he sat beside Choi.

"Elder General Choi, I feel sad," the president said, pouring Choi another drink.[115]

"There is nothing to be sad about," Choi lied. "I think it is a pity that you will be surrounded by corrupt advisors after I, who have always given you honest advice, leave you."

The president soon walked away. Choi sat there, meditating on dusty aphorisms from Chinese philosophy: "Lumber should be cut along the carpenter's inking string to be useful; a monarch should accept honest advice," noted the *Scripture of Documents*. Did a dictator care about such wisdom?

"Pay a malignant person back with a virtuous deed," Lao-Tzu had instructed.

"Offer a foe a rational deed in return," Confucius advised. Would Choi? No, he could not attain that level of detachment; bitter feelings haunted his better instincts, and revenge peered behind pride.

After the party, Choi and Major Nam Tae-hi bid farewell to each other. They had worked together for ten years, training Korean soldiers and struggling to create a new martial art. While Choi flew to Malaysia in 1962 as Ambassador Extraordinaire and Plenipotentiary, South Korea parachuted Nam into Vietnam, where he began teaching soldiers how to do what he had done on a mountaintop during the Korean War — kill communists with his bare hands.[116]

Malaysia: The Foundations of Tae Kwon Do

After Choi and his family settled into Malaysia, Choi became obsessed with Tae Kwon Do, setting up an outdoor gym for himself in the front yard of the Korean Embassy, not caring who thought it unbecoming of an ambassador to jump around like a country boy. He wanted to spread Tae Kwon Do like wildfire. He hated the official duties of an ambassador, especially the formal events. At dinners, he would be mortified when he accidentally ate the bread of a guest sitting beside him or when he showed up in top hat and tuxedo when everyone else was dressed casually.

That year, he decreased his responsibilities as ambassador and devoted more time to expanding his 1960 Tae Kwon Do book into an English-language version. During formal events, he would talk about Tae Kwon Do every chance he could. To create new patterns (*hyungs*), the dancelike series of techniques that mimic a martial arts fight, he used the embassy's typists and squirreled away every spare hour from his diplomatic duties. Unknown to Choi, one of the Korean councillors at the embassy noted this and told the KCIA that Choi was abusing his position.[117]

A few months later, Choi found a white envelope on his desk. It contained a letter from his elder brother, who he had not seen in more than fifteen years and who he assumed was dead in North Korea. Choi was elated but suspicious: Could it really be my brother's writing? he thought. Or had somebody imitated the handwriting of my brother to entice me to join communism? Perhaps the KCIA had set this up to accuse him of being a communist? North and South Korea were still technically at war, with covert operations replacing outright war, and any contact with a North Korean, even a family member, was grounds for treason in South Korea — a crime punishable by death. Scared that someone would tip off the KCIA, Choi read the letter and ripped it to pieces.

Soon after, he met the man who had snuck the envelope into the embassy, and Choi obtained another letter and a photo from his brother. He forwarded them to his mother, who lived in South Korea with Choi's first wife and first daughter. When his mother saw the photo, she wept for many days, because she had not seen her eldest son since the Second World War. She died within a year, and Choi, stuck in Malaysia, was unable to visit her. He was devastated, haunted by memories of her, his brother, and their childhood in North Korea; he was also oppressed by guilt that he, his mother's runt, was an unfilial son. In later years, he would silently cry for his mother's forgiveness, but in those raw days, he fled to his martial art.

Choi filled 1962 to 1964 with building Tae Kwon Do's foundations, starting associations in Malaysia and Singapore (only the third and fourth associations in the world at the time, after Korea's and Vietnam's), and creating most of the martial art's patterns, his second major innovation. (The first innovation, in the late 1950s, had been his Theory of Power.) In 1962, Tae Kwon Do still looked like Tang Soo Do, and Choi still practised the Karate patterns, but he was creating twenty-four of his own patterns with the help of some of Tae Kwon Do's pioneers.[118] He treated the athletes like surrogate sons; he dreamed and they flew. "He wrote the moves and we physically demonstrated them until they looked good," said C. K. Choi, one of the pioneers.[119] Ambassador Choi called the twenty-four patterns *Ch'ang Hon*, his pen-name for calligraphy and books. He said that he stopped at twenty-four to acknowledge the hours in a day, which was a symbol for our short life on earth.[120]

In 1964, Choi suddenly left Malaysia — people accused him of embezzlement — and his return to Korea shocked martial arts leaders who thought they had forever jettisoned the name Tae Kwon

Do. Choi rounded up his athletes from the Oh Do Kwan and Chung Do Kwan for a new mission: to promote Tae Kwon Do and to publish a new book. His men gave him advice about techniques and posed for the photos of the patterns that he had created in Malaysia. They altered Karate hand techniques (highlighting the back fist for example), encouraged more dodging, and experimented with flying and jumping versions of Karate kicks.

Jong-Soo Park, for example, had just won a national sparring championship in Korea and told Choi about a kick that he liked. Park had been Nam Tae-hi's student and was probably the best technician in sparring in his generation; he taught police officers in Seoul while helping Choi with the book, and he lived with Choi in those years, which is what the main pioneers often did. Park showed Choi that he could swing his back leg 180 degrees and strike a jaw or solar plexus with the heel. If done with a straight leg, the kick contained the same powerful momentum as a swung bat. If he bent the leg and maintained the momentum, then the kick struck like a whip. In both cases, the heel hit the opponent's head. It was a risky kick, because it took time to spin 180 degrees, but it could be devastating — a knock-out in sparring, if timing and distance were right.[121]

Choi was so impressed that he asked Park to do it again. The kick required maximum speed and perfect balance, Choi realized, and the momentum of the 180-degree spin added extra power to the heel. That night, Choi roused Park from sleep and asked him to do the kick yet again. Park crawled out of bed and demonstrated the technique over and over, while Choi tried to think of a name for it. Over the next ten days, Choi asked him to perform it more than a thousand times, and eventually Choi had a eureka moment: the name would be "reverse turning kick" (*Bandae Dollyo Chagi*). Tae Kwon Do already had a "turning kick" from Karate, but the new kick shot out in the opposite direction, so Choi added "reverse" to "turning kick."

The kick was not a new technique, because Park's senior, Woo Jong-Lim, had developed it a while ago. Woo had developed many of Tae Kwon Do's reverse kicks in the 1950s.[122] Athletes such as Park, however, were applying the techniques during competitions, taking risks in the air with basic punches and kicks, and gambling with 180-degree versions, too. None of the basics were new — a kick was a kick — but an airborne or 180-degree version was new, and risky, and extremely impressive when it knocked out opponents during sparring. Choi had never seen such techniques in action, and he inserted them into his book one by one. This was how some of Choi's champions, such as Park, made it into the footnotes and some instructors, such as Woo Jong-Lim, did not. It was also how Choi came to regard himself as the creator of the techniques.

Choi was a master at organizing and pushing his athletes to do impossible-looking techniques and an expert at explaining and naming the movements. Park said that Choi often had eureka moments for Tae Kwon Do names. "Sitting stance" (*annun sogi*) came from a demonstration in Lebanon, when Choi saw a circus act in which a clown remained sitting when someone pulled away a chair.[123] In West Germany, Choi saw a traffic-

Choi overlapped four photos into one to show Jong-Soo Park executing a reverse turning kick.

Photo courtesy of Choi.

light pedestrian symbol and "walking stance" (*gunnun sogi*) popped into his head for a Karate stance that he wanted to rename. Choi avoided animal names for Tae Kwon Do — there is no "horse stance" or "cat stance," no crouching tigers and hidden dragons, as in other martial arts. He was obsessed with developing a martial art based on scientific principles for the human body. A horse stance was a "sitting stance" and a cat stance was a "rear-foot stance." A tiger was a tiger, and dragons belonged in parades.

In 1965, one of Choi's prison mates from the Second World War, now a smuggler, financed the publication of Choi's new Tae Kwon Do book that showcased complicated jumping, spinning, and flying kicks. For the average person, the near-impossible kicks would be hard to believe without the book's step-by-step photos, which Choi laid out as if a strobe light were capturing the in-between moves. The flying kicks, in particular, were astounding. For example, around 1954, Nam Tae-hi had been one of the first to demonstrate the flying side kick. As eleven men crouched in a row, Nam ran,

Choi's books were full of strobe-like photos to highlight the in-between moves of jumping kicks. This one shows Jong-Soo Park doing a flying side kick. *Photo courtesy of Park.*

flew over all eleven lengthwise, and broke a board on the other side. A photo of that kick landed in Choi's book. At the time, martial artists were focused on perfecting ground techniques — on fundamentals such as front kick, side kick, and spinning back-kick, but even the spinning kick was rare — yet there hung Nam in mid-air, and there sprung Jong-Soo Park on the 1965 book cover, floating at head level. Was it any wonder that martial artists revered ancient *hwarang* warriors?

After Choi published his text, he was accused of copying a Karate book,[124] because Choi had continued to borrow heavily — but the new text clearly pointed in a new direction, usually up. Martial artists were supposed to leap and spin from every angle (kicking and punching along the way) and land with perfect poise. They were to rely on T'aekkyŏn-inspired leg techniques, a lead leg shooting out as fast as an arm for example. And they were supposed to memorize scientific formulas and know exactly what they were doing in every tenth of a second of a technique. Tae Kwon Do was becoming insanely athletic.

Vietnam: A killing art

While Choi laboured in Malaysia, Nam trained soldiers in Vietnam.[125] Just as Karate had grown popular during the Second World War, Tae Kwon Do exploded in Vietnam's jungles and gyms.[126] Nam did not fight on the front lines but trained those who would, picking sixty martial artists and athletes from the Korean army, training them for six months and sending them out to teach others. This was only a start. Korea would eventually post 647 Tae Kwon Do instructors in Vietnam.[127] Funded by the Americans, South Korea would send approximately 300,000 personnel to fight communists there (and many Korean soldiers would suffer from postwar trauma in the process).[128] The United States had been backing South Korea against North Korea for twenty years, and South Korea would return the favour in Vietnam for the next ten. Korea sent the Blue Dragon Division, Tiger Division, and the fanatically anti-communist White Horse Division, which was supposedly full of third-degree black belts.

The Blue Dragon marine corps were the first Korean soliers in the Vietnam War. They were tough mercenaries, bought by the Americans to fight the Viet Cong. But the communists massacred the Koreans, who had not been trained to fight in the jungle; every night, military planes were full of Korean bodies flying back home. In response, the Korean government set up a special boot camp that simulated Vietnam's jungles, and provided better uniforms, boots, and martial arts training for the soldiers. The Korean marines learned more than self-defence however; they learned a killing art. They practised what to do when they were surprised in war, or when they were completely surrounded, or when they had no time to pull a trigger.

Among the first experts to train soldiers after Nam returned to Korea was a Vietnamese officer, Nguyen Van Binh, who hated communists as much as Choi and Nam did. He began teaching martial arts in his Oh Do Kwan in Saigon in 1962. He told me that in his gyms, the first in Vietnam, approximately 60,000 students (2,000 of them black belts) trained from 1962 to 1975.[129] Overall, a million civilians and soldiers studied Tae Kwon Do in that time, he estimated. Soldiers kept fit and learned specific skills. "In close combat, or even far away, it was better when they knew a martial art," Van Binh told me. The soldiers who trained in martial arts moved faster, had better reflexes, and built up their confidence, even after six months of Tae Kwon Do training.

Those who trained longer could kill with their bare hands. I asked Van Binh how someone could do that, because it seemed impossible. "If you punch to the temple, you can break the skull. You cannot kill a man with a punch to the forehead, but if you punch the nose or mouth, for example, you can break the face easily," he said.

Many stories circulated about how Koreans used Tae Kwon Do in combat during the Vietnam War. In 1966, a *Time* magazine reporter wrote: "To Westerners, the process sometimes seems as brutal as it is effective. Suspects [the Viet Cong] are encouraged to talk by a rifle fired just past the ear from behind while they are sitting on the edge of an open grave, or by a swift, cheekbone-shattering flick of a Korean's bare hand. (Every Korean soldier from Commanding General Chae Myung Shin on down practices for 30 minutes each day Tae Kwon Do, the Korean version of Karate.) Once, when the mutilated body of a Korean soldier was found in a Viet Cong–sympathizing village, the Koreans tracked down a Viet Cong, skinned him and hung him in the village."[130]

An American officer in Vietnam, A. S. Bolcar, read the *Time* article and sent a letter to the publication: "Sir: We of the special liaison group have lived and worked daily with the Korean Tigers since their arrival in Viet Nam. They rank professionally with any fighting unit we've known. We find them 'brutally efficient,' but nowhere have we seen any grave sitting, Tae Kwon Do cheekbone splitting, or mutilation by skinning. Had the Tigers done these things, 695 Viet Cong would never have surrendered."[131]

Still, a rumour began that the Viet Cong had orders to move as close as possible to U.S. ground forces but were to avoid close combat with the Koreans.[132] One reason was a battle from the night of Valentine's Day, 1967, when 1,500 Viet Cong soldiers attacked approximately 250 Korean marines in the Blue Dragon's 11th Company. In a Communist stronghold in Quang Ngai Province, the Koreans were entrenched in a heart-shaped camp studded with barbed wire and concrete barriers near Tra Binh Dong village. With flamethrowers and cannons, including 120-millimetre mortars that elephants had carried down the mountains, one Vietnamese battalion blasted into the Korean camp from the southeast, beating drums, blowing whistles and screaming *"Tai Han ra di, ra di!"* ("Come out, Koreans!"), while a second Vietnamese battalion burst through the wire from the north, overwhelming the trenches in waves, and attacking so fast that the Koreans were often unable to shoot.[133]

As the communists overran them, many Korean soldiers fought like ambushed tigers. Bodies piled in the trenches. One Korean rushed into a hole and lobbed out grenades as Vietnamese soldiers chased him. A second ran through flames to attack a Viet Cong fighter holding a flamethrower. A third Korean exploded a last grenade while jumping on a group of the enemy, committing suicide in the process. After the hand grenades ran out, the Koreans had no choice but to lash out with rifle butts and Tae Kwon Do. In the trenches, it was hand-to-hand and knife-to-knife combat, with the Vietnamese soldiers pushing and pulling the trapped Koreans deeper into the camp.

Two hours after the start of the attack, the communists controlled about one-third of the camp, and the Koreans faced annihilation as fog and rain prevented Americans from flying to their aid, but one of the few things going right was Korean artillery fire — and the soldiers' fighting spirit. When the Vietnamese faltered in the middle of the battle, Captain Jung Kyong-gin ordered a daring move that would decide the battle: he counterattacked. One of his platoon leaders led a courageous charge into a breach that the Vietnamese had made earlier in the battle. The commander shot five enemy soldiers with a pistol, after which his squad pushed the Vietnamese back into the breach, trapping the Viet Cong within the wire. A second group of Marines saw the counterattack and joined the fight, so that the Koreans soon surrounded their surrounders. Now the Koreans shouted, *"Ra di, ra di!"* ("Come out, come out!").

When the fog finally cleared, four American Skyhawks flew in to attack the remaining Vietnamese force. After the battle, the traumatized Koreans counted 15 dead companions and 104 dead Viet Cong inside the heart-shaped perimeter and another 140 dead Viet Cong outside of it, near the concertina wire.

Captain Jung's general flew to the site to congratulate him. Jung stood before him after the horrific battle and tried to report what had happened but ended up saying, "Commanding General, sir, I have lost too many men, so in no way am I entitled to your praise, sir," and he burst into tears.

Details of the battle flew into headlines in major Korean- and English-language newspapers. South Korea awarded Jung and one of his officers, Shin Won Bae, the *Tae Geuk*, Korea's Medal of Honour, and all the Korean soldiers in the 11th Company received a full-rank promotion. Jung's exceptional leadership in ordering a counterattack, along with his soldiers' bravery and their Tae Kwon Do training, had contributed to the communist defeat. Shin Won

Bae, who later commanded that same Blue Dragon unit (now called the 2nd Marine Division) told a Marine Corps publication in 2004:

> Even though tactics call for fixing bayonets to rifles during close quarters to neutralize the enemy, our weapon at the time, the M-1 rifle, was not a weapon that could be wielded quickly. In urgent situations, the Marine in the front would fiercely strike the enemy's face and vital parts using Tae Kwon Do, causing him to momentarily lose his will to fight. Then a second Marine would finish off the enemy with the rifle. Additionally, striking the enemy with an entrenching tool was highly effective in destroying the will to fight among the enemy's lead elements. While Tae Kwon Do demonstrated its practical effectiveness on the battlefield, more importantly, martial arts training instilled the confidence to defeat the enemy . . . I think this is the greater significance of Tae Kwon Do training.[134]

This "confidence to defeat the enemy" is embodied in two of the martial art's five tenets: Perseverance and Indomitable Spirit.

In November 1967, after the Valentine's Day battle, the Korean Marines won the National Tae Kwon Do Championship in Korea — winners on the battlefield and in the ring. In 1968, Marine headquarters included Tae Kwon Do training and tests in combat training. "The Marine Education Base, which oversaw initial training for noncommissioned officers, and enlisted Marines, initially established an objective of 85 percent of Marines earning the highest Tae Kwon Do certification," a Marine Corps publication noted. The soldiers also developed Mu Chuk Do (The Invincible Way), a more lethal form of Tae Kwon Do. "However, after teaching this form throughout the Corps for several years, the Marines reverted to Tae Kwon Do as the standard, reserving Mu Chuk Do for Marines assigned to reconnaissance units."[135]

American officers, such as platoon commander James L. Jones, were so impressed with the Valentine's Day win that they enrolled their soldiers in martial arts and began their own programs. Magazines published photos of Korean instructors training American soldiers in hand-to-hand combat. Jones later became U.S. Supreme Allied Commander in Europe and the Commandant of the Marine Corps, where he helped to create the Marine Corps Martial Arts Program (MCMAP), which still exists. He said that his marines had envied the skills of Captain Jung's soldiers.

Vietnam showcased Korean martial arts and was one of the main reasons that the art became popular. As word spread of Korean soldiers' fighting abilities, many Americans learned that the name of the art was Tang Soo Do.[136] Only some Koreans called it Tae Kwon Do. The Americans invited Korean instructors to teach in the United States, which soon hosted more Korean gyms than any country in the world.[137] One journalist estimated that there were twenty-five Korean masters in the United States in the early to mid-1960s, at the beginning of the Vietnam War. By the late 1960s, there were 800 instructors. As a result, the United States became a pillar of Choi's Tae Kwon Do in the 1960s, along with Vietnam, West Germany, Malaysia, and five other countries. Few people, however, were calling it Tae Kwon Do.

Chapter 7

THE ACE TEAM AND THE KOREAN CIA

Someone must have been spreading lies about Josef K., for without having done anything wrong he was arrested one morning.

— Opening line of *The Trial*, by Franz Kafka

Choi and his pioneers had been travelling and giving international demonstrations for years, but a 1965 tour finally caught the attention of foreigners at a time when the Vietnam War was making headlines. One of Choi's close friends was South Korea's ambassador to West Germany, who had been a major promoter of Tae Kwon Do since 1959.[138] He invited Choi and an "Ace demo team" to conduct a Tae Kwon Do tour in Europe in 1965.[139] Choi and four instructors (with bags of new Tae Kwon Do books) arrived in Italy, where they booked an Olympic arena for their first demonstration.

The South Korean ambassador for Italy sat among the audience members, most of whom were Italian soldiers. On stage, Han Cha-gyo, a member of the Ace team, jumped over two six-foot soldiers and broke two wooden boards on the other side. The audience yelled and clapped — and kept clapping, which Choi could not understand. Why did they continue? He assumed they were protesting. Perhaps they suspected that Han had tricked them, that he had performed some kind of magic.

"How on earth can they go on clapping for such a long time?" the General asked the ambassador.

"That means 'encore,'" the ambassador replied. "I think you had better demonstrate it again."

Choi motioned for Han to repeat the manoeuvre. After Han

sailed over the soldiers' heads and broke more boards, the audience went wild. It was not magic or a trick. This was the same Han Cha-gyo who, along with Nam Tae-hi, had amazed the South Korean president in 1954.

During the 1965 tour, Han and his three Ace team-mates, Jong-Soo Park, Joong-keun Kim and Jae-hwa Kwon, flabbergasted audiences in Turkey, Malaysia, Singapore, and West Germany. Choi had chosen the best fighters he could.[140] The demonstrations included sparring with audience members, partly because the team members had no choice; belligerent fighters, especially Karate

In 1965, General Choi (in shades) and South Korea's ambassador to West Germany Choi Duk-shin (other man in suit) led the Ace demonstration team of Jong-Soo Park (far left in white uniform), Jae-hwa Kwon (middle), Joong-keun Kim (far right) and Han Cha-gyo (not shown). *Photo courtesy of Choi.*

experts, would heckle them and publicly challenge them to fights. None of the Ace team members lost, or, if they did, no one publicized the losses. The team members had conditioned their limbs for breaking techniques also. In Germany, Joong-keun Kim broke a brick in half.

The Egyptians, however, were not impressed. At the headquarters of Egypt's ranger corps, as Kim prepared to break his brick, a man in the audience yelled, "I can do that!" Choi immediately ordered Kim to add another brick, because some of the men in the audience looked as big as Hercules — and maybe they could crack a brick in half.

"We can do that," yelled another man. Choi directed Kim to add yet another brick, bringing the total to three. The audience waited. Kim raised his hand and brought it down to smash all three bricks. Some audience members were impressed, but others tried to replicate what Kim had done, trying to break three bricks then and there. None succeeded.

After the demonstration, though, an Egyptian soldier approached the VIP area and asked his Egyptian commander, who was with Choi, if he could show him a technique. The commander agreed. The soldier removed an oblong stone from his pocket and broke it with one Karate chop. The commander was astonished and the proud soldier looked as if he had knocked down a mountain. Something had to be done, Choi thought, because everyone knew that a stone was harder to break than a brick, and Choi refused to lose this unofficial contest. He summoned the host of the demonstration to find a stone ten times bigger than the one the soldier had broken. After it was placed before the assembled VIPs, Ace team member Jae-hwa Kwon smashed it to pieces. The Egyptian soldier disappeared.

News about the demonstration spread through Egypt's military and police forces, and Choi took advantage of the goodwill to boldly announce that Tae Kwon Do was Korea's "national sport."[141] This, of course, was untrue. Martial arts leaders in Korea could not decide on a name, let alone pick a national sport, but Choi transformed Karate experts into Tae Kwon Do experts and set up associations in Egypt, West Germany, Italy, and Turkey, and he distributed his new books as gifts to them. Together, they reviewed patterns in the book and recruited one or two influential people for the associations. Many wondered how a martial art known as Karate, but mysteriously named Tae Kwon Do, could suddenly have whole associations in multiple countries, but the General was more than an opportunist; he was a PR man before public relations became a household term — and, more than that, he was a showman, a poet, and an ex-general. He knew how to push his supermen to perform what audiences wanted to see; he knew how to explain the powerful techniques; and he knew how to crush hecklers, bullies, and enemies.

People were used to the overwhelming power and speed of Karate and other martial arts, but Choi claimed that the height, dexterity, and power of flying kicks showed that the athleticism of Tae Kwon Do was unique. He wrote: "Certain detractors claim that flying techniques are both impractical and dangerous [in sparring] . . . Numerous Tae Kwon Do instructors, with years of experience, can testify that a well-executed flying kick conducted with speed is not only extremely devastating, but has the added advantage of surprise." He forgot to add that it was awe-inspiring; the wondrous thing about the martial arts is that you do not have to be an expert to admire a great technique, assuming you are not the victim.

In the 1960s, the demo teams showed off flying front-kicks, flying side-kicks, and the impossible-looking flying twin-foot kick. One variation of this last technique involved one foot kicking the face while the other simultaneously kicked the chest. Two other devastating kicks were the mid-air spin-kick (jumping and spinning 360 degrees or 540 degrees to kick the face) and Han Cha-gyo's specialty, the overhead kick (jumping over an opponent to kick someone on the other side). These flying kicks were nearly impossible to execute during sparring (Choi's detractors were correct), unless a black belt trained every day for years, and even then the timing and power had to be perfect.

Kong Young-il was a member of Choi's select demo teams in the 1960s, and, like the others, he trained day and night and could perform those kicks. He had begun in Shotokan Karate and Judo and later trained in Nam Tae-hi's Oh Do Kwan in South Korea.[142] Training was severe. In summer, Kong and his classmates would wring the sweat from their uniforms in the middle of practice. In winter, the floor was so cold that they did not stop moving. In the 1960s, a normal routine would be:

5:30 a.m.–6:30 a.m.: wake up and run for an hour
9 a.m.–12 noon: fundamental techniques

2 p.m.–5 p.m: sparring techniques
5 p.m.–9 p.m.: eat and teach soldiers and their families
After 9 p.m. (on demo tours): party

Choi treated his demo team members like surrogate sons, taking care of them and ensuring that they did not fly out of control at night. At bedtime, he would peek into the bedrooms of his men, making sure they were in bed, tucking in their blankets.[143] Sometimes, the martial artists would pretend to be asleep and sneak out to party after the General left. The problem with performing in the day and partying at night was that Choi would force them to wake around 6 a.m. no matter how much they drank and how jet-lagged they were. Since 1938, when he had begun Karate, he had been rising at 6 a.m. every day of his life, no matter what time zone he was in, no matter how hard he had partied.[144]

Usually, they would be jolted awake by Choi's morning meditation, which involved banging a callused fist against a hotel wall, knocking only the right fist. He kept the left hand sacred for Confucian values.[145] His son-in-law, Michael Cormack, a black belt who joined the international demo team later, said, "We'd be sleeping and we'd hear the wall: he'd be tapping his knuckles, thinking about what he's going to do, and the whole hotel would shake." Boom. "He was very focused." Boom. "We didn't need alarm clocks." Ba-boom.[146]

It was no wonder that the exhausted supermen sometimes failed to break boards or bricks — and sometimes dozed during demonstrations, in which case Choi would wake them with a punch in the stomach.

Not all went well between the men during the international tours. On the first day of the Ace demo tour in 1965, for example, Choi looked into a bag that Jong-Soo Park was holding and noticed that it contained a package of hot pepper that was leaking onto Choi's precious Tae Kwon Do books. Choi barked at Park for carrying the pepper with the books. Pepper stains were impossible to remove. But Choi's wife had given the pepper to Han Cha-gyo, Park's teammate, who had placed it in the bag for Choi and the team. They loved spicy food. Still, Choi was angry at Park, not Han. They were all walking to an elevator on that first day, and Park slowed down to allow a woman to enter before him, when Choi suddenly threatened to send him back to Korea for walking too slowly. This was too much for

Park. He had carried the heavy bag as a favour for Han, his elder, and had let the woman pass out of courtesy, but the enraged Choi did not seem to understand. Park put down the bag and glared at Choi, and the rest of the team said nothing as the elevator hummed. This was day one.

"I'm going back to Korea," Park announced and asked for his passport.

Choi was surprised, and turned his head away, which is what he usually did when someone displeased him. He looked at the wall, as if Park did not exist, as if Park had not spoken. Choi caused many conflicts in his life, but he rarely resolved them in a straightforward manner, face to face, unless he was certain of victory. On that tour, he refused to let Park leave, and the two men treated each other with more care after the Hot Pepper Incident. Park had figured out a secret about his general, one that few people had learned: you had to stand up to the belligerent Choi, no matter how scary the consequences seemed.

On the last day of the tour, after the stress of the demonstrations — the sparring, the breaks, the Karate taunts, the constant travel, the short nights — they were eating in a Hong Kong restaurant just before returning home. The team was worn out. After more than a month of travelling together, they were bruised, aching, tired, and irritable. A waiter placed two eggs on the table in front of Choi, even though he had ordered only one. He offered the extra egg to Joong-keun Kim, who in turn offered it to Jong-Soo Park because Park was much younger, Kim said. This was an insult, in Park's view, because Park was only one or two years younger; Kim was once again throwing his weight around, pulling rank, trying to make Park feel inferior. Han Cha-gyo had had enough of Kim a couple of weeks ago and, despite being Kim's senior, had almost pummelled him. Park slid into a quiet rage at the table. Then he ordered Kim to leave the room.

Kim began to shake. In hindsight, challenging Kim was not a good idea, as he was a key member of South Korea's presidential bodyguard and, in some ways, was Choi's superior, but Kim and Park had been avoiding a fight during much of the tour and Park wanted to finally settle it.

As the two men walked upstairs, Park seethed, and Kim foamed at the mouth. Park could see the white spit on Kim's lips. At that moment, Choi and Han jumped in, and Choi hammered them with a stern lecture. "We've lasted one and a half months together!" Choi said. "Why fight now?"

Kim apologized to Park and stuck out his hand. Park refused to shake it.

✗ ✗ ✗

Back in Korea, the international tour failed to impress other martial arts leaders, but Choi still had connections within parts of the government and the KCIA, and he hoped to consolidate his martial arts power. The South Korean president ignored him, busy with a potential famine, the Vietnam War, and an escalating covert war with North Korea, but Choi needed the president, because one of Choi's priorities was to unify the nine main gyms under the name Tae Kwon Do. Choi would never give up.

The KTA was still the Korean Tae Soo Do Association, and nearly every martial arts leader wanted to be KTA president. They planned coup d'états and counter-coups inside the KTA as often as their political friends planned them against the president of South Korea. In this context, Choi once again shouldered his way to the position of KTA president.

In 1965, during a meeting in which a martial arts leader accepted the name Tae Kwon Do in public and then refused it in private, Choi grabbed the man by the shirt, dragged him up the stairs, and, in the presence of other martial arts leaders, knocked his head against a wall.[147] "It is impossible to find such a wicked scoundrel like him," Choi said. "We had better get rid of him." Choi watched him shake.

Even though he and the South Korean dictator hated each other, Choi continued to threaten powerful men and manoeuvre politically as deftly as his Ace team did physically. Somehow, he convinced the dictator to accept the name Tae Kwon Do, and, under Choi, the KTA became the Korean Tae Kwon Do Association once again — but few martial arts leaders got along with Choi, especially one of the most famous in the country, Hwang Kee.[148] And everyone continued teaching Korean Karate patterns, avoiding the *Ch'ang Hon* patterns that Choi and his men had developed in Malaysia.[149]

Soon after, martial arts leaders organized a martial arts coup d'état to oust Choi. Another famous leader, Lee Chong-woo, head of the Jidokwan (one of the nine main gyms in the country), later

Many martial arts leaders partied as hard as they trained. Here, in 1965, Choi sticks a cigarette in the mouth of Hwang Kee, Choi's beloved enemy and head of the powerful Moo Duk Kwan. Han Cha-gyo, member of the Ace team, is second from the right. *Photo courtesy of Choi.*

Hwang Kee and Choi Hong-Hi, 1965. *Photo courtesy of Choi.*

told two martial artists, "Choi Hong-Hi was like an authoritarian dictator, so Uhm Woon-kyu and I had to kick him out. One morning we went to visit him at his house in Hannamdong [near Yong San] to ask him to resign, but Choi Hong-Hi begged us to allow him to remain as KTA President for six more months. We told him he would have to choose between three things: Money, Position or Honor. We told him that if he chose Honor and resigned, we would help him make his own private International Taekwon-Do Federation [ITF], but we wanted him to resign immediately and get out of the Korean Tae Kwon Do Association." Lee, Uhm, and others labelled Choi a "permanent troublemaker."[150]

Choi could not care less. He resigned from the KTA and created the ITF in 1966, in the Rose Room of Seoul's Chosun Hotel.[151] As promised, Lee and Uhm helped, landing on the executive. Meanwhile, Tae Kwon Do slowly grew overseas, thanks to Choi's diplomatic connections, Nam Tae-hi's students, and the first wave of pioneers who had started their own gyms. The ITF now contained nine founding countries, mainly the ones that Choi had visited during the Ace tour of 1965.

Within two years, the ITF spread to thirty countries and Tae Kwon Do expanded in South Korea when the Ministry of National Defence issued an order for the armed forces to train in the martial art.[152]

But the ITF and the KTA became competitors, even though the "T" in "KTA" now stood for Tae Kwon Do. The competition was a dangerous game. Choi had split from the KTA's umbrella group, the Korean Athletic Association, which ran its own building;[153] the ITF met at the Chosun Hotel instead. The physical split meant that the ITF had to root itself somewhere else, because anyone who wished to succeed in South Korea needed deep roots somewhere in the dictatorship. While a few gyms clung to the Ministry of Education and others to the KAA, Choi boldly connected his ITF with the notorious Korean CIA, despite the reports of torture and human-rights atrocities that surrounded it.

In an effort to gain influence with the dictatorship, Choi appointed the KCIA's creator as the ITF's honorary president; he also included KCIA agents in the ITF's leadership. It was a classic Choi manoeuvre: audacious and risky, and with the violence lurking out of sight. The KCIA had become a state within a state, launching hundreds of espionage operations against North Korea and becoming known during the Cold War for its ruthless pursuit of enemies, both real and perceived.[154] It had modernized Korea's Confucian values, replacing ancient vagueness with massive files and dynastic worship with modern secrecy, and it planned many of the government's legislative ideas, shook down millionaires, spied on its citizens, and supported theatres, an orchestra, and a large tourist centre.[155] In turn, Tae Kwon Do modernized ancient *hwarang* warriors; some martial artists were now soldiers and spies.

One problem, as Choi saw it, was that the KCIA was increasingly harassing and torturing its own citizens. Running missions against communists was one thing, but torturing a Korean politician or a civilian simply because you did not like his opinion was another. Koreans heard about KCIA interrogators clubbing people with metal pipes and suffocating them with wet towels.[156] But Choi maintained connections with the KCIA; while thousands of innocent Koreans were incarcerated in 1966, for example, a former Korean CIA director hosted a drinking party for Choi at a *kisaeng* house.

But Choi soon realized that he could not play in the same league as the KCIA. In 1967, two of his Tae Kwon Do executives, Kim Kwang-il and Lee Gye-hoon, were involved in a mission to abduct 203 Koreans from seven countries, a surreal operation that jolted even General Choi.[157]

The East Berlin Incident

It began early on June 17, 1967, in West Germany, where a South Korean official telephoned well-known Korean composer Isang Yun at his home in West Berlin and asked him to visit the embassy. Yun travelled to Bonn, and once he was inside the embassy, officials grabbed him, stuck him in an attic, and for two days peppered him with accusations about being a spy for North Korea. The composer denied the charges, but officials transported him to a Hamburg airport and slipped him onto a Japanese Airlines plane bound for Seoul — even though he had no passport or plane ticket.[158]

Meanwhile, in Heidelberg, rumours of missing South Koreans trickled into a German police station after a letter arrived from a student studying at the University of Heidelberg. The letter explained that the student found himself "in the situation of K," the man in Franz Kafka's *The Trial*, a book that follows a man who is arrested, tormented, and forced into a courtroom for reasons he never finds out. The Korean student felt the same way. When Korean agents arrived to escort him, he tried to escape and discovered that they knew Tae Kwon Do, judging by the way they roughed him up. They hustled him onto a plane and deposited him in Seoul, where the KCIA put him on trial.[159]

In West Germany, officials heard more stories: a Korean student in Heidelberg was invited to dinner and kidnapped; a lecturer vanished from a Frankfurt university; a doctor, painter, poet, and several newspaper reporters were missing, all of them Korean-Germans. In total, more than forty-five Koreans were missing in Germany, eight in France, and 143 in Austria, the United States, the U.K., Australia, and South Korea. What was going on?[160]

A KCIA chief in Germany, Yang Doo-wan, knew. Undercover as an embassy councillor, he was leading the German part of a massive operation run by the KCIA's third branch (in charge of counter-intelligence and rounding up spies) and the sixth branch (devoted to dirty tricks, sabotage, and assassinations).[161] Yang was arresting rebellious students and artists, all of whom the South Korean president and the KCIA disliked. This was the turbulent 1960s; anti–Vietnam War students were demonstrating in the United States and Europe, the Cold War was peaking, and the KCIA had fabricated and exaggerated allegations that students in Europe were moonlighting as North Korean spies.[162] Yang had imported fifty extra KCIA agents and had recruited Korean Tae Kwon Do instructors and Korean miners (who had been sporadically introducing Tae Kwon Do to Europe over the years). He had organized a plane to fly the abductees from Germany to Seoul, where agents deposited them in Namsan, a wooded hill in the city centre that contained the KCIA's headquarters, the basement of which was equipped with torture devices that could do anything except turn men into women and women into men.[163]

General Choi eventually discovered that Tae Kwon Do was involved in the mass abductions. During the week of the kidnappings, thirty-one-year-old Kim Kwang-il, a Tae Kwon Do pioneer who had lived in Stuttgart for many years, traveled six hundred miles from city to city, showing Korean officials where students lived. Lee Gye-hoon, a second Tae Kwon Do pioneer who was involved, was a KCIA agent at the end of 1966 and an executive of Choi's International Taekwon-Do Federation. Choi was powerless to stop the use of Tae Kwon Do officials in the kidnapping mission.[164]

In Germany, one student managed to escape on the way to Dusseldorf airport and made it to a police station, where he filed a desperate report. The German police were baffled at first. Mass kidnappings? Women luring students to abductions? Martial artists forcing people into cars? The police believed him, and Germany issued an official protest, calling the operation "a grave breach of international law" and offering police protection to the remaining 4,200 South Koreans in West Germany. People assumed that German intelligence knew about the operation and that it had allowed the Koreans to carry out the mission with the proviso that Korea would return the students to Germany, but it was obvious that no one expected everything to spin out of control.

The kidnappings were dubbed the East Berlin Espionage Incident, because students had supposedly visited North Korean agents in that city. The KCIA accused the students of receiving espionage training, starting a socialist revolution, and accepting $200 to $1,000 each for the work. The incident occurred during a time when North Korea was launching hundreds of assassination attempts and commando raids on South Korea, so it was extremely unwise for any South Korean to visit North Korea. Still, $1,000 seemed a paltry amount to start a revolution.

The international scandal landed in newspapers around the world, and South Korean President Park Chung-hee faced a barrage of criticism. He was livid. The KCIA was supposed to have quietly "encouraged" suspected communists to fly to Seoul, but the world now saw a thuggish part of South Korea that it usually associated with North Korea. As the outcry grew, Germany expelled three South Korean diplomats and suspended aid.[165] Police arrested a Korean miner and a Tae Kwon Do instructor, Kim Kwang-il, and France delivered a formal protest to South Korea, where an uproar had begun, partly because of the kidnapped composer, Isang Yun.

Agents in Seoul treated him as badly as they treated the other abductees. They bound his feet and hands, covered his head with a wet towel, suspended him from a pole, and kicked and beat him with wooden sticks, insisting that he confess to being a spy. He fainted repeatedly but finally agreed to sign the confession because he was afraid of dying.[166] Under the National Security Law and the Anti-Communist Law, he and his cell mates faced death sentences.

The composer had been through this before, during the Second World War, when Japan arrested and tortured him for resisting the Japanese occupation, something General Choi would have understood. Choi had resisted the Japanese empire and devoted his life to empowering his military with martial arts; Yun had rebelled and devoted his life to writing music about justice and humanitarian concerns. The KCIA had kidnapped Yun because, in 1963, he had visited an ancient Koguryŏ tomb in North Korea, looking for a possible setting for a new composition, but the KCIA had no time for artistic whims and convicted him of treason. A worldwide petition led by Igor Stravinsky and Herbert von Karajan was presented to the South Korean government; the KCIA responded by allowing Yun to compose an opera on the floor of his cell.

Choi heard about Yun's incarceration and learned that the mastermind of the global operation was the KCIA director himself, the notorious Kim Hyung-wook, an officer during the Korean War whose unbearable arrogance was surpassed only by his appetite for bribes. Just that spring, Choi had enlisted his help to convince the South Korean president to build a Tae Kwon Do centre in Seoul, but the lobbying had failed.[167] Kim's nickname was "Wild Boar," and he held an unimaginable amount of power: he swayed elections; controlled parts of the economy; stole tens of millions of dollars; promoted cultural, religious, and athletic events; and launched espionage missions anywhere on the planet.

After the German kidnappings, the Wild Boar laughed about a compliment circulating in Seoul that James Bond could not have arranged a better abduction of the 203 Koreans. "Our people," he told *Der Spiegel*, "were already home by the time the story first appeared in the press." The operation was "impeccably unobservable," he said.[168] His arrogance may have been fuelled by the support of the American CIA, which had also "encouraged" three South Koreans in the United States to return to Seoul.[169]

As part of the operation, the Wild Boar arrested powerful people in South Korea: politicians, religious leaders, and, for some reason, the secretary of one of his adversaries, Park Chong-kyu, who was not only the head of the Presidential Security Force (PSF), but a third-degree black belt in Hapkido and Judo. Park Chong-kyu would later be known as "Pistol Park" in the Olympics and Tae Kwon Do. In the sixties, he oversaw his own intelligence missions outside of the KCIA and ran a small empire that competed

In Seoul in 1967, Koreans await trial during the East Berlin Incident.

Photo courtesy of Choi Hong-Hi.

with the KCIA and the Prime Minister's Office. These were the three spheres of power — the KCIA, the PMO, and the PSF — that spun around the dictator, supporting him while at the same time protecting their territories from each other.[170] Shortly after the Wild Boar arrested the secretary, "Pistol Park" aimed a gun at the Boar's forehead and demanded that he release her. The KCIA director hesitated, then relented.[171]

It made us deserve to be called savages, Choi thought of the East Berlin Incident.[172] He suspected that the story was worse than the publicized version, and that the KCIA had tried to force the South Koreans into becoming spies (or counter-spies) and had kidnapped them when they had refused. At best, the KCIA had exaggerated the North Korean spying accusations in a fit of paranoia or simply as a warning to all those demonstrating against the regime. Two of Tae Kwon Do's tenets were Integrity ("able to define right and wrong") and Courtesy ("a sense of justice"), but now the world was reading about the art's link to a surreal KCIA mission that was as unjust as it was bizarre.

It is likely that Choi raged not only at the mission's brazenness but at the KCIA for failing to notify him — in West Germany of all places! His close friend was Korea's ambassador there. Why had he kept Choi in the dark? As it turned out, the West German ambassador had had no advance notice about the abductions, and the KCIA had supposedly tortured *him* — South Korea's own ambassador.[173] Afterwards, the ambassador asked his government to relieve him of his duties, and he became a religious hermit.

Worldwide protests and diplomatic pressure helped the 203 victims in South Korea; the vast majority of abductees were released — including the Kafka student — but not composer Isang Yun. Korea charged him with spying and executed two of the kidnappees. In spite of an international campaign to release Yun, the composer languished in jail for two years.

Back in Germany, police released Tae Kwon Do instructor Kim Kwang-il. A year later, in 1968, he was back in the ITF, promoting the martial art and building a West German ITF organization where he played a leading role until 1971.[174] A Tae Kwon Do colleague of his, C. K. Choi, guessed that Kim Kwang-il had not been physically involved in the abductions and, in fact, had perhaps helped the German government to obtain more information about what the KCIA had been up to in 1967.

KCIA agent and Tae Kwon Do pioneer Lee Gye-hoon was also back on the job for Choi's ITF a couple of months after the mission. In Tokyo, he introduced Choi to the renowned Karate master Masutatsu Oyama, a Korean who had become Japanese and was famous for punching out bulls. Choi tried to convince the famous Oyama to switch his citizenship from Japanese to Korean and to jump from Karate to Tae Kwon Do, but to no avail. The KCIA agent helped them to become blood brothers anyway and later rose to become the KCIA's deputy director.[175]

In 1969, the Wild Boar finally agreed to release composer Isang Yun, threatening to kill him if he did not keep quiet.[176] Yun returned to a West German opera house to open *Butterfly Widow,* the piece he had composed on the floor of his cell. He also opened a second work, *Dreams,* which was based on Taoist parables that sought inner freedom. One of the librettos lamented: "What has passed returns to nothingness if one gazes back at it . . . Today is spring; tomorrow the flower wilts."[177]

After the East Berlin Incident, Choi was wilting in Korea, despite his KCIA connections, successes in Vietnam, and international Tae Kwon Do demonstrations. He suspected that the South Korean dic-

Hong-Hi Choi (on the left) shares a gift with Oyama as Lee Gye-hoon (second from left) looks on.

Photo courtesy of Choi.

tator wanted Tae Kwon Do to become a powerful muscle in the dictatorship.[178] Choi faced two choices: either surrender to the injustice or criticize the dictator. He chose the latter — criticism was one of Choi's strengths, of course — but he was fighting above his weight category. Even though the KCIA had messed up in Germany, the South Korean president himself was transforming into a darling dictator of the West, a Cold Warrior who faced down North Korean, Chinese, and Soviet communists while running one of the most successful capitalist economies in the world. Choi wanted to control Tae Kwon Do, but he knew that he could not defeat President Park and the three spheres of power circling the dictator, each of which had connections to the martial art.

Financially broke and politically weak, Choi began negotiating for $2 million from a North Korean agent — a crime punishable by death, but nothing came of the talks. Given what had happened to composer Yun for a simple visit to North Korea, Choi had risked too much. Afterwards, he found out that the South Korean president and "Pistol Park" had approved a special KCIA agent, Kim Un-yong, to take control of Tae Kwon Do.[179] Kim was to merge the martial arts gyms and, along the way, deal with Choi.

Part III

SELF-CONTROL

Mr. Kim is a mountain, and he stood alone and many times remained quiet. However, because he is a mountain, he has a correspondingly large valley, and he has the capacity to accept much bitterness, which is a lesson for juniors.

— From an introduction to Kim Un-yong's 2002 memoir

극

기

Chapter 8

ENTER THE CLOUD DRAGON

Choi considered Kim Un-yong to be both a subordinate and a "close friend," which is about the same as saying that you like someone while kicking him in the kidney. Who was this new rival, Kim Un-yong, whose last name meant "gold" and whose first name meant "cloud dragon"?[180] I should fully introduce him, as he would conjure more success for Tae Kwon Do than Choi and Nam put together, and the subtle workings of his heart and mind would nearly destroy Choi and many other Tae Kwon Do pioneers.

Kim was born on March 19, 1931, in the year of the Ram, in Taegu, a town that lived inside him like the clear water of a brook, as he once recalled it.[181] Even at the age of seventy, he would remember that his hometown, in those days, did not trouble itself with the three obsessions of Money, Position, and Honour. If there was one overriding theme in Kim's life, one word that explained his trajectory from small hometown to political stratosphere, it was "timing," as he put it — good timing and bad timing.[182] When Kim Un-yong was three, his father, Kim Do-hak, worked as a journalist for a Japanese newspaper and introduced his son to a provincial premier who wore a gold-embroidered uniform. I will wear the same uniform if I become a premier, thought the boy. That meeting had been good timing and would stick in Kim's mind for the next seven decades. When he was six, his father died from pneumonia in the year in which penicillin was invented. Bad timing. Kim had only one photo of his father.

After the death, Kim's mother moved the family to Seoul. She was a modern woman, educated, and her ancestors had grown from a royal family, which, if you know Korea, means they were of the *yangban*. They were rich in the 1930s, a time when many Koreans went hungry. Kim's family owned a mine, land in five places, and buildings in Seoul and Taegu.[183]

Before and after the Second World War, his mother enrolled Kim in schools that were predominantly Japanese. Kim was a good student and an athlete, training in Judo, boxing, Kong Soo Do, skating, and running, but he dreamed of being a diplomat, the pinnacle of achievement for many Koreans in those days. When Kim was nineteen years old, six weeks before his final civil service examination, northern communists flowed into South Korea, and the Korean War began. His nose was deep in his books — he took breaks only to eat and go to the washroom — and he missed the last train out of Seoul. Bad timing. The next day, he, his friend, and his friend's mother hunkered down to survive the bombardment of the city. Afterwards, as North Koreans swarmed over Seoul and most of the country, drafting young men along the way, Kim hid in the mountains for more than two months, until South Korean and American forces reclaimed the city.

The communists shattered Kim's life, but he pieced it together in the military, just as Choi had. Kim joined the army when he was nineteen and studied in the United States at an infantry school in Georgia and at a university in Texas, which cost a fortune. Although both men were in the military, they could not have been more different. Kim had come from the aristocracy while Choi emerged from peasant stock. Kim lived with childhood wealth and Choi with poverty. Kim lived within an aura of sophistication and Choi lived by his fists and a heart that was bigger than his mouth. In short, Kim was cloud and Choi, rock — and both men could absorb an enormous amount of punishment and still keep moving.

Kim married a wealthy woman in 1958 and retired as a lieutenant colonel ten years after joining the army.[184] During the 1961 coup d'état in which Choi participated, Kim despaired as he watched his country's liberal party crumble in one bloodless morning. "Soldiers should never be allowed in politics," he later lamented. Always a survivor, he used his personal army connections to begin working as an interpreter and protocol officer for Korea's leaders, and he worked for the South Korean dictator himself in 1961.[185] Good timing there.

He ended up in the Korean CIA by 1963 and was posted to the United States.[186] As far as I know, he has never written about this secret journey. Officially, he was a diplomat, a project officer for Cultural Activities at the South Korean Embassy in Washington, DC. Unofficially, however, he was agent "Mickey Kim." He was a linguist who spoke perfect English, as well as Japanese, French, German, and Spanish, and he was a classical pianist; he quickly learned how to bridge cultural differences with eloquent words and Frédéric Chopin.[187] He must have travelled a lot, because besides his embassy role in Washington, he was a councillor with the Korean Embassy in London, England, and with the Korean Mission to the United Nations — and he had time to complete graduate work at George Washington University in 1964.[188]

He claimed that he helped to open Tae Kwon Do gyms in the United States and England around that time. "I loved sports and maintained good relationships with martial arts instructors when I was a diplomatic official and helped them as much as possible," he wrote in his memoir. "I busied myself when there was a tournament, and I financially helped instructors to open martial arts gyms."[189] In the United States, he said that he paid rent for instructors and helped them to negotiate bank loans and organize competitions and, in England, helped to establish a Tae Kwon Do association.[190] These were huge contributions, at least symbolically, because Tae Kwon Do was then unheard of and instructors needed money to get started.

A Tae Kwon Do pioneer named Jhoon Rhee knew Kim at the time and told me that Kim was not involved with the martial arts in 1964. "Later, he might have done something, when he went to New York, but when he was in Washington, no. He didn't have any idea about martial arts, he wasn't related to martial arts, and he never mentioned it."[191] This is an important point, because many people have wondered how Kim became involved in Tae Kwon Do. At the time, Rhee was one of the few Korean instructors in Washington and he was leading a wave that would popularize the art; he befriended Bruce Lee, trained national champions, and became known as the "Father of American Tae Kwon Do" in the process. He also befriended Kim, the future leader of Olympic Tae Kwon Do.

Mickey Kim wrote that he had once studied Kong Soo Do — Korean Karate, but he does not look like a martial artist. The best often do not. You can spot a martial artist two blocks away: the way he swaggers or, more likely, the way his body moves with ease, betraying the power in his limbs. On closer inspection, you might notice the hands callused like hills, the forearms knotted with muscles, the lean cheeks, the near-invisible scars. Kim did not look like that; his face was slightly pudgy, his lips big, and eyes piercing. He had the face of a businessman — his scars internal, perhaps.

From 1963 to 1971, Mickey Kim worked on various KCIA operations in the United States and Asia, including, in 1964, working with a group in Washington called the Korean Cultural and Freedom Foundation.[192] The group organized high-profile events and, beginning in 1970, became part of a Korean network to bribe and seduce U.S. Congressmen. Jhoon Rhee had helped to set up the foundation, but he did not know that the KCIA and illegal activity was involved.[193] The Washington embassy had two important missions in those days: receiving U.S. economic and military aid and improving Korea's image.[194] The foundation helped with the image part even after the KCIA infiltrated it and Tae Kwon Do became entangled.

Rhee had helped one of Kim's secret-service colleagues to establish the bizarre foundation on behalf of Reverend Sun-Myung Moon, leader of the Holy Spirit Association for the Unification of World Christianity.[195] Many called the followers of this church "Moonies" and considered the church itself a cult. Moon's followers, however, thought that Moon was the second coming of Jesus Christ and that the foundation would help to further his work. That Kim, Rhee, the KCIA, and Tae Kwon Do became involved is a surreal part of history that deserves attention, because Kim and Rhee would go on to become leaders in global Tae Kwon Do.

Kim's secret-service colleague was Rhee's cousin and Reverend Moon's right-hand man, Pak Bo-Hi, who helped Rhee to open one of the first Tae Kwon Do gyms in the United States — Rhee's Karate Institute in Washington, DC.[196] Both Rhee and Pak were committed to Moon, and they invited Rhee's martial arts students to religious services.[197] Rhee joined the board of trustees of Moon's church and the board for Moon's Radio of Free America, a radio station that broadcast anti-communist propaganda and, unknown to Rhee, raised money for intelligence activities.[198] Rhee denied that he was a secret-service agent and, in fact, had been surprised to learn that Mickey Kim was co-operating with the foundation and the radio station.[199] Rhee was an ardent follower of Moon until 1965 — when he was confronted with the movement's limitations, one of which involved restrictions on marriage. "I married in 1966," he told me. "You know, if I had remained in there, I could not have married; I would have had to wait for their blessings."[200] He began to fade away from the organization, but, as his Tae Kwon Do became successful, he donated hundreds of thousands of dollars to Moon's followers in the 1960s. He finally quit when all hell broke loose among the Moonies, the KCIA, and the American government in the 1970s.

Meanwhile, Mickey Kim, who would soon become president of the Korean Tae Kwon Do Association, was powerful at the South Korean embassy, talented at organizing people and large sums of money for complicated projects. Besides helping with the radio station and the foundation (hosting a meeting at his house for example), he lent a hand with two other Moon initiatives: the Little Angels, a group of Korean children whom people thought were orphans and who travelled the world singing for heads of state; and the Asian Peoples' Anti-Communist League's Freedom Centre, which distributed propaganda about South Korea.[201]

The powerful American celebrities and politicians who lent their names to these Korean projects — supporters such as former presidents Dwight Eisenhower and Harry Truman — did not know that KCIA agents had infiltrated the projects, that Moon was heading them, and that the initiatives were raising money for covert operations.[202]

In spite of the intrigue — or perhaps because of it — Tae Kwon Do continued to do well, and in the mid-1960s Rhee's Karate Institute became the hottest thing since *Seven Samurai*. He had started the institute in 1962 after a martial arts open house, during which he jumped eight feet in the air and broke three wooden boards. Within three months, he had 125 students.[203] There would soon be pioneers like him in Canada, the U.K., Australia, Iran, and in many other countries. Many of the pioneers would be challenged by local martial artists wondering who the new Korean hot shots were.

A Judo instructor challenged Rhee soon after the institute opened. "There were no local Karate or martial arts schools in Washington; I was the first one, except for a Judo school. He came in, and it was very obvious from his body language that he came to embarrass me. In the middle of a class, he walked to the middle of the floor and said, "Let me ask you, if I punched like this, how would you defend yourself?" and I blocked and kicked him as hard as I could. I knocked him to the floor. He immediately surrendered in front of all my students. That brought a lot of publicity — word of mouth — from my students, and he, the Judo instructor himself, sent many people who wanted to learn Karate . . . I was quite good at the time, because I had already taught in Texas for four years, sparring against all these big people, so I had confidence, and he could see that."[204]

Within two years, in 1964, Rhee's first black belt in Washington, Pat Burleson, won Rhee's First National Karate Championship in the United States. Rhee knew powerful people in Washington: the Moon foundation's vice-president sent a note to the South Korean ambassador reminding him of the championship.[205] Rhee's sparring was extremely tough, as if the military mindset had parachuted from Asia to the United States. All the Karate sparring on the open circuit in those days was tough. Burleson, for example, had studied Shotokan Karate in 1957 while stationed with the American military in Japan and was already a strong fighter when he met Rhee and Rhee's star pupil, Allen Steen.[206]

"We got the fundamentals from Rhee, and he improved my kicks 500 per cent," Burleson said. "The Japanese had poor kicks compared to the Koreans. We kicked to hurt: short, sharp kicks." The kicking was the main reason for the Korean art's rising popularity.[207] "We called it Karate," Burleson said. "I coined it 'American Karate,' because Tae Kwon Do was the least known martial art in the United States. Chuck Norris called it Tang Soo Do." Only later would Choi Hong-Hi convince Rhee and others to rename it Tae Kwon Do.

No matter what it was called, the bare-knuckled sparring was tough, with no safety gear except tape around injuries. "It was supposed to be non-contact, but we sent each other to the hospital right and left," Burleson said. He lost most of his teeth in sparring in those years, which was similar to the fights in the mixed martial arts today, minus the ground fighting. "Do you remember the Jean-Claude Van Damme movie *Bloodsport*? The movie was not a true story — a Hollywood lie — but those were the types of matches we had."

Long before the martial arts craze, Rhee, a good businessman, had predicted the high entertainment value of his competitions and had persuaded NBC's *Sports in Action* to cover his second national championship in April 1965, the first tournament to receive national television coverage. In the semi-final, Burleson lost to Mike Stone in what Burleson described as a "grudge fight."[208] "I had beaten his teacher in 1964. It was a tough fight. Afterwards, Mike and I remained good friends." No one was hurt badly, but Stone, who had learned Karate when he was a soldier in the United States, knocked out Burleson with a ridge-hand to the head. NBC's producers, surprised by the aggression, especially the tournament's final, bloody showdown between Stone and Walt Worthy, broadcast only excerpts. Sitting in the audience were the Korean ambassador, the U.S. White House chief of secret police, leaders from the KCIA-infiltrated foundation, and Reverend Sun-Myung Moon himself.[209]

The tough sparring spread across the United States, and despite no-contact rules by schools like Rhee's institute, the wicked matches were a major reason for those martial arts becoming popular among fighters in North America. Burleson and Steen opened gyms, and Rhee's empire grew.

"But the public didn't understand Karate," Burleson added, "not like today, with Tae Kwon Do in every neighbourhood and mixed martial arts around the world. Americans thought it was a mythical, spiritual thing. I can't tell you how many times I was challenged by men walking into my gym to fight. Our shortcoming in those days was that we didn't go into the character-building as much as we should have; we were too busy showing that it worked, and our goal was to make a national champion out of anyone who walked through the door." Burleson's experience was typical in Tae Kwon Do gyms in North America.

Burleson, Steen, Rhee, and others toned down the aggression. "The rules softened in 1969 or 1970, and I moved to California to train with Chuck Norris," Burleson explained. "There, we played the same game but added rules to protect the face. And I went to see Steen and told him that we were all going to jail sooner or later because someone was going to die. We used safety equipment after that, and added a point system."

Rhee introduced sparring equipment after a sparring match in 1970, when a competitor landed a wheel kick on a champion's face, smashing his cheekbone. "The injury made me nervous," Rhee said.[210] He realized that someone was going to get crippled or killed during sparring. In fact, someone did get killed — in the Dominican Republic. The intense sparring motivated Rhee to develop safety gear, and he added a safety-equip-ment factory to his empire, help-ing to end the blood-and-guts era — or, more accurately, helping to send it underground.

Rhee taught future champions Skipper Mullins, Fred Wren, Roy Kurban, and Jeff Smith. Mike Stone was not Jhoon Rhee's stu-dent, but he became a famous fighter, especially after Elvis Presley hired him to teach Karate to his wife, Priscilla, with whom Stone began an affair.[211]

In the 1960s, Chuck Norris sauntered onto the scene, com-bining Korean kicks with Japanese hand techniques, and he was known for his devastating reverse punch. He had learned Korean Karate in the early 1960s while stationed as a soldier in South Korea and befriended Rhee and Bruce Lee in the United

In later years, Choi awarded a ninth-degree black belt to Chuck Norris, making Norris a Tae Kwon Do grandmaster.

Photo courtesy of Choi.

States. Norris won many prestigious U.S. tournaments and appeared in the 1972 Bruce Lee movie *Way of the Dragon*, in a scene that ranks as one of the best in martial arts movie history.

Thanks to Lee, Rhee himself starred in a martial arts movie, *When Tae Kwon Do Strikes* (renamed *Sting of the Dragon Masters*), which was about a Korean rebellion against Japanese rule. The trailer for the movie begins with a thundering narra-tor's voice as a bare-chested Jhoon Rhee kicks, punches, and screams his way through hordes of thugs: "Here comes a unique and devastating force! Tae Kwon Do! A very lethal form of Kung Fu! Jhoon Rhee is called the Father of Tae Kwon Do in America. See why five million people worship this amazing grandmaster!"

This was a fitting introduction for a martial art that was storming into movies and competitions like a tornado. As cham-pions showcased all that was wondrous and dangerous about the first wave of Tae Kwon Do, they did something else, too: they generated money. It was in America where people realized they could apply big-business principles to Tae Kwon Do, which in the late 1970s was becoming as popular as Karate. As the two arts borrowed from each other, Rhee and his champions began affiliated clubs and promoted their gyms as much as Choi Hong-Hi promoted Tae Kwon Do during international demonstrations.

Ironically, Rhee's nationally televised 1965 competition contributed to Americans discovering the truth about the KCIA and Moon's foundation. That year, well-known supporter Robert Roland ordered the foundation to remove his name from the structure of the organization because he could not support a "fanatical pseudo-religious group." Roland wrote that the group "proclaims through its teachings, Divine Principles, that their 'leader' is the fulfillment of the Biblical prophecy concerning the coming of the Messiah . . . To substantiate my position you will find attached excerpts from the official publication of The Holy Spirit Association, *The New Age Frontiers* published in San Francisco. These will show the apparent affiliation of the Korean Cultural Foundation with The Holy Spirit Association and its affiliates; the Karate Institute of Washington, DC, and the 'Little Angels' of Seoul, Korea."[212]

Roland went on to quote Reverend Moon from an April 15, 1965, issue of one of Moon's publications: "Then back to Arlington for a rest and a bite to eat before driving in several cars to the Karate Tournament under the auspices of the Korean Cultural Foundation and the Jhoon Rhee Institute of Karate. About the Karate Tournament: NBC was there and the officials were excited about this new art or sport of Karate, and said they would certainly televise it every year. It will be on a national hook-up May 16."

The president of Moon's foundation, a well-known American general, resigned after receiving Roland's letter, and a mass exodus of high-profile supporters followed.[213] Few Americans wanted to be connected to Moon. Rhee followed the exodus, and, later in life, he would create his own martial arts philosophy to change the world and to help people become humanly perfect, as he put it. He called it the "100-21 Club," which stood for hundred years of wisdom in the body of a twenty-one-year-old.

Meanwhile, Moon's foundation continued to grow well into the 1970s, and Rhee became friends with Olympic Tae Kwon Do's future leader, Kim Un-yong, teaching him how to drive a car in Washington.[214] Those were the good old days, before Kim became heavily involved in the martial arts, before Rhee grew to hate what Kim did to Tae Kwon Do, before they became enemies.

✗ ✗ ✗

Choi Hong-Hi knew about Kim's secret-service background and, in the early days, was not impressed with Reverend Moon and the Unification Church, but Jhoon

Jhoon Rhee and Choi Hong-Hi in the early seventies.

Photo courtesy of Choi.

Rhee was important, and Choi always worked with important people. In 1966, he invited Rhee to help negotiate a merger between Choi's newly created International Taekwon-Do Federation and other martial arts associations in Korea.[215] The merger talks failed, but three years later, Choi helped Rhee and other pioneers in America start a Tae Kwon Do association.[216]

Soon after, Rhee visited Choi's home for dinner and, during the meal, could not believe it when Choi began crunching pheasant bones in a soup.[217] Everything was a battle or a contest for Choi, even eating. He ate things no one else touched: fish heads, roasted grasshoppers, pig's feet and tail, even an entire pig's head half-crushed with hot stones to squeeze out the fat. Choi would eat these "delicacies," as he called them, while his daughters screeched in horror.[218]

During the pheasant dinner, Rhee watched him destroy the bones. "How can you eat that?" he asked, finding the bones nearly impossible to swallow.

"There's nothing to it," Choi replied and continued crunching.

Rhee turned to Choi's wife: "For sure, he is a special person," he said. The former general was five inches shorter than Rhee, who was five-foot-five, but Choi was very tough, Rhee thought.

Choi would one day ask Rhee to replace him as ITF president, and Rhee would politely decline.[219] "Why should I take over a headache?" Rhee said. He had watched the ITF mess up the ranking system, especially in Europe, where Choi had randomly bestowed high black belt ranks.

In the late 1960s, the South Korean president forced Choi to negotiate with other martial artists to unify the various factions —

with the KCIA facilitating — which in Choi's eyes meant interfering. The KCIA interfered with almost every activity in Korea, but Choi did not want anyone to take over the ITF. They took over anyway, as in the wretched poem where a magpie builds a nest only to catch a pigeon hatching an egg in it, Choi thought. He had wanted the president to announce that Tae Kwon Do should follow the techniques being practised in the army or the techniques already well known internationally. Instead, President Park wanted not only the nest — he wanted the eggs, the branch, and the entire tree.

The power balance between the ITF and Korean Tae Kwon Do Association had shifted against Choi. He had never had much support from the president, but now Choi no longer had strong support within the three spheres surrounding the president: the KCIA, the Prime Minister's Office, and the Presidential Security Force at the Blue House, which is what Koreans call the presidential mansion.

In 1968, Pistol Park called Kim Un-yong in the United States with an urgent summons: "The Blue House needs a first-class secretary to handle American issues. Please return immediately." That January, more than thirty North Koreans dressed in South Korean army uniforms had rushed thirty miles from the border to the Blue House, where they came within eight hundred metres of assassinating the president. Two days later, North Koreans seized a nearby American spy ship, the USS *Pueblo*, and the Americans' first reaction was to consider dropping a small nuclear bomb on North Korea.[220] Relations between the three countries had never been worse, and the South Korean president apparently needed Kim's talents and connections in Washington and New York.[221]

But when Kim arrived in Korea, he was assigned to be an adviser to a group of Blue House security personnel who were undergoing special training with the American air force. Kim became disillusioned. "My title was first-class secretary in the Blue House dealing with American affairs," Kim wrote, "but my real mission was to organize security-office members involved with the U.S., and doing interpretation and other protocols. I was not happy with this mission, which was not suited for me."[222] He spent many days in agony, especially after his mother died in 1968. (Moon's foundation in the United States sent a monetary gift to Kim to show its sympathy.)

He began working as director of an academic group but discovered he did not like it. "At that, I was in a deep dilemma," he wrote. "I lost my hope in life and felt mental emptiness and I fought an internal struggle. I started thinking that it is time to leave the public service and start a new career."

However, Kim Un-yong was working with the most powerful men in Korea. He was now assistant to the head of the Presidential Security Force, Pistol Park, who had maintained connections with the Moon foundation and who was helping to organize a massive KCIA mission in the United States.[223] Former intelligence officer Philip Liechty, who served with the American CIA in Korea in the late 1960s, explained the PSF to a journalist this way: "You have to understand what kind of people were recruited to the Presidential Security Force, President Park's personal bodyguard . . . It was a time when there were several carefully planned paramilitary assassination attempts on the president, attempts by teams dispatched from North Korea, and so he surrounded himself with proven killers. The important thing is that the man who protects the president in a country like that has to have demonstrated that he is willing to kill without hesitation for his boss, to do anything the president asked him to do."[224]

Kim was the number-two man in that security force. In 1970, Pistol Park — or perhaps the South Korean president himself — gave the okay for Mickey Kim to take over Tae Kwon Do.[225] Kim said it was an unexpected request and he did not want the job, partly because of the turmoil between Choi and martial arts leaders. "At that time, Tae Kwon Do was embroiled in an internal struggle and the position of president of the Korean Tae Kwon Do Association was vacant," Kim explained. "I was deeply depressed." He had jumped from the position of KCIA agent to presidential security officer to head of a troublesome martial art that needed a lot of money during a time when there was little money to be found in Korea. Nevertheless, Kim, a wealthy, well-connected man, became Tae Kwon Do's new leader, the KTA president.[226]

South Korea's leader told Choi that he should move to an honorary position in Tae Kwon Do and let younger men, such as Kim, take over.[227] Choi did not appreciate that sort of honour, but Kim was powerful within the KTA, along with Uhm Woon-kyu and Lee Chong-woo, the two martial arts leaders who had once called Choi a "permanent troublemaker."

In January 1971, Kim took office, and Uhm became vice-president.[228] Kim accused Choi of allying the ITF with North Korea, but there was no evidence of that back then. "Tae Kwon Do was like a pearl in the mud," Kim wrote. "Depending on how it is led, it will shine or stay in the mud."[229]

It was an odd statement to make, as Choi, Nam, and the pioneers had turned Tae Kwon Do into one of the hottest martial arts on the planet, with membership in the tens of millions. The KTA claimed to have 1.3 million members but acknowledged that Choi's ITF was flourishing: 360 major gyms, most of them ITF, had mushroomed in Seoul from the original nine *kwans* in the 1940s, and the Korean military practised the ITF techniques that Choi and his men had developed in Malaysia.[230] The ITF contained more than thirty national associations and, in the United States, it had become as popular as Japanese Karate and was part of a martial arts craze led by Bruce Lee, Chuck Norris, and Kim Un-yong's friend Jhoon Rhee. Surely, all this was the "pearl" part.

The "mud," perhaps, was in the South Korean dictatorship, despite the extraordinary economic boom there. In 1971, South Korean President Park announced that "Tae Kwon Do" was *Kukki*, which rhymes with "spooky" and means "national sport."[231]

Caught between an angry Choi and a powerful dictator, KTA President Kim did not have an easy job. He said that he felt anguish and he avoided threats from people who warned him to stay away from Tae Kwon Do. Kim later admitted on a television show, "I accepted the position of KTA President because the Korean government told me to correct the way Tae Kwon Do was at that time."[232] He was indirectly saying that he took the job because he had no choice. But Pistol Park and the South Korean president were behind him — and with friends like that, who gave a flying kick what Choi and the ITF threatened?

Kim's primary responsibility was to raise huge amounts of funds for a new Tae Kwon Do Centre and a world championship; he kept his powerful day job as assistant to Security Chief Pistol Park and maintained his KCIA ties to Moon's foundation in the United States, ensuring that the KTA benefited financially on the way. As usual, the connections between all these leaders and groups were convoluted and hidden — not to mention bizarre. It was a state of organization that was a specialty of the omniscient Korean secret service.

In 1970 and 1971, for example, when Kim promised to put together a World Tae Kwon Do Championship in Seoul, Moon's foundation sent cheques to Kim and the Tae Kwon Do association. Naturally, when the story leaked to the media, people wondered why a Moon organization (infiltrated by the KCIA) would give money to Tae Kwon Do. It was an odd financial relationship, and, in later years, the American government would officially look into the matter; U.S. investigator Howard T. Anderson would ask the foundation's head, Pak Bo-Hi, about foundation money flowing to Korean government officials and KCIA operatives, including Mickey Kim.

Investigator Anderson asked about three cheques to Kim ($200 on February 10, 1970; $300 on April 30, 1970; and $300 on June 14, 1971) and a number of other cheques to Kim's Tae Kwon Do association.[233]

Mr. Anderson: Do you recall what these payments were for?

Mr. Pak: I think this was a payment, an assistance to his publication known as the *Korean Observer*.

[Pause]

Mr. Pak: The indication we have here is, scholarship and research. We classified that [as] scholarship and research.

Mr. Anderson: Scholarship and research?

Mr. Pak: Yes, scholarship research, a grant, probably.

Mr. Anderson: To Mickey Kim?

Mr. Pak: Yes.

Mr. Anderson: But he was a Korean government official at that time, was he not?

Mr. Pak: At that time? What was it, 1971? I don't know . . . I remember one or two times we gave a research grant to the *Korean Observer*. This may be granted for that purpose.

Mr. Anderson: There are also — I won't show them to you, but the inspection of some of the records show that there were checks to the Korean Tae Kwon Do Association. Does that have any connection to Mickey Kim?

Mr. Pak: I think so, because he was president of the Korean Tae Kwon Do Association. This is a giant cultural and sports organization, nonprofit, that the Koreans are very proud of, and apparently they had some international event. They needed some funds contributed by various organizations. I think we contributed to that because the same cultural [sic] and field of workers. It is fitting into our purpose of the foundation.

Kim's work with the *Korean Observer* does not appear on his resume. Under his guidance, the KTA moved quickly to contain Choi's Tae Kwon Do. In 1971, South Korea's president announced that 360 martial arts gyms in Seoul needed permits. Most of the gyms were part of the ITF, and the rules for obtaining the permit were so strict that 80 per cent of gyms failed to get it. Afterwards, the South Korean president decreed a new, large tax on businesses, including a tax on gyms.[234] How were Choi and the ITF pioneers to raise money for all these taxes? They probably saw the money grab for what it was: extortion. This was a country where millions in bribes flowed from the three spheres of power into Swiss bank accounts or into a cabinet behind the South Korean president's desk in the Blue House.[235]

While Mickey Kim promised to use the martial art to improve Korea's international image, and Tae Kwon Do became part of the curriculum in Korea's primary and secondary school systems, Kim tapped his connections within the Presidential Security Force to raise a small fortune for a Tae Kwon Do building, the Kukkiwon. He collected 200 million Won, equivalent to more than U.S.$1 million today, and gathered donated building materials. Choi would be no problem, presumably.

For four years, Choi and the ITF had been causing trouble for the Korean Tae Kwon Do Association, but Kim seemed to know something that no one else knew. In December 1971, alluding to the hostility between him and Choi, he told a reporter, "All the major and minor problems and troubles created during the early development of Tae Kwon Do will be resolved through the efforts of people who are quietly looking into the matter."[236]

Chapter 9

AS IF IN A
BRUCE LEE MOVIE

Tae Kwon Do! Those who use it, take command! Those who don't, die!
> – Narrator in the trailer for Jhoon Rhee's 1973
> movie, *When Tae Kwon Do Strikes*

Internationally, the battle between Choi and Kim became more serious in 1971. Kim's organization sent instructors to countries that already had ITF instructors, a direct challenge to Choi. It sent thirty-one-year-old Yoon Kum-joong to open a new gym in Malaysia, for example, where ITF schools had been thriving for years. Within ten months, he was dead, shot in the chest and abdomen in his home.[237] The killer was never found.

The intrigue between Choi and Kim, between their two martial arts, was as secret as it was disturbing. A summary of facts from 1962 to 1971 makes the point:

• **Kim Un-yong (Mickey Kim)** worked with a Moon foundation that was partly staffed and financed by the Korean secret service. The foundation sent money to the Korean Tae Kwon Do Association and to its president, Kim.

• **Choi Hong-Hi,** head of the International Taekwon-Do Federation, accepted $2 million from North Korea, only to reject it at the last minute. Still, he was communicating with North Korean agents, which was punishable by death in South Korea.

• **The Korean** CIA budgeted money for the Korean Athletic

Association to participate in covert missions in the United States. Two of Kim's bosses were leaders of the missions and were involved with the Moon foundation that occasionally sent money to Kim and Tae Kwon Do.

• **Jhoon Rhee,** the father of American Tae Kwon Do, was a friend of Choi and Mickey Kim's, donated to Moon's followers, and sat on the board of Moon's foundation. Rhee's cousin was Moon's right-hand man Pak Bo-Hi and had helped Rhee to set up a martial arts institute in Washington, DC, one of the first Tae Kwon Do schools in the United States. Pak was implicated in a massive KCIA mission in the U.S.

The American government, when it eventually admitted to knowing about the covert mission, dubbed it "the Plan," an operation that resembled the East Berlin Espionage Incident in 1967 — only ten times bigger. The Plan's overall goal was to reverse the United States' decision to drastically reduce American aid and troops in South Korea, and it outlined how to bribe, seduce, and influence more than a hundred members of the U.S. Congress, infiltrate the American Joint Chiefs of Staff, bribe and intimidate American academics and the press, and along the way buy off, harass, and threaten Korean-Americans who criticized the South Korean dictatorship.[238] When U.S. politicians found out about the Plan, they suspected that parts might be illegal, while other parts, such as Moon's attempt to build an M-16 machine-gun factory, were worrisome.

The situation unnerved Choi and his pioneers. As I list their adversaries in the early 1970s — Kim Un-yong, the KCIA, and the other special Ks — I marvel at Choi's ego and his limitless desire to control global Tae Kwon Do. His ITF was thriving, but Choi had entered a game that promised to annihilate him.

The game began in the autumn of 1970, when South Korea's president held meetings in the Blue House to co-ordinate the Plan. It had probably begun long before that, but that year the president assigned responsibilities for the mission to Pistol Park, Kim Un-yong's boss.[239] The mastermind behind the Plan in the United States and Canada was KCIA agent Yang Doo-wan, who had moved from West Germany to Washington, where he was now KCIA Station Chief. Yang had been in charge of the East Berlin Incident in

Germany in 1967 and now oversaw all KCIA activities in the United States. His alias was still "Lee Sang-ho," and he was a close acquaintance of people in the KCIA-infiltrated Moon foundation.[240]

I assume that Yang imported many of his best agents and martial artists to do the KCIA's dirty work, just as he had in Germany. A British journalist, Andrew Jennings, quoted a former American CIA officer, Philip Liechty, regarding allegations that "the Korean CIA used taekwondo schools as bases for operations and cover for its overseas officers, particularly here in the U.S. There was a period when some of these people were allegedly involved in kidnapping and covertly removing Korean students, protestors against the Park regime, from the U.S. back to Korea."[241]

The Plan contained nine points, the ninth of which was "To intimidate 'uncooperative' Korean residents in the United States through their families, relatives, and close friends in Korea."[242] In the 1970s, KCIA collaborators seemed to be watching everyone in Korea — such was the KCIA's aura of omniscience — and families survived by not talking to anyone, including their own families, about anything.[243] The KCIA exported this attitude to North America: in the Plan, under the heading "Operations Relating to Korean Residents," the KCIA targeted the "U.S. Branch of the Korean Athletic Association" because the branch was an "Anti-Communist Organization."[244] Korea's secret service had become adept at staffing, financing, and controlling large Korean organizations, such as the KAA.

This was the same KAA that contained Kim Un-yong's Korean Tae Kwon Do Association, the KAA that Choi had avoided when he began the International Taekwon-Do Federation in 1966. The Plan provided details for South Korea's diplomats and secret-service agents about what to do with the KAA: they should formulate "an organizational network of anti-communist fronts" that involved an unnamed, ex-marine association based in Los Angeles and eighty collaborators in five U.S. cities.

For years, General Choi had been warning about such activities and now it was too late. Between 1970 and 1976, the Korean secret service budgeted $50 a month to ten KAA collaborators each in San Francisco and Chicago, and twenty each in Los Angeles, Washington, and New York City.[245] As in the 1967 kidnappings in West Germany, KCIA agents and collaborators, including Tae Kwon Do instructors, would threaten Korean-Americans who criticized the South Korean regime or would "invite" them to visit Korea.

By 1973, American officials were hearing complaints from terrified Korean-Americans. Agents were ordering people to stop criticizing South Korea, were threatening them on the phone at night, and were spreading rumours about family and friends interrogated in South Korea.[246] An editor of a Korean-American newspaper, someone known to be against the regime, was on his way to give a public speech when he was kidnapped.[247] A professor committed suicide in South Korea during KCIA interrogations.[248] As the years went on, the reports became worse: anonymous phone callers threatened to kill children in the United States and Korea, and family members were tortured and imprisoned in South Korea because they were related to the regime's critics in the United States.[249] At first, the American CIA and FBI largely ignored the complaints — Korea was a U.S. ally during the still-raging Vietnam War — but a small number of American politicians in Washington and Seoul, including the U.S. ambassador in South Korea, were appalled.

Korean-Americans turned to them for help, and they relied for information on courageous publishers, such as Song Sun-keun, a newspaperman who published the *Korea Journal*, a small community paper in San Francisco. Song was a friend of Kim Dae-jung, the democrat who had nearly defeated the South Korean dictator in a presidential vote in 1971 (in spite of a manipulated election). Song and his newspaper had been criticizing dictator Park Chung-hee for more than a year when KCIA agents tried to buy out his paper. Song refused. KCIA operatives then forced Korean-American advertisers to stop advertising in the *Korea Journal*, thereby draining the paper of its revenue. Song kept the paper going anyway, a voice of dissent during a time when journalists were bribed or threatened into supporting the dictatorship.[250]

Then, on a Tuesday in 1974, Song received a phone call: "You will be killed Sunday," said a sinister voice in Korean. The caller claimed to be a reader of the *Korea Journal* and accused Song of being a communist.

"You don't read my paper," Song replied. "We are strongly against Communism, just as we are against Park's dictatorship."

The caller hung up, but Song had recognized the voice based on the man's accent from a southern province of South Korea; the man was both the Consul for the San Francisco area and a KCIA agent.[251] Song had received past death threats but he did not often report them to the police, because he believed that "You will be killed" in Korean was sometimes not as serious as in English. He did report this threat to the police, though — and to the FBI, which responded with a few light interviews of suspects.

The Consul did not kill the journalist, but the KCIA tormented Song with death threats and scared advertisers until Song ran out of money. He published a story in which he described the threat, and he named the Consul as the culprit, which meant that the political conflict became a personal vendetta. Soon after, Song discovered that the KCIA planned to send a thug from Los Angeles to run him over with a car, but the car never arrived, and Song's articles became more critical than before.

In 1976, one of Song's friends overheard the Korean Consul arrange for a Seattle-area martial arts master to kill Song by running him over with a car. The friend also overheard a martial arts instructor discuss a plan to kidnap Song and take him back to Korea. That year, Song said that the Consul himself attempted to ram him with a car and the journalist moved out of the way just in time.[252]

If these situations had not been so terrifying, they would be farcical, like a series of scenes from *Kill Bill*, but this was reality and Song, worn out and broke, gave up publishing. I find the story unnerving, not only because it obliterated everything good for which my martial art stood, but because it was typical of what was happening in those days. It was one of the few stories that was publicized.

Relentless KCIA campaigns, such as the one against Song, kept many Koreans silent and fearful around the world throughout the 1970s, but not Choi Hong-Hi. True, Choi had once used the KCIA to help Tae Kwon Do, but the crucial difference was that he put Tae Kwon Do first and South Korea second. For him, the KCIA had been a tool to expand and protect his martial art. For his enemies, the country came first and the martial art second; Tae Kwon Do was a tool of the state.

Few people believed Choi's warnings about the regime, calling him paranoid, jealous, and a troublemaker. From a martial arts perspective, one of the most disturbing parts of the Plan and the investigation that followed was that the names Kim Un-yong (KTA president) and his boss, Pistol Park (chief of the Presidential Security Force), kept strolling into the oddest places. Pistol Park, a martial artist in Judo and Hapkido, was one of the most powerful men in the dictatorship and headed many illegal activities that raised money for covert activities:

– In 1970, he convinced the South Korean president to sign 60,000 fund-raising letters for a bogus charity in the United States.

– In 1971, he stole $200,000 from a KCIA operative who was supposed to use the money to bribe U.S. Congressmen.

– In 1973, he and his brother, who was president of a South Korean university, were part of a plan to buy off and pressure American academics.

– In 1974, one of his aides handed an envelope stuffed with $10,000 in cash to John E. Nidecker, special adviser to Richard Nixon, one of many bribe attempts from Pistol Park to Nidecker.[253]

Did Kim Un-yong know about these transgressions? I do not know, but while he led the Korean Tae Kwon Do Association in 1971, he was part of an effort to collect donations from American companies for a South Korean election that year. The KCIA wanted $100,000 to $150,000 from Colt Industries, maker of the M-16 machine gun, and Kim Un-yong was the man to get it. In the mid-1960s, while he had been a KCIA officer, Kim had set up an important meeting between a Colt official and the South Korean president, who had wanted to build a gun factory in Korea.[254] In 1971, acting for Pistol Park, Kim asked Colt Industries for a campaign contribution for the election in a few months.[255] At the time, in South Korea, Kim was raising 200 million Won (more than U.S.$1 million today) for the Kukkiwon, a majestic Tae Kwon Do centre in Seoul.

Colt officials authorized a cheque for $100,000, payable to Kim Un-yong, but on the advice of lawyers withdrew it because they discovered that such donations were illegal in South Korea. Still, the KCIA deftly raised at least $8.5 million in "loans," "pre-paid fees," and "commissions" from American firms, which were all sent to President Park Chung-hee for his dubious 1971 election.[256] The dictator defeated his rival, Kim Dae-jung, by a small margin, and, later, a U.S. Congressional report would conclude: "Given the fact that Kim Dae-jung lost the 1971 presidential election by less than 8 per cent of the vote . . . the possibility exists the $8.5 million, when co-mingled with funds from other [American] sources, accounted for the difference in votes . . ." Following the election, the South Korean president announced an emergency decree; for the average Korean, the consequences of this "emergency" and all the "fees" and "loans" was the most politically repressive period under the South Korean dictator.

The KCIA not only required huge amounts of cash and man-power, but it also needed poison. The KCIA Station Chief in Washington smuggled much of the illegal money in and out of the United States in Korea's diplomatic pouch.[257] American intelligence once discovered a secret shopping list from the pouch, a list that included "electronic surveillance equipment" and "poison," which the regime needed in South Korea.[258] Choi Hong-Hi had heard that a preferred method of murdering political opponents was to poison their liquor during social engagements.[259] Since hearing that, he had always checked his drinks at the *kisaeng* houses; often, a rival would drink first to show that the liquor was not spiked.

In 1971, Choi must have known how insane things were getting with the KCIA and Tae Kwon Do, for he still had many connections within the secret service. He knew the two instructors who had been involved in the 1967 kidnappings, and he continued working with Jhoon Rhee, who was a friend of Kim Un-yong's.

At the same time, a martial arts movie craze was sweeping the world. In 1971, the movie *Billy Jack* contained Karate and Hapkido sequences and soon became a hit, followed by *Red Sun*, starring Charles Bronson and Japanese acting legend Toshiro Mifune. Then Bruce Lee, who learned a lead-leg side kick from Jhoon Rhee, released *The Big Boss* in 1971, *Fist of Fury* and *Way of the Dragon* in 1972, and *Enter the Dragon* in 1973, all of which turned him into a household name in Asia and the West.[260]

The show I remember, however, is the television hit *Kung Fu*, starring David Carradine, which merged marital arts mayhem with Eastern philosophy in the American Wild West. A recurring theme for Carradine's character (called "Grasshopper" by his blind teacher, Master Po) involved maintaining a just and peaceful atti-tude amid violence, crime, and people who regularly insulted him.

Tae Kwon Do's pioneers faced the same dilemmas but with no

commercial breaks. In South Korea, the secret police were more powerful than the Prime Minister's Office, and, in North America, Korea's ambassadors reported to the KCIA's station chiefs. Choi could barely keep up, but never scared of a fight, he concluded that, as usual, he should take matters into his own hands. In 1972, two KCIA men, former subordinates of Choi's, visited him at home for a friendly chat.[261] At first, Choi treated them like friends, complaining that the South Korean president was abusing the situation in Tae Kwon Do by pitting Mickey Kim's organization against Choi's. The two agents agreed with Choi and, in that moment, he suddenly remembered a passage from Han Fei, a philosopher in the third century BCE: "Watch for the enemy within your group."

One of the men, a former KCIA branch director, patted Choi on the back and said, "Sir, wouldn't it be better for you to do your best from abroad, considering the current situation?"

"Never!" said Choi, realizing that they were fishing for information. "Why would I live abroad? I need to straighten what is going on in the field of Tae Kwon Do." With that statement, the KCIA relaxed its surveillance of Choi — and within a week, he and his right-hand man, Nam Tae-hi, fled the country on a plane to Canada.

Chapter 10

THE EXILES

The fifth element that is essential for the Tae Kwon Doist is accuracy in throwing kicks and blows. In a time of crisis you get one chance. If you miss, you cannot step back . . .

– Duk-Sung Son, founding member of Tae Kwon Do[262]

Choi and Nam transferred the headquarters of their Tae Kwon Do organization to Toronto, Ontario, but Choi left behind his family and arrived in Canada with no money, no reputation, and no power. Why Canada? It was located between Europe and South America, where Choi wanted Tae Kwon Do to expand; Jong-Soo Park, one of his best pioneers, lived here and ran a growing network of gyms that were generating world champions in sparring. But more importantly, Canada was a relatively neutral country politically: a Canadian passport would give him access to both communist and non-communist countries. Choi had well-hidden hopes to introduce Tae Kwon Do to communist nations.

But adapting to a culture where Money meant more than Position — and Honour had a low exchange rate — was a fall for a man who had once led 100,000 soldiers. He had told people that he used two names: one was "Choi Hong-Hi," given by his father, and the other, "Tae Kwon Do," given by heaven — but how could he become immortal in a Canadian suburb, a cultural wasteland by his standards (and not a *kisaeng* house in sight)?

His martial art saved him once again. On the way to Canada, he and Nam had stopped in Hong Kong to pick up Choi's newly published Tae Kwon Do book — yet another book — which contained

518 pages of old and new techniques. It featured Nam Tae-hi and Jong-Soo Park on the cover and finally proved that Choi and his men had developed techniques that were different from Karate. An example of Choi's obsessive detailing was "Finger Belly," which referred to the inside part of one's hand, between the palm and the fingertips, used to support a back fist in certain strikes. He had plucked the name "Finger Belly" from a dream.[263]

A more dramatic addition was Choi's section about T'aekkyŏn, an innovation that distinguished Tae Kwon Do from Karate. He had continued claiming that Tae Kwon Do rested on Korea's ancient art of T'aekkyŏn, a lie repeated so many times by so many people that most believed that Tae Kwon Do was thousands of years old. It was only natural that Choi finally got around to adding T'aekkyŏn techniques to Tae Kwon Do. He entitled them "Foot Technique Sparring" (*Jokgi Daeryon*) in the 1972 book, and, in later books, simply "Foot Sparring" (*Bal Matsogi*). Most of the T'aekkyŏn techniques required extraordinary leg agility and power. One of the easier moves involved a defender kicking the ankle of an attacking leg in mid-air and immediately kicking the attacker's head with the same leg, a one-two move that forces the leg to be as fast as a punch.[264] Choi's T'aekkyŏn techniques mimicked those from ancient times, promoting dodges and circular attacks, which was completely unlike Karate's linear strikes, blocks, and counter-attacks.[265]

Even though Nam Tae-hi dominated the cover of Choi's book and the martial art, the two men were drifting apart. Nam did not know anyone in Toronto — and perhaps he had become disgruntled with Choi's cantankerous ways — but Nam's former star assistant, Han Cha-gyo, was running a successful gym in Chicago, and Nam and Han began a new martial arts organization, the U.S. Taekwon-Do Federation.[266]

In moving to North America, Choi and Nam had landed in the heart of the KCIA's Plan to bribe U.S. Congressmen and threaten Korean-Americans. Choi had heard stories about the KCIA harassing his ITF instructors in North America and their families in Korea. After the KCIA transferred one of its agents from Washington to Toronto in order to heavily pressure the Korean Consulate to take "action" against activists, the Korean Consul applied for refugee status.[267] Years later, a colonel would tell Choi that that same Consul had directed Jong-Soo Park, Choi's disciple, to kidnap Choi before the Consul applied for refugee status.[268] Park denied the charge.

Accusations such as these festered in Choi for years, as did the one about Korea's ambassador to France, Lee Soo-young, who had helped Choi to send instructors to France and worked with him to promote Tae Kwon Do. Two months later, the KCIA suicided Lee.[269]

✘ ✘ ✘

Choi was not the only Korean who fled his homeland. Also in exile was Kim Dae-jung, the democrat who likely would have beaten President Park Chung-hee in the 1971 South Korean election if the election had been fair.[270] Park was overseeing one of the hottest economies and most brutal regimes in the world, and he began a new wave of repression, partly because of Kim Dae-jung's mass support in 1971.[271] Travelling around the world, Kim denounced the dictatorship and become a hero. Koreans love their philosopher-kings, and Kim embodied Korea's resistance to decades of military dictatorship.[272] Moreover, this Confucian gentleman was toughened by years of harassment and he courageously stood for all those Koreans who had never wanted to collaborate with dictators and thugs.

In 1973, President Park found Kim's overseas activities intolerable. Kim was to begin a fellowship at Harvard University in the United States, where he regularly visited high-level American officials. Part of the KCIA Plan was to follow him everywhere he went — anywhere in the world.[273] In South Korea in 1971, Kim had survived a house bombing and he had been severely wounded when a truck almost ran over him.[274] Now, in 1973, the KCIA was looking for an opportunity to quietly kidnap and kill him.

Tae Kwon Do black belts became involved whether they knew about the Plan or not. One of the few episodes that landed in the local media occurred in 1973 as Kim Dae-jung prepared to speak in San Francisco about his three-stage idea to reunite North and South Korea. The South Korean Consul in San Francisco directed the Plan in the area, overseen by a KCIA chief in Washington.

The Organization of Korean Studies in Berkeley, California, had booked Kim to speak in a hall in the International Student Centre at 7:30 on the evening of May 18, 1973.[275] The hall was extremely tense, mainly because a dozen dubious characters wandered in and out of the lobby. Who were they? The KCIA chief, Yang Doo-wan, knew. He had sent a KCIA operative, Bae Young-shik, from Los Angeles to the San Francisco hall. Bae was both vice-consul of the Korean Consulate in L.A. and a KCIA agent. (As in the case of Kim Un-yong, it was normal practice for South Korea to secretly assign KCIA agents to government positions overseas.) KCIA Chief Yang himself was not in the hall, but he directed the operation from the Hilton Hotel, where he was staying — the same hotel where Kim Dae-jung had checked in.

A Korean journalist and family friend of Kim Dae-jung, Song Sun-keun, was in the Berkeley hall and later wrote an article in the *Korea Journal* about the events that followed. He noted that ten martial artists were in the room.[276] At 8 p.m., a security guard was keeping an eye on them as they stood in front of the hall and discouraged people from entering. The guard followed them upstairs, where he confiscated a large shopping bag that contained ten ketchup bottles and a dozen eggs, and returned downstairs to hand the bag to the event's director. The master of ceremonies stood at the podium and held the ketchup and eggs before the audience. "Someone with these things tried to disrupt our orderly meeting tonight," he said. The audience booed.

They livened up when Kim Dae-jung entered the hall, accompanied by four bodyguards. Also in the hall was a Tae Kwon Do instructor, Rhee Min-hi, who had trained in Kong Soo Do at the Jidokwan, one of the nine important gyms in South Korea. Rhee was a powerful man in the San Francisco area, especially after South Korea awarded him with one of its highest medals for his services in the Korean community in the United States in the early 1970s. In San Francisco, he oversaw a martial arts gym on Polk Street, ran a travel agency, and was head of a broadcasters' association. Some people suspected that he was a KCIA operative, but Rhee denied it. However, he did not like Kim Dae-jung's criticism of Korea and he hated Kim's proposal of reuniting North and South, an idea that smacked of communism. Also, Kim had been claiming that the South Korean government was out to assassinate him — a ridiculous allegation, in Rhee's view, because if Korea had wanted to kill Kim, then why had it allowed him to leave South Korea?

Rhee did not know that there were ten other martial artists in the hall. He installed himself at the back while Kim Dae-jung walked up to the microphone and the crowd clapped heartily. As Kim began speaking, Rhee interrupted him.

"Why do you criticize the head of our nation?" Rhee yelled, marching to the front. "You should fight in Korea! Don't stir up good compatriots here!" Rhee did not want Kim to say negative things about Korea, and he climbed onto the stage, making it to the podium. Bodyguards rushed at Rhee and pushed him away, and the hall erupted into yells.

Scarier than the melee was the fact that there was a man taking photos and filming the audience with a camera. People knew that KCIA agents in the United States routinely filmed controversial public events. Agents would note the names of Korean audience members and mail the lists and the film to Seoul, where the KCIA would threaten families of those who had been at the events.[277] The man taking photos in the hall was a KCIA agent.

The master of ceremonies, who was near Kim, pointed at Rhee and said, "Whoever this man may be, he is definitely disrupting our meeting, which is being conducted in a democratic manner. Therefore, all those who are in favour of dismissing him from this room, may you please clap your hands." The audience cheered and clapped.

"All those who don't wish to hear this speech, follow me," Rhee suddenly announced. No one rose, and Rhee once again dashed at Kim near the podium.

"Please be excused," Kim told him. Rhee stood there.

"Get lost!" yelled someone from the audience.

At that point, San Francisco police officers with guns and clubs entered the hall and arrested Rhee. While police escorted him out, Bae Young-shik, the KCIA agent from Los Angeles, walked up to police officers and flashed an identity card: "I am an official of the Korean government," he told them. "This is a Korean meeting. We will manage our own affairs." The police ignored him.

As police drove Rhee away, he explained that he was simply expressing his opinions to Kim. In South Korea, communists were not liked, Rhee explained, and people could not walk around holding a North Korean flag. Police advised Rhee not to return to the meeting, and they released him.

Meanwhile, one of Bae's compatriots was on the phone to KCIA Chief Yang at the Hilton, telling him what was happening. This level of organization was impressive, and I am guessing that Yang quickly updated someone in Seoul. Viewed from a vantage point from outer space somewhere between San Francisco and Seoul, the scene looked like this: as martial artists harassed Kim Dae-jung and police arrested Rhee, an agent was simultaneously reporting the blow-by-blow to Yang at the Hilton, who, in turn, reported to Seoul. Why such organization? Because the South Korean government wanted to silence Kim, and the KCIA was looking for an opportune time to kidnap him.

Back in the hall, Kim continued his speech, explaining that the unfortunate incident with Rhee had taken place as if everyone in the hall lived in South Korea. They had just witnessed the kind of politics that was typical in Korea, he said. "This incident tonight, however unfortunate, can prove a point I've been making all along" — that political disagreement should not degrade into physical conflict and terror, he explained.

A year and a half later, in 1974, when FBI agents finally got around to speaking to Rhee Min-hi about the incident, he admitted to disrupting the speech but denied being a KCIA agent — and claimed that the KCIA had never approached him.

More than thirty years later, I Googled Rhee and discovered that his sons, Simon and Phillip Rhee, had become martial arts movie stars, known for *The Best of the Best* movie series from 1989 to 1998. Their father, Rhee Min-hi, had advised them on the films, which featured Tae Kwon Do techniques. Simon Rhee told me that the brothers had never been involved in their father's political work, and that the Rhee-Kim confrontation ended up in a thirty-second spot in a well known Korean television series, *Hourglass*, in which an actor playing his father confronts Kim.[278]

"I later apologized to Mr. Kim," Rhee Min-hi told me on the telephone. "I said I wasn't against him as a person, but I didn't like his policies." Rhee added that only after the 1973 confrontation did he learn that Korean consulate members and KCIA agents had attended the talk in the hall. Three people reported to the FBI that Rhee had probably been a KCIA agent, but Rhee told Kim that the rumours had been wrong — the KCIA had never ordered Rhee to confront Kim.[279]

"I was maligned for so many years," Rhee lamented. A couple of years ago, he and Song Sun-keun, the journalist who had written about the Rhee–Kim confrontation, met at a party in Seoul, and they patched up, Rhee said. And Rhee met Kim Dae-jung many times, too, both men working out their past differences. One day in 1998, Rhee stood at a podium beside Kim — this time as an invited VIP — in spite of the whispered gossip.

✗ ✗ ✗

The KCIA failed to stop Kim Dae-jung in the United States in 1973, but agents constantly shadowed him, looking for the right place and time.[280] Koreans in North American cities felt like they were living in surreal South Koreas, with consulates, not the U.S. government, running communities, and KCIA agents, not American police, enforcing laws. But kidnapping Kim in the United States became less feasible as American intelligence services increased their vigilance. For years, the Americans had been tracking the KCIA, and they were becoming more annoyed with its boldness and blunders on U.S. soil.[281] Most American intelligence leaders and government officials did not seem concerned that the KCIA was harassing and threatening Korean-Americans, but a high-octane kidnapping of Kim Dae-jung involving martial artists would lead to bad publicity for American policies in Asia, where American leaders needed the Koreans on-side in the Vietnam and Cold wars. In the early 1970s, the Americans were constantly telling the KCIA and South Korean government to control themselves in the United States and get their agents in order, especially the collaborators who were not officially listed as KCIA agents but acted like they were. In short, the KCIA would have to kidnap their man in another country.[282]

The KCIA finalized that plan in July 1973, and picked Tokyo, Japan, as the place. One of Kim Dae-jung's people would later tell the FBI that, just before the kidnapping, Rhee Min-hi flew out of San Francisco to Asia.[283] But Rhee laughed when I asked him if he had flown to Tokyo for this mission. "I never knew about a KCIA plan to kidnap Kim Dae-jung," he said. "It's all nonsense."

The FBI heard that an assistant instructor at a martial arts school and a martial artist from the Wha Rang Karate Institute flew out of San Francisco just before the kidnapping. In addition, KCIA operatives flew from the U.S.: one from San Francisco, two from New York City, and two or three who accompanied KCIA Washington Chief Yang to Tokyo. Twenty-four KCIA personnel were on the kidnapping team — from South Korea, Japan, and the United States — all of them coordinated by the sixth branch of the

Kim Dae-jung and Rhee Min-hi in 1998,
25 years after their famous confrontation.

Photo courtesy of Rhee.

KCIA, the one in charge of assassinations.[284]

On August 8, Kim Dae-jung was staying at Tokyo's Grand Palace Hotel, which was spiked with KCIA agents. After lunch with a Korean official, who turned out to be part of the plot, Kim stepped out of his hotel room and agents grabbed, drugged, and stuffed him into a car trunk and raced to Osaka. An uproar immediately followed in Japan, where police, who had been tipped off about the plot, had been following KCIA agents in the days before the kidnapping.

The day after the abduction, agents transferred Kim to a high-speed boat that zipped at thirty-five knots back to South Korea. During the explosive international reaction, the Seoul station chief for the American CIA told the American ambassador of South Korea that the KCIA was behind the kidnapping. The ambassador jumped into a car, drove to the Blue House, and demanded that South Korea's president release Kim.[285] On the boat, agents tied down Kim with weights and were preparing to throw him into the Sea of Japan, when aircraft buzzed overhead with a message to release him. A couple of days later, the KCIA let him go in Seoul, only to deposit him in prison the following week. The fiasco refused to die down, however, especially after Japan downplayed the operation and South Korea denied that the KCIA was involved.

✗ ✗ ✗

In 1974, the Americans had had enough of the James Bond scenes. The FBI, the U.S. Department of Justice, and the American CIA, which had been tracking KCIA agents and had supposedly bugged the South Korean president's meeting room in Seoul, thought that the Plan was a nuisance from the day it started. Koreans who were neither diplomats nor KCIA agents were handing cash to baffled U.S. Congressmen, assigning agents to infiltrate the U.S. government, and offering women to politicians. Meanwhile, rogue martial artists jumped in and out of various surreal and scary scenes. Some U.S. politicians accepted the bribes and the stories began crawling through the newspapers. For American intelligence leaders, the entire operation had grown embarrassing, but to honest Tae Kwon Do instructors and other Koreans around the world who knew about the threats, kidnappings, and torture, the whole thing was more than unjust; it was terrifying. It did not help to hear that the American CIA was busy training torturers in Chile, Brazil, Uruguay, and Argentina.[286]

Still, the Americans quietly kicked KCIA Station Chief Yang Doo-wan out of the country in 1974, because the U.S. State Department considered him responsible for the harassment in the United States, and he and his Plan had become an embarrassment.[287] Back in Seoul, the South Korean president immediately promoted Yang, who continued overseeing the Plan. Officially, the KCIA reduced its operations in the United States, but, covertly, it expanded the Plan. This meant that day-to-day nondiplomatic persons had more work to do; the KCIA became nearly invisible but it continued threatening Koreans in North America.

Choi Hong-Hi was talking himself hoarse warning people about South Korea.[288] He said that the South Korean government was harassing his martial arts pioneers, and he became more worried about his own life. Many thought he was exaggerating, but he knew the truth. Newspaper stories about tortures in basements and calls at night were intimate, individual reminders of the larger repression in South Korea and in other American CIA–backed dictatorships.

Choi and Nam Tae-hi knew the game; after all, they had once worked with Korean and American intelligence leaders.

One day, when Choi was organizing a tour of Europe and the Middle East — and planning to get on a plane the next day — a Tae Kwon Do instructor called to say that he had flown from South Korea to the United States with a message. "In Korea, I was able to sense that they are planning some scheme against you," he told Choi. "As you know, they kidnapped the opposition leader, Kim Dae-jung. They would not leave you alone. I am calling because I care about you, so please consider and delay your schedule instead of leaving tomorrow."

Choi knew the instructor, and, as usual, had to determine quickly whether he was a friend or foe. He suspected that Kim Un-yong's organization had sent him with the message, which Choi interpreted as a threat.

"Thank you very much for flying thousands of miles to tell me about the scheme," Choi replied. "But I would not stop or even change our plan."

The next day, Choi got on a plane, along with his demonstration team of Jong-Soo Park, C. K. Choi, Kong Young-il, Pak Sun-jae, and Rhee Ki-ha. They were all seventh-degree masters, beginning a 1973 world tour. It was unlikely anyone would mess with them, but they were only five men. What Choi had not told the Korean caller was that he had some muscle behind this tour. Thanks to an American CIA agent, Robert Walson, who was a high-ranking black belt, the CIA was financing the tour, because Choi's International Taekwon-Do Federation desperately needed money. Choi had also avoided mentioning that the American CIA had sent agents to provide protection for the team at overseas airports.[289]

In this context, Choi began new Tae Kwon Do branches in five countries. In Egypt, more than 100,000 people watched the ITF team's demonstration.

Chapter 11

From Spooky *Kukki* to WTF

Tae Kwon Do is not just for self defence (hoshinsul) but must also be used to straighten up humanity, as well as set discipline for an upright and honest society.

– Kim Un-yong (a.k.a. Mickey Kim)

I now know that whenever a martial artist becomes a history expert, it is time to reach for the Scotch. From the beginning, Tae Kwon Do has had high ideals and fought violence with violence (and sometimes fought justice with violence, too), but the history of the martial art has always hidden the painful truths about this violence. Millions of people, including Koreans, do not realize that the tall tale about Tae Kwon Do being an ancient martial art is more than a neat story: the creation myth sells the meditation while hiding the brutality, points to heaven and ignores the blood. In the 1950s and 1960s, Tae Kwon Do needed ancient mumbo-jumbo to hide its Karate roots and, in the 1970s, it needed ancient, invisible warriors to promote a wicked regime.

Choi's myth about 1,500-year-old dynasties and *hwarang* warriors had a deep and practical purpose in the early 1970s: the sketchy "historical research" that embedded Tae Kwon Do in Korea's old culture grew into a legend as hardy as an ancient gingko. It came as no surprise, then, that the Korean Overseas Information Service published a booklet, *Taekwondo*, which opened with: "Taekwondo is a martial art unique to Korea developed about 2,000 years ago."[290] But the nation borrowed more than Choi's creation myth. To his amazement, it stole the name of his martial art, Tae Kwon Do, and it assigned Kim Un-yong to merge the nine martial-arts gyms (*kwans*).

Kim believed that the *kwans* had been monkish in their isolation, medieval in their segregation, and simply vicious during tournaments. Uniting them and raising money for a world Tae Kwon Do headquarters, the Kukkiwon, were Kim's most important projects. In fact, political and martial arts leaders chose him as KTA leader in 1970 partly because they thought that he could raise huge amounts of money.[291]

At Kim's first press conference, a journalist asked him if he would indeed build the Kukkiwon as promised.

"Yes," Kim replied.

"How much will it cost?" the journalist asked.

Kim froze, because he did not know. He knew that he wanted a Kukkiwon and, coming from a rich family, he had thought "where there is a will, there is a way." He turned and whispered to Lee Chong-woo, a martial arts leader who sat nearby.

"Say that 300 million Won will do," Lee whispered back. In those days, that was an enormous sum, equivalent to U.S.$1.5 million today.

"I think we need no more than 200 million Won," Kim said, not wanting to alarm people with the larger number. Korean newspapers reported the amount.

Kim wanted the Kukkiwon built in the old style, "to give the impression of tradition, like the Korean Palaces, for instance, or the magnificent homes of the Confucian high officials," he said. For the roof, he chose a traditional Korean tile: the blue *kiwa*, the same type of *kiwa* on the Blue House, the country's presidential mansion. In the old days, the making of blue *kiwa* was a respected, secret art, passed from father to son. There is a saying in Korea: "He is as secretive as a *kiwa* merchant."

Kim could not find land in Seoul for the Kukkiwon, so he approached a friend, the mayor of Seoul, who offered him a flat patch.

"I need the highest ground in Yoksam-dong," Kim countered.

"You can have lower ground," the mayor insisted. "I don't understand why you need a place on the top of the mountain."

"This martial arts gym will have a monumental meaning," Kim said. "I also have a feeling that a Tae Kwon Do miracle might occur if we build it at the summit."

Kim received his mountaintop miracle, and construction began in November 1971, "financed with my personal property," Kim wrote, "and donations from my acquaintances — large companies like Samsung."

One year later, the Kukkiwon was inaugurated by Kim Chŏng-p'il, Kim Un-yong's former KCIA boss, who was now Prime Minister of the country.[292] The beautiful, three-storey building rested on a two-acre lot and contained studios, an auditorium, a dormitory, a recreation room, and the distinct aura of ancient history around its blue *kiwa* roof. The Kukkiwon would unite rival martial arts factions by forcing them to conduct black belt promotions and Tae Kwon Do business in the Kukkiwon itself.[293] The building would be more market than monastery.

Many martial arts leaders refused to unite, but they soon had no choice. With the iron support of the Korean regime, Kim transformed part of the Korean Tae Kwon Do Association into the World Taekwondo Federation, which sounded nearly identical to Choi's International Taekwon-Do Federation.[294] Also, the acronym "WTF" sounded like "ITF" in English. Choi, in a rage, warned them not to use the term "Tae Kwon Do," but everyone ignored him and South Korea severed all ties to the ITF in Canada.[295] The war between Choi and Kim entered a new phase.

The timing of the WTF's birth seemed inauspicious — it was created between the month of May (when the KCIA targeted Kim Dae-jung in the United States) and the month of August (when the agency stuffed him into a car trunk in Japan) — but creating a global Tae Kwon Do group was a smart move for the dictatorship, which needed Tae Kwon Do to improve the nation's image overseas. At the time, South Korea was running an economic powerhouse, generating self-confidence along with self-reliance. This was an achievement for a tiny nation that had been overshadowed by Japan and China for much of its modern history. Promoting Tae Kwon Do was a physical manifestation of Korea's confidence. Kim Un-yong wrote: "By practicing Tae Kwon Do, one can build up the spirit of self denial and perseverance, gaining confidence in tackling whatever difficulties one may face, a mental attitude which leads to composure and generosity. In other words, a Tae Kwon Do man knows how to be modest . . ."[296]

After the Kukkiwon was constructed and the WTF launched, Kim focused on another impossible and modest goal: globalizing the new brand of Tae Kwon Do.[297] But Choi had already globalized it and the ITF had skyrocketed in popularity, so Choi was appalled at the irredeemable bluntness of Kim's campaign. Choi worried that people around the world would confuse his Tae Kwon Do with the new one: "Wild panic grass, easily mistaken for wheat or rice, can actually prevent the growth of the genuine article," he wrote. "I cannot help but despair over the tainted image of Tae Kwon Do . . ."

In May 1973, Kim hosted a world championship for thirty countries at the Kukkiwon, "the first official universal match of the art held 20 or 23 centuries after Tae Kwon Do began to be practiced," Kim announced.[298] South Korea ranked first at the tournament and the United States, stocked with Korean Karate champions, ranked second.

Choi responded with a 1974 ITF world championship in Montreal, Canada, that Nam Tae-hi and Dong-Ja Yang helped run. Under immense pressure in those days, Choi insulted Nam and accused him of a plot. Paranoia and threat hung around Choi like a dark cloud, so Nam was not surprised by the accusation. "We were very close in the army," Nam told me, "but he thought I was doing things against him." Nam had led much of the teaching in the ITF in the early days; senior instructors had become closer to him than to Choi, and Choi had grown paranoid as a result. Nam added that he had never seen Choi do much martial arts in all the decades he had worked with him. In Nam's view, Choi's relationships with his pioneers seemed to follow the same pattern: "What I found was that, when he started, he said very good things about a person. In the end, he always disparaged that person — talked bad about him."

Choi heard that the South Korean president had expressed shock when he discovered that Choi lived in Canada. Politicians tried to persuade Choi to return to Korea, but he assumed that the invitations were a set-up for a kidnapping. A rumour began that the volatile Choi was dead and that his ITF had fallen apart.

Meanwhile, Choi's family lived at the whim of the KCIA's fifth branch, which was in charge of finalizing passports. In Canada, he was in the middle of a process to obtain Canadian citizenship when he heard that Korea would not issue a passport to his adult son, Jung-Hwa, and daughter, Sunny.[299] Choi's wife and a second daughter, Meeyun, had already joined him in Canada, thanks to help from Jhoon Rhee, who had helped Choi's wife sneak to the Dominican Republic.[300] She flew to Canada from there. But Sunny and Jung-Hwa were still stuck in South Korea, and Choi believed that they were hostages.

Many stories were circulating about the KCIA hustling people to the dreaded Namsan torture chambers in Seoul. Choi knew the stories and worried about his children, but he refused to fly to Seoul. He was sacrificing them for Tae Kwon Do, as he saw it, and he fell into a bottomless agony. He had miscalculated how fast his power would wane while in exile. Night after night, he cried in bed, facing a wall. He feared that one wrong move might end their lives, that the KCIA would murder his children because of him. He tried to muffle his sobs so that his wife would not hear.[301]

A year later, in 1974, South Korea allowed Jung-Hwa and Sunny to leave. They arrived at Toronto's airport, where their father stood waiting for them. The Choi family did not normally show much emotion in public — no hugs, handshakes, and loud words when greeting each other — and feelings were usually kept below the surface, because Koreans of Choi's generation were like that, restricted by a hundred rituals. In private, Choi could be funny and talkative, but at the airport, he greeted them in the manner he usually did in public, as if nothing dramatic had occurred. He simply looked at his son and daughter and said, "Good."

✗ ✗ ✗

The World Taekwondo Federation was already writing Choi out of Tae Kwon Do history and elevating Nam Tae-hi as founder of the now-famous Oh Do Kwan, the only military gym in the mid-1950s that had practised Tae Kwon Do.[302] The status of other martial artists rose as Choi's fell. Uhm Woon-kyu and Lee Chong-woo, who had called Choi a "permanent troublemaker" in the mid-1960s, helped to create and lead the WTF and the Kukkiwon, which is still the WTF's governing organization today. The WTF claimed that no one had written down the rules of Tae Kwon Do, ignoring Choi's five books from 1959 to 1972.[303] Lee, with Uhm's help, wrote the WTF's first book of techniques, *Taekwondo Textbook*, published in 1975.[304]

Uhm, Lee, and a pioneer named Hyun Jong-myung, who had attended Tae Kwon Do's Naming Committee meeting in a *kisaeng* house in 1955, helped to develop the WTF's patterns, which contained techniques similar to those in Karate and the ITF. For example, *Taegeuk Il Jang*, the WTF pattern for white belts, used the same punch and two blocks that Choi had inserted into his first pattern, *Chon-Ji*, which, in turn, was based on the *kihon* pattern from Karate.

A new sparring rule in the WTF surprised everyone however: punching an opponent in the face was no longer allowed during sparring. Martial artists laughed, because it made no sense; how could you spar and not hit the face? A punch was fundamental in the fighting arts.

None of this stopped Choi's men from deserting him and joining the WTF. A common criticism of Choi is that his martial arts instructors, most of them anti-communist soldiers, left him because he co-operated with North Korean communists, which, in those days, hit the same triggers as the term "al Qaeda terrorist" today. In reality, his instructors began leaving him long before he formally co-operated with North Korea. They left him partly because South Korea increased the pressure on ITF pioneers and instructors, a pressure that became unbearable for many in the 1970s. They also left him because he was difficult to work with.

The first major defection occurred in 1971 in West Germany, where conflicts between the German Tae Kwon Do leader Heinz Marx and Kim Kwang-il (the pioneer who had been involved in the KCIA's East Berlin Incident) flared into a scandal. Choi sided with Kim, and the entire German association left the ITF and joined Kim Un-yong's WTF two years later.

The second loss occurred in 1974 when the organization in Turkey also jumped to Kim's group, mainly because Choi had failed to solve an alleged corruption problem with a pioneer, See So Cho. After those two defections — two pillars of the ITF gone — the losses came fast and hard, and Kim continued to globalize the Korean regime's martial art. In 1974, the South Korean regime convinced and forced thousands of gyms, ITF or not, to line up behind Kim's WTF. Also, the Amateur Athletic Union in the United States accepted the WTF, not the ITF, as a member. Choi lost high-calibre instructors to the WTF, men such as Jae-Hun Kim, who ran gyms in Boston and whose father was in the South Korean government, and brilliant sports administrators like Dong-Ja Yang, who later ushered the WTF into the Olympics.[305]

Most depressing for Choi, in 1975, was that the General Association of International Sports Federations (GAISF) seemed to favour the WTF over the ITF for membership. Being part of the GAISF was a major step toward joining the Olympics, and Kim Un-yong had lobbied hard to have Tae Kwon Do included, but Choi's ITF and a Japanese group of Karate leaders had also applied. The GAISF, however, could choose only one martial arts group.[306]

On the day of decision at a GAISF conference in Montreal, Canada, the Japanese argued that Tae Kwon Do was a part of Karate and that so-called Tae Kwon Do instructors had, in fact, opened Korean Karate gyms in North America and elsewhere. For his part, Choi argued that his Tae Kwon Do was the original and legitimate art. Kim knew they were right — Choi had named Tae Kwon Do and Jhoon Rhee had been only one of many famous Tae Kwon Do pioneers who had run "Karate" gyms before changing the name to Tae Kwon Do — but Kim spent two hours driving around Montreal, telling a key GAISF official that Tae Kwon Do was distinct from Karate and listing the serious problems with Choi, whom he thought was "squirrelly."

"I gave official examples of basic techniques, told him the origin, and explained the difference in rules," Kim said. "Of course our conversation was in English. That time, I thanked God that I had linguistic talent."

Kim spoke again inside the GAISF conference. "The history of Tae Kwon Do goes all the way to ancient times," he purred. Choi was "greedy" for trying to "privatize" Tae Kwon Do, Kim believed, and added that martial artists had ejected Choi from the Korean Tae Kwon Do Association in 1966, that Choi did not follow financial rules, and that Choi lived in limbo with regards to citizenship. Kim no doubt neglected to mention that South Korea was harassing and threatening Choi and his pioneers and that Choi was ruined financially, while Kim had access to a sophisticated network of financing. In short, South Korea wanted to eradicate Choi's ITF from the world. At the end of the GAISF meeting, Kim's martial art won over Choi's and Japan's — and Choi's Tae Kwon Do continued its slide.

Meanwhile, in the mid-1970s, everyone was riding the martial arts film craze started by Bruce Lee and others. Even boxer Muhammad Ali learned Tae Kwon Do: Jhoon Rhee taught him the "accupunch" that Ali used to knock out Richard Dunn in 1975.[307] But political forces pushed Rhee around in spite of his successes. He did not join Kim Un-yong's WTF, but a Korean newspaper reporter told U.S. officials that Rhee had received money from the KCIA to open martial arts schools. The Internal Revenue Service investigated and cleared Rhee of any wrongdoing, but Rhee told me it was an extremely stressful time.

Back in South Korea in 1975, Tae Kwon Do was booming and

Kim Un-yong had awarded himself an eighth-dan black belt that placed him one level above a master and meant that in only four years he had accomplished what other martial artists took decades to do. Kim noted that 721 Tae Kwon Do experts taught in 48 countries, with more than two-thirds of the instructors teaching in the United States, Canada, and West Germany. In South Korea, three million students, including 300,000 black belts, were training in Tae Kwon Do.[308]

In Canada, Choi announced that twenty million students were members of the ITF around the world.[309] South Korea had one of the hottest economies on the planet and, building on Choi's and Nam's twenty years of sweat and yells, now boasted one of the hottest martial arts.

But Choi's ITF ran out of money once again, and he realized that Kim had obtained too much, too fast. Kim lobbied for the WTF's inclusion in three international events: the Asian games; the South American Pan-Am games; and an international soldiers' sports competition.[310] A cunning strategist, Kim was registering Tae Kwon Do with these big-name organizations so that in one swoop he would marginalize Choi, raise the value of Korea's martial art, and gain access to bigger budgets. In North America, the KCIA continued bribing and threatening Koreans, including Choi's pioneers, who drifted from the ITF to the WTF.

It did not help that Choi was homesick. Canada allowed him to travel everywhere — it was his new home — but he recalled a saying from Lao-Tzu: "The ideal society is where one can live comfortably in one's home town from birth to death." He envied his friends in Korea, who woke up to the crowing of roosters and went to sleep to the barking of dogs. Choi loved rural areas, but in Canadian cities, roosters were illegal and dogs were not supposed to bark at night — and people kept to themselves. Choi said that he had not laughed in a long time.

South Korean officials harassed Choi and his Tae Kwon Do bodyguards at airports, trying to stop them from travelling and occasionally threatening them, according to General Choi. One of his pioneers, C. K. Choi, told me: "The South Korean government was backing the WTF. Because of that, the ITF was dissolved in Seoul, Korea . . . Most of the time, these diplomats abroad went after the Tae Kwon Do pioneering instructors. That is well known."[311] South Korean pressure on the instructors began as mild complaints about the ITF, followed by bribery attempts, followed by threats.

Choi could not turn to the Americans for help. A U.S. CIA agent, a black belt, had helped the ITF once, but other than that, American intelligence agencies and politicians were ambivalent when it came to criticizing their South Korean allies. Choi had reason to be scared, although I doubt he would ever admit it. The U.S. Justice Department, the American CIA, and the FBI knew about the KCIA Plan, but they investigated as little as possible.[312] By this time, thanks to news reports, the world knew that South Korea was a criminal enterprise and that its agents threw human-rights advocates off bridges and ran them over with cars, but in the view of the Americans, South Korea was an important ally in the Cold War. In 1973, the United States had promised that it would "not interfere" in Korean internal affairs. In fact, it committed $1.5 billion for a modern militarization program.[313] U.S. Secretary of State Henry Kissinger knew about the bribery, threats, and illegal activities in the United States, and in 1974, after a particularly violent crackdown in South Korea, the U.S. Ambassador in Seoul suggested to Kissinger that the United States should counsel moderation.

The ambassador would not forget Kissinger's reply: "Why counsel moderation?"

"If you were where I am, you would want to do so," the ambassador replied.

"No, I wouldn't," Kissinger said. "I don't think we should be involved. So why counsel?"

In Korea, the ambassador expressed concern anyway, privately. Kissinger ordered that a cable be sent to him to "tell him to get off their backs."

Understandably, the South Korean president interpreted this American attitude as support, and the Korean regime became stronger.

Kim Un-yong became an indomitable force against Choi as rumours continued to haunt Choi and his ITF pioneers. One time, Choi discovered that the KCIA had approached a black belt with an assignment to kidnap him. Another time, in the hours before flying to a Tae Kwon Do event in Chicago in 1975, he heard that demonstrators were gathering at a church of Reverend Sun-Myung Moon. A U.S. CIA agent tipped off Choi, but he flew to the event anyway and there was no demonstration.[314]

✗ ✗ ✗

How does one fight an indomitable force? With indomitable spirit.

In Washington, DC, on June 10, 1975, a former Korean Embassy attaché, Lee Jai-Hyon, sat at a witness table in a large hearing room of the House International Relations Committee and became the first of many Korean officials to expose South Korea's secret Plan in the United States and Canada — "Koreagate" — a Plan that involved Tae Kwon Do leaders and instructors at various levels. That year, a journalist reported that the Los Angeles president of the KAA — of which Tae Kwon Do was a member — beat up Koreans, raided their businesses, and threatened to massacre their families. "The pampering attitude of Korean government authorities encourage and condone a long record of violent activities of the officers of the Korea Amateur Association [KAA] of America," the journalist wrote.[315]

Angry and scared, Lee told U.S. Congressional investigators: "I will testify on other aspects that have not yet been touched upon."[316] Out poured details in five years of hearings, but it was too late for Choi, too late for Tae Kwon Do, and too late for the Koreans already in prison. It was time for drastic retaliation, in Choi's view.

He began negotiating with his long-time enemy, North Korea, in the gamble of his life. For thirteen years, off and on, he had been talking to agents from the Hermit Kingdom, flirting with the idea of visiting and accepting money. Now, he published an open letter to the South Korean president, listing reasons why "Choi Hong-Hi is the one who would cut his throat."[317] His list included the regime's violation of human rights and its role in turning Tae Kwon Do students into gangsters. Choi sounded like a martial arts hero — or a vigilante.

One month later, in 1975, a North Korean advised him that he could meet his brother, whom Choi had not seen in thirty years. Choi and the North Korean picked a date and a place — Sweden, a politically neutral country during the Cold War. On the day when Choi finally met his brother, the elderly man was sitting in a car with North Korean agents. Choi climbed in. Overcome by emotion, neither Choi was able to say anything, so they simply clenched hands and allowed themselves to be overwhelmed by all the grey hair and wrinkles, overwhelmed by how time and struggle had ground away their spirit.

At the North Korean embassy, with agents hovering nearby, they talked about their parents, who were dead, and their younger sister, friends, and relatives — a conversation that spread bitterness through their hearts like bad liquor. The North Koreans brought out the real stuff, and the North Korean ambassador to Sweden joined them in drink after drink, with the conversation inevitably veering into politics. Choi announced that the two Koreas should unite and he listened to an eager explanation about the superiority of communism, but all he craved was to be left alone with his brother. The ambassador picked up the cues and left the room, and Choi and his brother talked all night — and all day and all night again, with North Koreans popping in to invite him to his hometown, discuss Korean unification, and meditate on the possibility that Choi could distribute Tae Kwon Do in North Korea.

On the third day, his brother asked him to visit Yongwon village, their hometown in North Korea, right then and there, because relatives and friends were waiting for them. Choi refused. He did not want to risk being labelled a communist and jeopardize his chances of becoming a Canadian citizen. Not knowing whether they would see each other again, Choi and his brother embraced, lamented, cried — and everyone in the room cried with them. Someone declared that the Koreas should be united soon to avoid such family tragedies.

Emotionally exhausted and sleep deprived, and numb with drink, Choi lost track of how he ended up at his hotel. He stumbled to an airport, where officials did not allow him on the plane, and he settled into a waiting area to sleep off his grief. His luggage departed without him.[318]

Part IV
COURTESY

Courtesy: consideration, co-operation and generosity in providing.

— Webster's Dictionary

예

의

Chapter 12

WHAAA!

In 1977, the politics of the Cold War thrived in Tae Kwon Do like a disease, and the martial art burned in Choi like an obsession. Since the coup d'état of 1961, he had succeeded in working against the president, devoting his life to saving his martial art from Kim Un-yong, as he saw it. Humiliations had swallowed every success, but Choi had recovered and the successes had built like calluses. By 1977, however, rage and ambition plagued Choi's better instincts and he turned to his long-time enemy, North Korea, with an ambitious campaign to expand Tae Kwon Do around the world and challenge South Korea and Kim the Cloud Dragon in every arena he could. North Korea had been giving Choi money to publish a Tae Kwon Do encyclopedia set, but the volumes were not complete.[319] The books — fifteen volumes eventually — contained more technical details than all Choi's past books put together and were being published one or two at a time, but Choi needed more money and power.

For easy money, he turned to his old enemy Kim Hyung-wook, the Wild Boar of the KCIA, who in 1967 had organized the mass abductions of the East Berlin Espionage Incident. Because of the international outcry generated by that operation, the South Korean president had fired the Wild Boar, who had fled to the United States in 1973 and taken with him at least $15 million, along with details about the KCIA's Plan, which he leaked to U.S. officials and the media.[320] Some of the Wild Boar's stories sounded outlandish — one American official wrote, "They were willing to pay him not

Choi Hong-Hi clinks glasses with North Korean leader Kim Il Sung during a 1980 Tae Kwon Do tour. *Photo courtesy of Choi.*

to reveal his knowledge of things in Park's past, like what he might say on the murder of a *kisaeng* girl, her involvement with Park and other government luminaries."[321] South Korea sent men to bribe and threaten the Wild Boar, giving him a taste of his own KCIA tactics.

In the summer of 1978, Choi engineered a meeting with him to ask for funds for South Korea's democracy movement (and for Tae Kwon Do, of course), hoping the Wild Boar had evolved into a being similar to the famous Ho brothers in China. The brothers had made their fortunes in counterfeiting and, when they were older, had donated their money to public works, such as Singapore's Buddha Heaven and the Ten Courts of Hell.[322] In return for the Boar's donations, Choi would supply him with Tae Kwon Do body-guards and possibly a post in Choi's Tae Kwon Do organization.

But Choi and the former KCIA director ran out of time; as the American investigation into its ally's illegal activities — called "Koreagate" by the press — petered into nothingness (probably because Koreagate scampered too close to Congressional Democrats), Choi met the Boar only once before the KCIA in France abducted its former director in 1979. The story goes that the Wild

Boar "(1) had his head cut off and sent to Park Chung-hee in the diplomatic pouch, or (2) was secretly shipped back to Seoul where Park personally executed him 'by shooting him twice at point-blank range' in the basement of the Blue House."[323] The Boar's body was never found, and since then, no high-ranking Korean official has ever testified about Korean wrongdoing in the United States.

Around that time, Choi unveiled an impossible-sounding campaign to North Korea, an operation that seemed more reckless than his poker game in Yongwon almost forty years before. The KCIA's Plan had continued expanding in North America, in spite of investigations and press coverage, and Choi's men had continued switching to Kim Un-yong's WTF. Choi's mission promised to counter this. He had applied military tactics to Tae Kwon Do sparring and he seemed to be applying them now to martial arts politics: "You must create opportunity, assess your opponent and his weapons, assess his techniques and habits, and press them to your advantage," he once explained.[324] His new mission would take him to North Korea, train large numbers of new instructors, and post them around the world, countering and cornering the WTF everywhere.

Very few instructors understood the political mission, but some defended him. "General Choi had to go to North Korea, because the South Korean dictatorship was taking over all the ITF," explained Michael Cormack, who was Choi's son-in-law and an official in the International Taekwon-Do Federation at the time. "ITF instructors were getting knocked off the master's list so fast . . . you need to have some funds to propagate Tae Kwon Do. It was a bad situation for him."

Still, ITF masters and instructors worldwide did not like Choi's operation, because South Korea was technically at war with North Korea. Choi ignored their pleas. Everything was a mission for him, including trying to marry off his daughters to Tae Kwon Do instructors, which showed that he challenged even the power of love.[325] Once he set his mind on a mission, on this North Korean operation, he would not give up; he would order his best pioneers to North Korea.

And what would he give in return?

He and the North Korean dictator, Kim Il Sung, shared several common points in their histories: both had been born in northern Korea long before the Americans and Russians split the nation; both had survived the Second World War and Japanese colonialism and would never forget the scars; and both hated and respected Japan and the United States. For a Westerner, it is difficult to comprehend the bitterness within these men's hearts, where history was measured in millennia, not decades. Most Koreans of their generation had considered Japanese rule not only illegitimate but humiliating.[326] For centuries the two nations had been equal in terms of geography, Chinese culture, and economic development, so Japan's dominance in the nineteenth and twentieth centuries was galling. North Korea's leader demonstrated his infinite loathing in 1977 by running a covert mission in which agents abducted Japanese children and couples from Japan's beaches and whizzed them on speedboats to North Korea, where they were forced to teach Japanese culture, mannerisms, and language to North Korean agents.[327]

Choi would be soon co-operating with such agents, because he wanted all North Koreans to practise Tae Kwon Do, especially in the military. The nation's soldiers trained informally in a martial art called Kuksul, but martial arts were not popular, and there was no Karate or Tae Kwon Do.[328]

Very few of Choi's men could fathom their General's mission. Michael Cormack agreed to go, as did Choi's son, Jung-Hwa, but most of the General's disciples and surrogate sons were shocked that he wanted them to visit communist Korea at the height of the Cold War. One story demonstrates how psychotic tensions could get: the Tree Cutting Incident, or Axe Murder Incident, in 1976, involved twenty or thirty unarmed North Korean guards attacking twenty or so American and South Korean soldiers who were pruning a tree in the demilitarized zone, which lies on the 38th parallel between North and South Korea. Trimming this tree was supposedly a routine event, and neither side carried guns in the DMZ, which was a no-man's land. However, after an argument about the sacredness of the tree, the North Koreans used axes and clubs to beat to death two Americans; the whole thing was filmed by a corporal on the South Korean side. Three days later, in retaliation, the Americans and South Koreans rounded up approximately sixty Tae Kwon Do experts and special forces soldiers to cut down the sacred tree in front of hundreds of North Korean guards, daring them to start a military rumble. The South Korean black belts provided protection on the ground while bombers flew overhead, but the North Koreans did not attack.[329]

Stories like this made Tae Kwon Do masters, most of whom had been soldiers, wonder if the General was losing his mind. Was he really planning an operation in North Korea? In South Korea, criticizing the country to a foreigner was punishable by seven years in jail — and talking to a North Korean was punishable by death.[330]

Among the first masters whom Choi contacted was Kong Young-il, one of Jung-Hwa's teachers from years ago. Kong was running a gym in the United States and was one of Tae Kwon Do's finest masters. He had begun studying martial arts in 1952, had trained soldiers for the Vietnam War, and had demonstrated Choi's art in 127 countries.[331]

Acting like a general, Choi called Kong and got right to the point: "You have to come with me to North Korea," Choi ordered.

Kong listened to the mission's goals and replied, "I cannot go." It was the first time he had ever refused the General's order.

"You have to go!" Choi yelled.

"Think about my family; think about my school," Kong said.

"Whaaa!" Choi yelled and slammed down the phone.

He called back immediately. "You have to go!"

"No, sir," Kong said.

"Whaaa!" and the receiver hit the phone again.

Kong picked up the ringing phone two more times, refusing again and again. Saying no to the General, his mentor, leader, and father figure of more than a decade, was one of the most painful experiences of his life. Choi was a generous, giving man, but if you did not follow his orders, then he became angry, cut you off, and considered you a nobody. Kong and Choi stopped speaking to each other for many years.

Nam Tae-hi, Choi's right-hand man, had had personal problems with Choi in the past, but the final split between them was due to Choi's North Korea. Nam viewed the mission as a colossal betrayal. "General Choi didn't do bad things, but he always betrayed other people," Nam said.[332] "I fought the North Koreans and Chinese. I killed many of them." Because of the North Korean mission, he never spoke to Choi again. Kim Un-yong's WTF later awarded Nam a ninth-degree black belt and turned him into a grandmaster equal to Choi.

Jong-Soo Park, who had helped Choi and Nam with books and world tours, also refused to go. He had been one of the few to find out that Choi had visited his brother with the help of North Korean agents in 1975 — and he did not like the current mission. Park's relatives lived in South Korea, so KCIA threats were possible. Choi accused him of collaborating with Kim Un-yong. At the time, Choi was trying to get the Canadian government to recognize the ITF, and here was his Canadian pioneer joining ranks with the enemy, in Choi's opinion. Park and Choi would not talk to each other for the next twenty years.

As more South Koreans learned of Choi's mission, the KCIA increased the pressure. The agency's tactics had become more subtle over the years — less physical torture and more covert pressure and infiltration.[333] Choi heard that the Consul General of Los Angeles, who was part of the KCIA's notorious Plan, had told Master Choi Sunduk of Arizona that his relatives would face trouble in South Korea. In another story, someone visited the mother of one of Choi's pioneers, Han Sam-soo, telling her that Han might be kidnapped.[334]

"There were scenarios where the KCIA approached many instructors or non-Koreans, first-degree to third-degree black belts," said Michael Cormack, who overheard phone calls and private conversations with masters. "If your brother was in the army or air force, he'd lose his commission; he'd be out of the army." There were other penalties. "This was heavy-duty pressure," Cormack told me. By 1980, out of hundreds of top-notch Korean instructors, only about a dozen remained with Choi.[335]

He and his martial art fell into the ITF's worst crisis. He felt like he was losing his sons. In his view, how could so many of them worry about their own families and jobs after Choi's sacrifices, including his own children? He continued with the mission anyway, wearing judgments like military badges and threats like medals. He taught techniques to new supermen, such as the agile Park Jung-tae, who could complete five kicks in mid-air and could jump over a car.[336] Park also represented a calmer, dignified approach to the art. Choi taught him for six months in the basement of the Choi house in Canada and gathered a team of fifteen martial artists who were brave enough to visit North Korea: seven Korean instructors from the United States, England, Greece, and Yugoslavia; seven instructors from Canada; one American master; and a photographer to record the event.[337] If Choi was obsessed before, he was possessed now.

And he was sixty-four years old. Time had flown like an arrow, but he had to start over, had to produce hundreds of instructors and disperse them around the world very quickly to compete with Kim Un-yong and the WTF, especially in Sweden, the USSR, and the communist countries that South Korea had been avoiding during the Cold War. "He felt he was making history," Cormack explained. "He felt he was doing something that would profoundly change Tae Kwon Do for the better. There would be problems, there would be adversaries from it, but with General Choi, you know, he always liked attention. There's a book called *Thriving on Chaos* — I don't know if you've read or heard of it — but he thrived on chaos. It gave him momentum and energy to take Tae Kwon Do further. Through all the deficits associated with this infighting within Tae Kwon Do — WTF, ITF, the politics of Park Chung-hee and North Korea, and everything — it did give him the impetus to drive harder, to work harder, to build and spread Tae Kwon Do faster."

"He was an extremely energetic, driven man — extremely focused: Tae Kwon Do was his life," Cormack added. "I mean, there are not many human beings like him anymore. You have to understand that for a son like James [Jung-Hwa] and a son-in-law like Michael Cormack, he was very difficult. We'd be watching a movie at home on Sunday night, after dinner, and we'd be into the plot, and we'd be right at the point where the action's starting, and the whole family is there. We'd look in the corner and see General Choi going, 'Is it W-shaped block going "into" or going "towards"?' He would be doing his seminar and asking us to word-smith for him! So, we would laugh and chuckle, but General Choi couldn't even get into a movie, although he did like comedy once in a while."[338]

To others, however, he seemed drawn to tragedy. Choi felt excitement and doubt about the mission. Would the North Koreans accept him and his Tae Kwon Do? Would they forgive all the words spilled about hateful communists? Would they allow him to visit his hometown? Would they even allow him to return to Canada?

What few people knew was that Choi had been planning this mission for years; he took only calculated risks and knew that the outcome of the mission would be good.[339] Kim Il Sung had officially summoned Choi for a visit in 1979.[340] The route from Canada to North Korea, then, had been as convoluted as Choi's life: a plane from Toronto to Vienna, then to Hong Kong, then a ship to Macao, where he had met a North Korean agent, then both flew to Beijing, where a private airplane flew them to North Korea's capital city. On the day of the meeting, Choi's car crept around a lake surrounded by low hills. The car stopped in front of a summer-house, where Kim Il Sung waited in a doorway. The gesture touched Choi, who had met many presidents and prime ministers; here was a leader whom Choi had possibly shot at during the Korean War waiting on his front step. Inside, the two men settled into a meeting room, where they smoked and talked as if they were friends — about the Cold War and about Kim's wish to unify North and South Korea. They clinked glasses.

✗ ✗ ✗

That same year, in 1979, after yet another round of torture and murder of striking workers, South Korea exploded in protests, and its president, Park Chung-hee, went to a safe house with his KCIA chief. During dinner, an argument erupted with the president's bodyguard, a man known for his ability to kill with his bare hands.[341] The KCIA chief shot the bodyguard and then, for some reason, shot the president, too.

Many Koreans celebrated. Choi and his men heard about the assassination while on a Tae Kwon Do tour in Argentina and raised a glass of champagne, but the party mood did not last long, because a new general took over South Korea and sentenced to death the man who could have been president, human-rights activist Kim Dae-jung. South Koreans took to the streets, and Generalissimo Chun Doo-hwan, the new leader of South Korea, declared martial law. Soon after, in Kwangju city, he ordered a crackdown that resulted in a slaughter of hundreds of people (some reported thousands): the May 1980 Kwangju Massacre became a new low in South Korea's modern history.[342] It was Korea's misfortune that each time a dictator fell, another rose to take his place, often worse than his predecessor.

In 1980, in the year of the Monkey (a year of erratic geniuses and cheery opportunists), South Korea's newest dictator received good news: the International Olympic Committee had granted recognition to the WTF, which was another step toward Tae Kwon Do becoming an Olympic sport. The news, coming two months after the Kwangju Massacre, focused the regime on the Olympics and Tae Kwon Do; South Korea began using sports to improve its image. Olympic hopes also focused the martial arts gyms that had been in turmoil since

1978, when the Korean Tae Kwon Do Association had abolished the traditional *kwan* system, merged all gyms under the World Taekwondo Federation and demanded that gyms send black belt test fees directly to the KTA and WTF's Kukkiwon. Various martial arts leaders delicately wondered why they should give away most of their money and power, but the KTA was unsympathetic: "Even though you sacrificed much for Tae Kwon Do, it is wrong for the *kwans* to ask for compensation for their sacrifices. We need to give up the old idea of *kwans* in favor of the new system, for standardization purposes."[343]

So much for ancient tradition. How could one argue in a country that had perfected the arts of veiled threats and subtle extortion?

✗ ✗ ✗

In September 1980, as Kim Un-yong and the WTF began their unlikely climb up the Olympic ladder, Choi and his team climbed off a plane for what seemed to be a suicide mission in North Korea. A historian once described the nation as "the most astounding garrison state in the world," which meant that the specialists in violence were the most powerful group in society.[344] North Korea had had a history of fighting half a century of Japanese colonialism and another thirty-five years of fighting the United States and South Korea, and every North Korean man completed eight years of military service. The North Koreans were more than ready to learn combat Tae Kwon Do. At the airport, a brass band and a thousand people greeted Choi and his team, who had long hair and wore bright suits with bell-bottomed pants and collars as wide as kites, because Choi had instructed the team to show off western trends.

The speeches began, followed by martial arts demonstrations. Did Choi mention that North Korea was running one of the world's most sophisticated prison gulags?

No, but he noted that North Korea was self-sufficient in agriculture, and during a Tae Kwon Do demonstration, he watched Park Jung-tae jumped over a man on a motorcycle.

Did he notice that North Koreans called their leader *urŏrŏ patta*, which means "to look up to and receive" the way Christians look to Christ?[345]

No, but he did give an obsequious speech to Kim Il Sung, who said that he was proud of Choi and that Tae Kwon Do would be taught in North Korea.

Did Choi mention North Korean human-rights atrocities?

No, but he was gratified to see that in the North the custom of respecting ancestors remained intact and that Kim Il Sung covered the entire cost of the trip — and offered Choi millions of dollars.[346] Nearly 30,000 people watched the team's demonstration.

Choi's speech contained a clear message: you are our friends. He told his North Korean hosts that Tae Kwon Do avoided violence, especially against communists, reassuring them that "Tae Kwon Do is not meant to kill or harm people, but is a defensive art and a people's martial art, which endows people with spirit and encourages a healthy body and a sound mind."

"They thought Tae Kwon Do was anti-communist," explained Michael Cormack, who was there for Choi's speech in North Korea. "They saw Tae Kwon Do instructors in Vietnam killing communists with it. General Choi, probably after a few Scotches, had written in a newspaper or had said, 'We will kill communists with Tae Kwon Do,' whatever. So, whether that was stated or not, they still had this nervousness . . . James [Jung-Hwa Choi] and the Koreans were extremely nervous, because they had been brainwashed that the North Koreans were the devil, the evil empire of the North."

Had General Choi sold his soul to the devil? No. He was accustomed to the aura of terror the way a Christian is to Sunday mass, but more to the point, he was in the middle of a wicked gambling game with Kim Un-yong and the South Korean dictatorship.

While in North Korea, General Choi, his son, and his son-in-law left the rest of the team to visit Choi's birthplace. He had last visited after the Second World War, when he had trudged into town to discover communists in control and his family gone. Choi visited his brother, sister, friends, and the house where he had helped his mother to grind tofu. The wrestler was no longer in the village. Everything was blue pine trees and Russian helicopters. The next day, they climbed into a helicopter and Choi's son-in-law, Michael Cormack, nudged Choi's son and pointed to a man inside who looked like Jong-Soo Park, only bigger. "Look," Cormack said. "It's Jong-Soo Park as a commie."

Some vendettas did not die easily.

One gift that Choi gave to North Koreans was a new pattern of moves that he called *Ju-Che*, which was the name of North Korea's ideology. He did this to jettison the *Ko-Dang* pattern, which had been the pseudonym of one of Choi's heros, Cho Man-sik, a Christian educator and an early North Korean leader until communists imprisoned him in 1946.[347] Now that Choi's friends were those same communists, *Ko-Dang* had to go. Expunging it and creating *Ju-Che* was a sell-out to the communists, even though Choi argued that the change was not political. The term *Ju-Che* is nearly untranslatable in English: it means self-reliance and independence and, deeper, everything that makes Koreans Korean.[348] As if to highlight this, Choi designed the *Ju-Che* pattern to be the most difficult out of the twenty-four, demanding a jumping split-kick and two techniques that were supposed to stop momentarily in mid-air, as if the attacker were floating. Today, in gyms and championships around the world, we yell, *Ju-Che* after the final technique of this pattern, saluting North Korea's ideology whether we like it or not.

A more important gift to the communists, however, was a change to "sine wave," a series of subtle movements that applied to all techniques. Good martial artists had always slightly bent their knees and rotated their hips before launching a technique (thereby creating more power), but Choi now wanted everyone to lower then raise the entire body, with no hip rotation, so that they could use gravity while driving downwards with a punch for example. Everyone had been practising a small sine wave (requiring a small knee spring and snapping of the hips) but Choi's gift was a big sine wave (requiring a big knee spring).[349] The differences sounded subtle, but, when put into action, they gave Choi's Tae Kwon Do patterns a distinct style — a slower, more rhythmic, bobbing-on-the-sea look that dramatically distinguished it from Karate and Kim Un-yong's Tae Kwon Do.

Just as dramatic were Choi's sudden announcements that North Koreans were practicing "pure Tae Kwon Do" (because they were doing a big sine wave) and that all the other instructors on the planet were "fakes." The majority of Choi's pioneers had disassociated themselves from him and his missions to North Korea, and Choi's reaction was swift. As my instructor, Mr. Di Vecchia, explained, Choi inserted a three-dimensional signature on the martial art (sine wave), handed it to the North Koreans and, in one move, disowned his wayward disciples, men who Choi viewed as disobedient and unfilial. In fact, disowning those surrogate sons was perhaps Choi's chief goal with sine wave. As everyone scrambled to adapt, Kim Un-yong's group continued to rely more on leg techniques and less on hand techniques during sparring.

What else did the North Koreans want? Power and access to the rest of the world — and the occasional martial arts assassin. "Believe me, Tae Kwon Do is a very powerful instrument, not just kicking," Michael Cormack told me. "They wanted access to the diplomatic tools, to be close to all those countries. They also saw Tae Kwon Do as part of their culture, and wanted to be involved with it."

You could say that the desperate General Choi had performed a 180-degree ideological kick. North Korea wanted to do what South Korea was already doing: use Tae Kwon Do for sports, culture, politics, espionage, and propaganda. Choi had disagreed with much of that in South Korea, but he was fine with it in North Korea, because he was in charge of the martial art in the North. Choi was politicizing what was supposed to be an apolitical martial art, or, to put it more accurately, he was hyper-politicizing a martial art that had always pretended to be apolitical, even though Tae Kwon Do had been born in the military and had grown up among dictators.

Choi's son, Jung-Hwa, co-operated in the venture to the North, even though he discovered that North Korean agents were becoming involved. "I had an inkling, because I saw that the ones who we trained were not going out as instructors, and strange guys who we'd never met were coming out as instructors instead." He saw a sophisticated motive in North Korea's involvement, especially when his father moved the ITF headquarters from Canada to Vienna, Austria: "Tae Kwon Do, to them, was a godsend, a present to them, because the *Ju-Che* idea was already dead; this was a way of getting into common people's minds, and they needed something that could replace *Ju-Che* philosophy. Tae Kwon Do, you can say, is a philosophy, and when they found how close the relationship between the instructor and practitioner was, they laughed and said, 'This is it!'" That relationship was a special bond — part militaristic, part fatherly — that agents could exploit. "They thought if the agent would be an instructor or the instructor would be an agent, then it would be a very easy way to control many people and infuse Korea-ism in their minds. Another thing is that Vienna is a way-station for many agents and many activities . . ."[350]

Within a year of the 1980 visit to North Korea, Jung-Hwa was co-operating with North Korean agents to assassinate South Korea's newest dictator, Chun Doo-hwan.[351] This chapter of the martial art's history is as difficult to explain as past chapters, but it is more clear-cut: the twenty-six-year-old Jung-Hwa met North Koreans who claimed to be the families of those killed in the Kwangju Massacre in South Korea in 1980, and the families wanted to avenge the deaths. Someone proposed an assassination plot. Jung-Hwa knew a couple of gang members in Toronto and agreed to find an assassin, deliver the funds, and act as a middleman between agents and assassins. The young martial artist felt cool in using gang connections for a worthy mission, but, more than that, he wanted to make his father proud. And he wanted to put his father's teachings into action — protect the weak from the strong — and rid the world of a sadistic president.

Chapter 13

OLYMPIC MANIA AND NORTH KOREAN MAYHEM

*Human perfection is defined as a person who never makes mistakes knowingly,
so if you balance strength in the body, honesty in the heart and knowledge in the
mind, then you are humanly perfect . . .*

— Jhoon Rhee discusses the Fifth Quality of his
"Seven Qualities of a Champion"[352]

On September 18, 1981, Korean Airlines Flight 901, scheduled for
Frankfurt, West Germany, sat for thirty minutes on the runway of
Gimpo Airport in Seoul, South Korea, as the crew waited for an
important last-minute passenger, Park Chong-kyu — also known as
Pistol Park, because he carried a pistol everywhere he went.[353] He
was a martial artist with deep connections in politics and sports; he
had helped to organize South Korea's military coup d'état in 1961,
was a member of the International Olympic Committee, and had
steered secret-service agent Kim Un-yong into Tae Kwon Do in
1970. Now, Pistol Park and Kim were leading Operation
Thunderbird, a mission to influence the most powerful people in
international sports — to convince them that South Korea should
host the 1988 summer Olympics, where Tae Kwon Do might make
a splashy debut.[354]

Wearing dark sunglasses, Park finally walked onto the plane.
The flight attendants were expressionless. He and Kim had gathered
a team of 107 elite Koreans from sports, business, government, the
secret service, and Tae Kwon Do, including Korea's education minister, two former ambassadors, and the KCIA's deputy director.
Flying from various countries, the 107 were to meet in Baden-

Baden, West Germany, for a crucial Olympic Congress, where the International Olympic Committee would vote for the country that would host the 1988 games. Along the way, Operation Thunderbird would provide security against plots by Choi Hong-Hi and his North Korean friends, because General Choi had threatened to disrupt the Baden-Baden meeting.

Pistol Park and Kim had launched the top-secret Operation Thunderbird in June 1981, when South Korea had been spinning in chaos. After the Kwangju Massacre, President Chun had continued his predecessor's policy of using martial artists to do some of the nation's dirty work in Korea, which consisted mainly of smashing unions. One third of political prisoners were workers, and the rest of the workforce took turns going on strike and protesting. Martial arts experts and plain-clothes police officers, called the White Skull (*paekkol*) strikebreakers, would pad themselves from head to foot and race on motorcycles to protests, where they would wade into crowds, breaking heads as they went.[355]

The new regime concluded that the fastest and most effective way to diffuse conflict, unite Koreans, and improve the country's image overseas was by hosting an Olympics. It was such a far-fetched idea that few people inside and outside the nation took Pistol Park seriously, especially because Korea had no Olympic-sized facilities and, as Kim soberly acknowledged, did not even have colour television. But the country had hosted the 42nd World Shooting Championship in 1978, and it had gone so well that Kim and Park, who was president of the Korean Shooting Federation, had dreamt that South Korea could host an Olympics. Perhaps sports would redeem their nation.

Korea was the underdog in the Olympic bid, so the objective of Operation Thunderbird was to entice powerful international sports officials to support the bid. That was the easy part when compared to the bid's two formidable opponents: first, Nagoya, Japan, which was the front-runner and had begun the enticement long before Korea, and, second, Choi Hong-Hi, who wanted to disrupt the important Baden-Baden vote. Park, Kim, and Operation Thunderbird would take them on directly, because Tae Kwon Do, Korean sports and their nation's prestige was at stake.

Nagoya in particular was a worry. Korea's martial arts leaders (and not only Choi) tend to become gently unhinged when comparing their martial arts to Japan's. Kim did not want Japan to win.

He recalled his days in Japanese schools when Japanese students bullied him. Pistol Park was "to take all available steps to win the support of IOC members." He and others contacted the president of Adidas (maker of sports equipment, including Tae Kwon Do gear), the Mexican president of the Association of National Olympic Committees and many other influential officials. Park worked backstage, gaining support from IOC members in South America and Africa. The KCIA also lent a "helping hand," and overseas Tae Kwon Do instructors lobbied thirteen IOC members in Europe and North America.[356]

The rumour that Choi planned an anti-Olympic demonstration for Baden-Baden shook the Korean Olympic Committee, which is surprising when you realize who was on that committee — some of South Korea's most powerful politicians, millionaires, martial artists, and KCIA agents. Kim did not believe the rumours but concluded that he needed bodyguards at the meeting, so he "called five Tae Kwon Do instructors in Europe to stand by the entire time," including Kim Kwang-il, the instructor who had been one of Choi's pioneers and who had once been arrested in connection with a KCIA kidnapping plot in West Germany.[357]

When the Operation Thunderbird team arrived in Baden-Baden, they had no idea where to start and how to spend their budget. Kim Un-yong switched hotels, staying with IOC delegates, instead of with his Thunderbird team, so that he could eavesdrop on what delegates said about Korea's chances before the crucial vote — and he reported the discussions to the Thunderbird team, who met their illustrious guests at French and Chinese restaurants in Baden-Baden. The Korean exhibit, with three Miss Koreas and five Korean Airline stewardesses dressed in traditional Korean dress, was inspiring compared to the staid Nagoya exhibit.

No one believed that the Koreans offered only ginseng tea and jade trinkets to IOC members, as Kim later explained. "Compared to us, Japan invited IOC executive members to Nagoya and gave Seiko watches as gifts," he said. Still, accusations of bribery would fly.[358] A *New York Times* reporter heard that someone had slipped "first-class airline tickets under the hotel room doors of I.O.C. members, expecting them to cash the tickets in, in order to curry their vote for the South Korean city."[359] The Korean team denied the charge.

Tae Kwon Do pioneer Kim Kwang-il and the other Tae Kwon Do experts stood guard in Baden-Baden. One instructor, Park Soo-nam, drove to the team's hotel with a trunkload of Korean food, because he knew that the members of Operation Thunderbird craved Korean home-cooking. Unfortunately, Prince Philip, the husband of Queen Elizabeth II, was staying at the same hotel and, security being tight, Park was kicked out of the hotel as a suspected terrorist. He re-entered only after explanations about *kimchi* and Korean delicacies.

Finally, on the day of the vote, Kim Un-yong entered the Baden-Baden meeting, sat down and fielded questions as if fighting in a war zone. Delegates carpet-bombed the Korean team with requests and criticisms, and Kim deftly handled them all. In the end, after the vote, when IOC President Juan Antonio Samaranch announced in French that the winner was "Seoul, Korea," the words rang in Kim's ears. Korea had soundly beaten Japan by fifty-two votes to twenty-seven, which amazed even the cheering Koreans.

"I wonder if the count was wrong," Samaranch said. It was right. The votes from the South American and African IOC members had tilted the vote in favour of the Koreans. Operation Thunderbird had been a success. Small Korea, the rabbit trying to be a tiger, momentarily rose above both China and Japan, and everyone forgot about the terror and torture under the South Korean dictatorship. Korea would host the 1988 summer Olympics. The whole thing sounded like a miracle, but it was not, Kim said, because victory does not come from miracles; it comes from hard work.

Just as sweet as the Baden-Baden win was the IOC's decision to include Tae Kwon Do as one of two demonstration sports at the 1988 games. Seoul had little experience organizing world-level championships, but Korea had accomplished a so-called economic miracle, leaping from Third World country to industrialized nation in only two decades, and it would perhaps pull off a sports miracle, too. "The Olympic Games were a turning point for Korea to move into the ranks of the world's advanced nations," Kim later wrote.[360] Tae Kwon Do would be part of the Olympics, and would show that Korea was not only powerful economically, but also physically and culturally. Olympic glory, power, and millions of dollars spread before Kim Un-yong and Korea, and President Chun picked "Harmony and Progress" as Seoul's Olympic slogan, a cunning cover for a dictator who was busy hoarding nearly $1 billion in "slush funds."[361]

Choi's men and the North Koreans did not disrupt Baden-Baden.[362] However, his son and North Korean agents continued the plot to assassinate the South Korean dictator. And, after his visit to North Korea, Choi began calling himself the "founder" of Tae Kwon Do more frequently. Before that, he had used "founding member."[363] If South Korea was going to steal a martial art that he had named, then it was better for people to know that the "founder" was not happy.

✗ ✗ ✗

In Canada, many people mocked Choi after his 1980 North Korea trip, calling him a communist.[364] Even Choi's friend at the American CIA headquarters, sixth-degree black belt Robert Walson, was worried — but Choi thrived within an aura of chaos and worry.[365] He did not publicize what he and the North Korean dictator had discussed, but within a year, he was training the North Koreans in hand-to-hand combat, and his son, Jung-Hwa Choi, was plotting with Michael Gerol and Charles "Chuck the Bike" Yanover, whom Jung-Hwa had met through a Tae Kwon Do instructor in Canada.[366] Jung-Hwa idolized secret agents, and he would party with tough men at Cooper's, a discotheque in down-town Toronto, befriending them in case he needed his back covered or his family protected.

At first, General Choi thought that the plot sounded childish. He told the North Koreans that he did not want his son involved, because it was extremely risky to involve his heir on such a danger-ous mission.[367] Jung-Hwa was the favourite in an ancient culture that structured society around the "three relationships" and the "five injunctions": honour your ruler, honour your father, and so on, for eternity. General Choi cared about his son, who was one of Choi's best Tae Kwon Do assets, and Jung-Hwa was his favourite in the family. When Jung-Hwa and his two sisters had been chil-dren, Choi would come home after a night of drinking and, think-ing the boy was asleep, would lovingly stroke his head. He would slip money under Jung-Hwa's pillow and whisper, "Don't tell any-body I gave you this, because I love you the best." Choi would do the same with his daughters, but they knew that Jung-Hwa, his only son, was the favourite.

In 1981, on a plane trip to Switzerland, the two men discussed the assassination plot and the elder Choi concluded that his son knew what he was doing. Choi gave him the okay, but he wondered if Yanover was capable of carrying out the killing.[368]

Jung-Hwa assured him that he was.

"Let's try him on Jong-Soo Park first," someone suggested.

Both Chois laughed. They were made of the same material; the elder Choi had taught the younger almost everything he knew, and they both believed that Park had betrayed the General.

As it turned out, the Choi men did not send Yanover after Park, and, to their surprise, they discovered that Yanover was more con man than murderer. Once, while in prison, Yanover had helped a former South Korean soldier to blow up Arviv's, a Toronto disco, because the owner wanted the $950,000 insurance money. You could say these men were ambitious and macho; the soldier would break ashtrays over his head or cut himself before a fight, saying "Let's go!" and Yanover was an international arms dealer once convicted of working with white supremacists to overthrow the government of Dominica. Yanover apparently planned to assassinate the South Korean dictator, possibly during a visit with Prime Minister Pierre Trudeau in Canada, but Yanover did not carry out the plan.

Jung-Hwa would never forget walking through Geneva, Switzerland, carrying an attaché case with a huge sum of money that North Korea agents had given him. He deposited it in an account. In Vienna, he interpreted for agents and gangsters, but after Yanover collected U.S.$600,000, someone tipped off the South Koreans, Yanover kept the money, and Jung-Hwa woke up to realize that this was no sparring match and that the plot put him and his young family at great risk.

The RCMP arrested Yanover in Canada. Meanwhile, his soldier friend, the one who broke ashtrays over his head, was in South Korea, where the KCIA arrested, tortured, and imprisoned him until the RCMP flew in to ask questions. Jung-Hwa suspected that he himself would undergo a similar interrogation if Canada shipped him to South Korea, where the KCIA wanted to interview him before the RCMP did.

"Bizarre Death Scheme," yelled the headline in the *Toronto Sun* after police announced the plot. Interpol in eight countries had helped the RCMP during a six-month investigation. The story also screamed from the front pages of the Korean-language newspapers: "The Assassination of Doo-Hwan Chun was Schemed at Choi Hong-Hi's." The RCMP raided Choi's house, looking for Jung-Hwa and evidence, but the younger Choi was already on a plane to

North Korea. As the police spent three hours searching the elder Choi's residence, he claimed he did not know about the plot.

The KCIA now had good reason to kidnap Choi and his son, and Choi found out that an assassin was assigned for the job. Most Korean-Canadians avoided Choi and KCIA agents called with good-night threats. Protests swelled in front of Choi's Canadian house; "Go away pro-North Choi!" they chanted. He did just that, moving to North Korea, where he lived until 1984, when the heat and threats finally dissipated.

In those two years in North Korea, wondrous and weird events transpired. He agreed to borrow $400,000 annually from the North Korean Tae Kwon Do Association,[369] and he created his last technique — the flying, tumbling kick — which involved jumping into the air while flipping backwards 360-degrees to strike an opponent with the heels.[370] He finished his fifteen-volume encyclopedia set during this dismal period, even as he felt a noose around his neck, even as he felt the South Korean government waiting for him. His adversaries were running a country that seemed intent on eliminating him.[371]

Much of the 1970s belonged to Choi's Tae Kwon Do, but the 1980s belonged to the World Taekwondo Federation and Kim Un-yong, who never looked back. WTF supporters did look over their shoulders however. That year, the North Koreans dispatched a unit to assassinate the South Korean president — yet again — this time in Burma. They narrowly missed him but killed most of South Korea's cabinet.

At the same time, Yanover used the $600,000 to buy diamonds and testified in court that his goal had been simply to steal from the North Koreans. A judge sentenced him to two years in prison for conspiracy to defraud, and it sentenced his accomplice, Michael Gerol, to one year. Jung-Hwa remained in North Korea and Eastern Europe.

✗ ✗ ✗

This was Tae Kwon Do in the early 1980s, when I first began studying the martial art: vigilantes; discos; KCIA agents; gangsters; assassination plots; and, somewhere in there, the time to create flying kicks and plan the Olympic Games. I did not know the extent of the intrigue at the time, but I now look back and remember that my uncle did repeatedly warn me about some aspects of the art. I had joined an International Taekwon-Do Federation gym near my house in Ottawa. One of Choi's pioneers, Park Jung-Taek, ran it. My uncle, however, had obtained his black belt from a WTF gym that was run by one of Kim Un-yong's right-hand men, Lee Tae-Eun. We had no idea what we were getting into, but my young uncle was from a war-torn country and knew something about the world. Being something of a father figure, he alerted me to the fact that I was betraying most of the values that my family held dear, because communists (in other words, maniacs and terrorists) ran the ITF. My uncle tended to be brash and melodramatic, and I, only sixteen years old, listened to him the way one listens to bad news on the radio, wondering when the songs would return.

Still, I scraped together a pound of courage to ask my instructor about the rumours. Grandmaster Park Jung-Taek was not around, so I bravely approached his second-in-command, Phap Lu, a gifted athlete who had been a student of an old Vietnamese master, Nguyen Van Binh. In Vietnam, Lu had heard stories about combat Tae Kwon Do during the Vietnam War, had trained at the Oh Do Kwan in Saigon, and had watched his martial arts friends become secret-service agents, but Lu landed in a Vietnamese prison, where he was tortured as an anti-communist.[372] He fled the country when released, arriving in Canada with waves of Vietnamese refugees, not knowing how closely his life mirrored Choi Hong-Hi's.

Lu set me straight. "This is traditional Tae Kwon Do," he said. He told me that the other one, the WTF's, arose decades later. The ITF was affiliated with North Korea, yes, but the WTF was based in a South Korean dictatorship. "Choi is the founder of Tae Kwon Do," Lu added, "and his Tae Kwon Do was the original one. We in the ITF practise a martial art, while they in the WTF train in a sport."

Chapter 14

THE OLYMPIC SUMMER OF LOVE

I am convinced that one of the most important roles the IOC plays in the quest for world peace is to provide a forum for dialogue and communication through sport events for countries having differing political ideologies.

– Cho Sang-ho, president, Korean Olympic Committee, 1981[373]

North Korea threatened a bloodbath if South Korea hosted the 1988 Olympics alone, and it demanded that the games be shared by both Seoul and P'yŏngyang.[374] After the Soviet Union agreed to join the Olympics, an overly excited South Korean government official blurted to the media that Russia's participation would act as "a strong shield against bullets." At the time, the Soviet Union was North Korea's ally and a Soviet official demanded an explanation for the outrageous comment. Kim Un-yong flew to the rescue, saying that the Korean official did not mean "shield" in the military sense. The bullets were metaphorical. Kim welcomed the communists with open arms and began teaching himself how to speak Russian. Korea, a small country that for centuries had been suspicious of foreigners — and for thirty-five years had waged a vicious covert war with communists — was opening itself to the enemy.

Choi Hong-Hi was already a couple of years ahead of them. He had been lobbying Olympic leaders to hold a joint martial arts event between his Tae Kwon Do and Kim's,[375] and Kim seemed to like the idea. The choice of Seoul as Olympic host had obviously struck a hard blow to North Korea, but there was hope of holding a joint Olympic Games, Kim believed, and South Koreans liked anything that pointed to Korean unification. At the very least, talking about a joint event was politically wise for both Kim and Choi.

But Choi, the tornado, had never been a good diplomat, while Kim was a masterful negotiator who could speak six languages. In 1985, Choi flew to Moscow to meet the Chairman of the Olympic Organizing Committee to warn him about "sham" Tae Kwon Do and the "phony" Kim, not knowing or caring that Kim had just been promoted to vice-chairman of an Olympic committee.[376] Choi's lobbying failed, and Kim succeeded in adding Tae Kwon Do to the 1986 Asian Games and the 1987 Pan American Games.[377] In the process, Kim became a member of the International Olympic Committee, transforming into a powerful man in international sports, and Choi, increasingly marginalized, could not compete with the rivers of money and favours flowing to and from South Korea.[378]

In 1987, the year before the Seoul Olympics, South Korea erupted after police tortured to death yet another student. Millions of Koreans took to the streets. With a long-needed revolution spreading across South Korea, the world wondered if Seoul would be capable of holding a peaceful games, but Korea promised "the largest and most successful festival of mankind in peace time."[379] The challenge was the "peace" part.

Kim Dae-jung and an ally, Kim Young-sam, decided that democracy should enter stage left, and they met in April 1987 to begin a new democratic party for an upcoming election. The KCIA and agents trained in Tae Kwon Do tried to stop them in what is now called the Yongpal Incident, named after the weightlifter who organized it. Politicians in South Korea's regime recruited Lee Sengwan, a Tae Kwon Do master, to hire fifty hoodlums to disrupt local groups trying to set up the democratic party. The thugs, backed by the KCIA and ultimately directed by the South Korean president, descended on twenty meetings, destroying furniture and attacking people with clubs. Lee had been a national sparring champion in 1964 and had become head of the Jidokwan, which had been one of the nine main gyms that had formed Kim Un-yong's World Taekwondo Federation.[380] Not much had changed since the regime's brutal tactics in the 1960s and 1970s; for his role in the 1987 attack on the democratic party, Lee was later sentenced to one-and-a-half years in prison.

In spite of the violent disruption and a ruthless dictatorship, the new political party grew and student protests continued. In June

1987, the South Korean president sent White Skull police (*paekkol*) to break student heads with clubs, but the protests went on, with four or five million Koreans marching through the streets. The president resigned at the end of the month and cleverly installed a replacement, another general, Roh Tae-Woo, who announced direct elections for 1987.[381] As if in response, North Korean terrorists planted a bomb on a Korean Airlines flight from Baghdad to Seoul, killing 115 people.[382] Many expected the North Koreans to target the Olympics, too, and the Americans filled Korean waters with warships.

Still, the games would go on, because the Olympics would unveil Korea to the world, just as the 1964 Olympics had unveiled modern Japan.[383] General Roh Tae-Woo won the Korean election in 1987 after the opposition split the vote, and went on to steal $650 million from Koreans over the years.

In 1988, as the promise of violence surrounded Seoul like a dark fog, Korea's secret service promoted and protected the Olympic Games, whose official emblem meant "progress through world understanding and peace." Kim Un-yong later wrote, "A total of 81,630 members of military and police forces were mobilized to provide security for 264 facilities."[384] They patrolled the ground, flew through the air, floated on the sea, and hid underwater, while American spy satellites watched the North Korean army's every twitch, everyone prepared for anything short of an invisible nuclear bomb.

✗ ✗ ✗

At 1 p.m., on the day of the opening ceremony, twenty massive balloons — ten metres each across — floated on the roof of Seoul's elegant Jamsil Olympic Stadium, which had been designed to reflect the curves of the Chosŏn dynasty's porcelain vases. The stadium was packed. For the first time since 1976, both the Americans and Russians were in the games, along with 157 other countries. North Korea and Cuba had boycotted. The balloons depicted huge, grotesque masks as dancers ran frantically to and fro carrying grisly and bizarre masks of their own. The masks were from Korea's ancient, shamanistic history: there was *Choyong*, which repelled bad spirits; *Yangban*, the aristocrat with the open, laughing mouth; and *Halmi*, the old widow.

Suddenly, flames leapt from the stadium floor between the dancers. Pandemonium. Were the North Koreans finally attacking? No, the dancers were performing "Chaos," followed by 1,008 "Taekwondoists," as they were called, who smashed boards, screamed through techniques, and forced order onto the bad spirits.[385] The Tae Kwon Do ceremony "symbolized the destruction of all barriers," Kim later explained.

After chaos and order on day one, the world watched 184 men and women from 32 countries participate in Tae Kwon Do, the demonstration sport, at Seoul's upgraded Changchung Gymnasium.[386] This was one of Kim's proudest achievements. He had turned a martial art into a sport and had showcased one of Korea's treasures. The "sport" part had always been one of his goals; he had aimed to take the "martial" out of the "martial art," to tone down the aggression, and to create a gentlemanly sport. He succeeded in 1988. At the end of the Tae Kwon Do competition, Koreans ranked first, with nine out of sixteen gold medals. Overall in that Olympics, South Korea won thirty-three medals, ranking fifth in the world, a spectacular finish for a small country.

But the lopsided Tae Kwon Do results worried many. Kim had miscalculated that few people would be interested in an Olympic sport dominated by South Korea, and people wondered why it should be an official sport for future games.[387] Viewed from afar, the entire competition looked like a battle between Koreans, because most of the Tae Kwon Do officials and coaches were Korean: Joon-Pyo Choi (who began in the Song Moo Kwan in 1956) coached the second-place Americans; Young Su Choung (from the Chung Do Kwan in 1962) coached Canada's team; Park Soo-nam coached West Germany's; and Young-Yul Oh was head coach for Australia, to name only a few.[388] The unspoken and perhaps unconscious worry was that Tae Kwon Do was racist — or overly ethnocentric, at best, favouring Koreans over non-Koreans, no matter what the skill level. In practice, it seemed as if non-Koreans faced an uphill battle in becoming international champions and, more tellingly, faced impossible hurdles in becoming international leaders in the organizations that ran Tae Kwon Do.

Also, rumours began that "branch trimming" (*gagee chigee*) had taken place in the combat sports at the 1988 Olympics and during the 1986 Seoul Asian Games.[389] "Branch trimming" refers to pressure on judges to rule against the strongest competitors in early sparring matches. The practice ensured that a few of the strongest fighters did not face Koreans in the final rounds. There would be no revelation of "branch trimming" until 2002, when a WTF vice-president would explain it to a journalist, but the rumours began circulating during the 1988 summer games in Seoul.

That first Olympics showed off Tae Kwon Do's kicks along with South Korea's economy and culture, but the International Olympic Committee did not choose Tae Kwon Do as an official sport for the 1992 games. In response, a desperate Kim Un-yong asked IOC President Juan Antonio Samaranch to consider Tae Kwon Do as an "exhibition sport" for 1992. Kim had created an elaborate plan, one that would have impressed his old mentor, Pistol Park, who had died a couple of years before.[390]

"For the growth of Tae Kwon Do it has to be chosen," Kim told Samaranch.

Samaranch's face stiffened, and he replied, "But we've selected the demonstration sports already, and only two are allowed." The IOC could not pick Tae Kwon Do as a demonstration again, because a sport could be a demonstration sport only once.

Kim explained his idea about "exhibition sport."

"Is it in the regulations?" Samaranch asked.

"No, it isn't," Kim said. "I made it up." He explained how Tae Kwon Do could benefit from the exposure at the 1992 Barcelona games and how the Olympics could benefit in the process.

"Is it possible?" Samaranch asked. "Did you think about the details?"

Kim had. He had a talent for details; it was not for nothing that the IOC had promoted him from member to executive member in 1988. First, he would reduce the number of weight classes in Tae Kwon Do, thereby decreasing the number of matches and completing the tournament in a day. Second, South Korea would pay for the players' security and expenses.

"All right. Let's try," Samaranch said, and he suggested that Kim approach IOC executive members individually to persuade each one to support the new idea.

As it turned out, the impossible occurred after Kim's intense lobbying: the IOC skipped the "exhibition" idea and, bending the rules, included the martial art as a "demonstration sport" in 1992 — and Kim was soon mired in one of the most publicized corruption stories in Olympic history. Before the press found out about the scandal, however, 128 competitors from 33 countries competed in Tae Kwon Do at the 1992 Barcelona Olympics.[391] Tae Kwon Do's leaders made sure that the Korean competitors did not dominate. The host country, Spain, did uncharacteristically well, which once again fuelled rumours about unfair judging.

Choi's reaction to the 1988 and 1992 Olympics could be summed up in one word — "phony" — and he was not referring to the rumours about cheating. Tae Kwon Do had officially become a "sport," but he wanted it to remain a martial art. Without punches to the head, without jumping kicks, without the hundreds of techniques that distinguished Tae Kwon Do, the Olympic sport was worse than Karate, in his view, but his view did not matter to the WTF, which now had tens of millions of practitioners while he had fewer than a million. Partly because of the turmoil between Choi and Kim and between the two martial arts, the Olympics rejected Tae Kwon Do as a sport for the 1996 games. Choi took that as a positive sign.

North Korea committed to giving Choi $10 million over ten years and he became more active.[392] No one knew about the money — neither his family nor his closest disciples, and certainly not his ITF executive, who struggled to cover the expenses of world championships that host countries usually financed. Choi's wife would tell her children, "I don't know if your father is rich or poor." With the money rolling in, some of Choi's prime instructors asked for a huge salary hike and, in response, he accused master instructors, such as Park Jung-tae and Han Sam-soo, of spying on him.

The accusations seemed bizarre. Park Jung-tae was Choi's top instructor in the world, and Han Sam-soo had been on an international demonstration team, but Choi accused Han of receiving "some direction for some task of the KCIA" and of being a double-spy since 1978.[393] In the war with South Korea's dictatorship and Kim Un-yong, it was unclear where Choi's boundaries lay between fear and paranoia, between generosity and greed. "He was a man of morals," explained Choi's former son-in-law and right-hand man, Michael Cormack. "Money corrupts. I never said General Choi never took the dollar that he shouldn't have, but I can say that when it comes to Tae Kwon Do, every dollar he got, he gave a hundred, in terms of time, effort, et cetera. He gave a thousand. General Choi, anytime, could have made way more money out of Tae Kwon Do if he wanted to.

That's obvious to anyone, that's why he's respected so much. So I think we can leave that alone."

✗ ✗ ✗

After all the threats in this martial art it seems petty to mention a problem in the 1990s: stealing, a gargantuan amount of stealing. With murder hanging in the air, why talk about bribery and extortion? Tae Kwon Do was not only enmeshed in the Cold War, it was scarred with corruption and gangsterism. The financial scandals that erupted in the martial art were significant because they finally got everyone to

Kim Un-yong (centre) with my ITF instructor, Jong-Soo Park (at Kim's right) and my WTF instructor Yoon Yeo-bong (at Kim's left). At far left is Chung Oh and at far right is Myung-Soo Son. *Photo courtesy of Park.*

acknowledge that not only was Choi Hong-Hi out of control, but Kim Un-yong, "the godfather of Korean sport," was, too.[394] The martial art was sinking into deep trouble after the 1988 Seoul Olympics.[395]

I did not know this when I joined Olympic Tae Kwon Do in the early 1990s, when Kim became vice-president of the International Olympic Committee. It was an exciting time, because the staccato ground kicks of the World Taekwondo Federation were as much fun as its Olympic fever. I had joined a WTF gym, run by Yoon Yeo-bong, because it had been close to my home. In those days, I still looked up to Choi Hong-Hi and his combat martial art in spite of the bad rumours, but I was also excited about Olympic Tae Kwon Do, joking with my uncle about training for the Canadian team. Every kid dreamed about joining the Olympics, a dream that fuelled phenomenal growth in the WTF.

Tae Kwon Do's leaders were involved in a number of controversies at the time. In a Korean article entitled "Need a medal? Come with money," a reporter discovered that one could hire Tae Kwon Do brokers with access to officially sanctioned black belts. One martial artist paid $10,000 to jump from a fourth- to sixth-degree black belt, which is one level below master.

Also, too many sparring matches were unfair. I entered martial arts competitions, both WTF and ITF, and quickly learned that judging was odd, at best, and that the behaviour of coaches, families, and the audience was a circus sideshow. I knew that Tae Kwon Do was not based on Buddhism or religious values, just as Karate had not been based on religion when Gichin Funakoshi brought it to Japan, but I did follow Tae Kwon Do's five tenets (Indomitable Spirit, Perseverance, Self-Control, Courtesy, and Integrity) and its five virtues (Righteousness, Propriety, Wisdom, Trust, and Humanity), but the competitions had sunk far below the standards of these ideals.

For example, fighters who drew blood in the ring were not disqualified even though the rules called for that, which made me wonder if a select few knew the covert rules while suckers like me continued pulling our punches. Coaches threatened fighters, and family members screamed like psychotics at child participants, which I found reprehensible. Worse, perhaps, were masters who argued with other masters who had apparently not shown enough deference in bows and comments. Then there was the boredom and the disorganization at the tournaments, the hours of waiting for late grandmasters, the audience walking through rings during sparring, and the high cost of everything.

In the late 1990s, I finally saw a couple of reasons for the cheating and chaos when journalists dragged the first big scandal kicking into the light of day. Kim Un-yong was implicated in a bribery incident during Salt Lake City's early 1990s bid for the Olympic Games. Since 1966, the Salt Lake City Olympic organizers had been attempting to win a bid to host the games, and in the early 1990s, they realized what they had to do to win: they heard people involved with the Olympics ask for favours — sex, gifts, money, and sweetheart business deals — so the organizers provided for what was known as The Club. In three damning books, Andrew Jennings and his co-authors wrote about "The Club of the Olympics" and the corruption swirling around them. "The games are controlled by a self-perpetuating oligarchy who travel the world like kings, most taking lavish gifts from cities desperate to cash in on the huge profits the Olympics can generate," Jennings noted.[396]

Kim and Tae Kwon Do stood at the centre of the Salt Lake City controversy — and would for the next fifteen years — but he saw the scandal as a smear campaign. The media reported that Kim's son, Jung-hoon (John) Kim, had been indicted in the United States for allegedly accepting $104,000 from Salt Lake City bidders for a bogus company job between 1990 and 1992.[397] The city's bidders, caught by U.S. officials, had been trying to influence Kim Un-yong, who was the most senior IOC official investigated in the scandal. "Federal officials have charged the committee with using an elaborate gift-giving scheme to court I.O.C. members who would vote on the site of the 2002 Winter games," reported the *New York Times*.[398]

Canada's IOC member, Dick Pound, later led an investigation of the charges and saw a side of Kim that was shocking when, in 1999, Kim confronted him and François Carrard, the executive director of the IOC. They were at an IOC executive board meeting in Lausanne, when Kim rushed back to the meeting after a phone call. Kim had thought that the Salt Lake City crisis was behind him, but another piece of evidence had arisen just as Kim was planning a bid to become IOC president. Bad timing, you could say.

"He just lost it," Pound told me. "He came storming back from where he got the phone call and encountered Carrard on the stairs — and did one of his martial arts poses. They didn't strike or anything like that. Carrard felt himself threatened. Kim came up to where we were, on the second floor, and he did the same thing. He said, 'Bastards! Bastards!' He had just lost it. He started doing that stuff. I said, 'Kim, calm yourself. Calm yourself!' Samaranch saw what was going on, intervened right away and said, 'Kim, go to my office and stay there.' Carrard went home or to his office; he was badly rattled by it. I said, 'Listen, I didn't join the IOC to be confronted by this kind of shit.'" Kim denied that he had struck a threatening pose. Pound said that Kim later sent written letters of apology.

For Kim's part in the Salt Lake City scandal, the IOC gave him a "severe" warning and a "reprimand" for a second deal involving benefits to his daughter.[399] Ten other IOC members — all supporters of Kim's — were kicked out of the IOC, a move that declared to the entire world that Kim was a survivor, because after every Olympic scrap, he was the last man standing. From Kim's point of view, the smear campaign had failed, but he was angry at the humiliation and angry that he had lost ten supporters, who were replaced by twenty people who did not support him.[400]

"He is a straightforward person, and he cannot hide his emotions," explained Lee Chong-woo, a WTF leader. "I can see through his thinking clearly, after serving him for a very long period of time. Un Yong Kim is a man with a strong desire to win and a strong driving force."[401]

After the severe warning from the IOC, Kim continued his climb up the Olympic ladder and his son left the United States.

Another well-known Tae Kwon Do son was also on the run around that time. After the failed assassination plot in the early 1980s, Jung-Hwa Choi, the son of General Choi, had moved to North Korea and Eastern Europe, where he had lived for ten years teaching Tae Kwon Do to instructors.[402] In 1992, South Koreans elected a civilian to lead the country and Jung-Hwa felt it was time to make a move. With help from Russell MacLellan, a Tae Kwon Do black belt and a Member of Parliament in Canada, Jung-Hwa cut a deal with Canadian police and gave himself up, knowing Canada would not ship him to South Korea for interrogation and torture. At the same time, coincidentally, his father flew to North Korea for fifty-two days, where he attended dictator Kim Il Sung's birthday party, thereby missing Jung-Hwa's trial in Canada.[403]

Jung-Hwa pleaded guilty and said very little during the trial, as per his father's orders. A judge sentence Jung-Hwa to six years in prison for counselling to murder a president. "Canada must not become or serve to become a place for mercenaries or terrorists," the judge said.[404] Jung-Hwa could have fought the charge, but he said he pleaded guilty to protect his father, who still denied knowing about the plot. Fighting the charge would have revealed more secrets about General Choi, and the older man did not want to get into those. Jung-Hwa wondered if his father had been some sort of spy. Had his father been a double agent for decades, pretending to work for South Korea but, in reality, co-operating with the North? The elder Choi had admitted to talking to North Koreans in 1962, 1968, and a couple of times in the 1970s. In any case, Jung-Hwa spent a year in a Canadian prison, where he worked as an English teacher and administrative clerk — and no one, not even Choi's family, knew that his father had known about the assassination plot.

Years later, Jung-Hwa said he felt no animosity toward his father, even though the elder Choi never visited him in prison. The principles of Confucianism, especially filial piety and filial duties, were paramount. "There is no such thing as forgiving, it's an absolute — you had to follow him," Jung-Hwa said. "Of course I was very hurt and had a shock that my own father would not visit me — and he would think of nothing of sacrificing his son." His father's rationale was that Jung-Hwa would inherit Tae Kwon Do in the end. "That's the only reason why he wanted a son," added Jung-Hwa, who knew his responsibilities. "Confucianism tells us that change is bad, we must conserve tradition. General Choi is from an era and his thought process is exactly the same as people who were 1,000 years old — very much old world. When we categorize the types of people and the people from different eras, in Korea, we say, 'There are men who studied with the brush, and there are those who learned with the pen.' Of course, now, people learn with computers. General Choi is a man who learned by the brush."

✗ ✗ ✗

Meanwhile, Kim Un-yong continued to dream big. After twenty-one years of struggle with Choi and other martial artists, and after decades of threats and negotiations with North Korea, Kim took credit for making Tae Kwon Do Korea's national sport, for globalizing it, and for making it part of the nation's identity. "It was like a dream," Kim wrote. The political benefits of Tae Kwon Do in the Olympics piled up with the gold medals. Winning athletes enhanced South Korea's prestige, increased tourism, and generated income for Korea. During competitions, millions of people heard the matches in Korean, the universal language of Tae Kwon Do.[405]

Kim now shot for a loftier goal: to lead the entire Olympics and replace President Juan Antonio Samaranch. Kim positioned himself as a brilliant alternative to the white Europeans who had always dominated the Olympics. A *New York Times* article explained that he "has been a master at rehabilitating his image, coalescing an apparently strong base in the developing nations of Asia, Africa and Latin America, and regaining enough political ballast that some insiders now consider him the favorite to succeed Samaranch. With Samaranch's Nazi-soldier past whirling around the Olympics, Kim pushed the fact that he would be the first nonwhite president of the I.O.C. in the more than 100 years of the modern games and the first from Asia."

A vote for Kim meant a vote for non-Western countries, for a former diplomat who was a master organizer, for someone who could negotiate billion-dollar contracts and tricky political mergers — a vote for a brilliant underdog who would take on a white hegemony. However, it also meant a vote for the Olympics's "perceived history as an autocratic, secretive, corrupt, elitist organization," which, by coincidence, mirrored the history of Tae Kwon Do's organizations. As one former delegate from India told the *New York Times* in 2001: "He has the wisdom of the East and the efficiency of the West."[406]

Chapter 15

"Branch Trimming" at the 2000 Olympics and the Street Fight Soon After

I believe that heaven helped us.

– Kim Un-yong, *Challenging the World* (2002).

Because the IOC had rejected Tae Kwon Do for the 1996 games, Kim Un-yong knew that selection for the 2000 games through formal processes had become nearly hopeless, so in 1994, he began a "007 operation," as he called it — an operation whose goal was to slip Tae Kwon Do into the Olympics at the last moment.[407] It was an intriguing name for the mission, since some people believed that Kim was still a high-ranking, secret-service agent. For the 007 operation, he would have to counter strong lobbying from martial arts groups in China and Japan, who, as usual, were lobbying for inclusion of their martial arts. Also as usual, Choi Hong-Hi's International Taekwon-Do Federation would attend the final, crucial meeting.[408]

There was no time for Kim to individually persuade members of the International Olympic Committee, and the direct support of IOC President Samaranch became crucial once again, this time at a showdown with Choi's people at an IOC General Meeting in Paris.[409] While Kim's fortunes had risen, Choi's had continued to fall, especially after the North Korean leader's death in 1994, when the north survived two years of floods and a summer of drought that killed an estimated half a million people.[410] Choi had been relentlessly lobbying the IOC to reject Kim's Tae Kwon Do.

"How will you calm opposition groups?" Samaranch asked Kim in 1994.

"I will make sure that there is no opposition until the IOC General Meeting," Kim promised. He had no idea how he would do this, but he had to portray complete confidence in front of Samaranch.

"Do your best," Samaranch said and agreed to the operation. He convened a special, executive committee meeting, where he asked the committee to add Tae Kwon Do to the final IOC General Meeting in France. There was no opposition and Samaranch added the martial art as the last agenda item.

On the day of the showdown in Paris, nearly 150 Tae Kwon Do black belts and Korean personnel waited for the IOC to decide if the martial art would become an official Olympic sport. Lee Chong-woo was there, as were other WTF executives, who were nervous about protests from Choi and the North Koreans. During the meeting, an IOC member from Slovakia turned to Kim and asked why there were two federations for one sport, and Kim replied with a long list of the WTF's international memberships. Afterwards, IOC members stood up to give supportive speeches, and eighty-five out of eighty-nine of them voted to include Tae Kwon Do in the 2000 Olympics. Kim felt proud.

The build-up to the 2000 games was rocky, however. Martial arts officials in Malaysia, for example, warned judges that they would take strict action if there were biased judging, and a riot broke out at the Asian Games after fans in Thailand disagreed with a judge in a semi-final match.[411] For Kim, though, South Korea had expanded Tae Kwon Do from a martial art to an international sport, and the mistakes in judging would be fixed. And he harboured bigger plans: he wanted to promote the martial art as an international symbol of courtesy and human respect — which, at first glance, strikes me as utterly surreal, because the art had grown during the Korean and Vietnam wars and was known as a killing art. His dream was understandable however; the power of martial arts generates awe and respect, and virtues such as courage, wisdom, and defending the truth have always surrounded Tae Kwon Do. Talks about reconciliations, mergers, and joint tournaments floated like whispers in a Korean geisha house.

While Choi Hong-Hi decreased his disruptions of Olympic Tae Kwon Do and North Korea reduced its attacks on South Korea, Choi felt that the dragon was not yet slain. He installed security cameras around his Canadian house and rallied his old grandmasters for the final mission of his life — a deal to reunify Tae Kwon Do and, while he was at it, reunify his homeland.

In that time, South Koreans appointed Kim Un-yong to their National Assembly in April 2000, and Kim-the-sports-leader became Kim-the-political-leader. There had always been an overlap between Tae Kwon Do and international politics, and, now, there was a stronger connection: Kim became a special adviser to the South Korean president, Kim Dae-jung.[412] The venerable Kim Dae-jung had battled dictators all his life, had avoided rogue Tae Kwon Do instructors, and had survived KCIA attempts to blow him up, run him over, and throw him into the sea. He had finally become president of South Korea and was now negotiating the Korean deal of the century: the Sunshine Policy, which promoted a long list of activities that pointed to reunification of the two countries. He chose Kim Un-yong, Tae Kwon Do's leader, to be on the North–South negotiation team.

That year, when the two leaders of a divided Korea met for a peace summit for the first time since the countries' creation,[413] Kim Un-yong was standing in the room. He found the North Korean leader, Kim Jong Il, to be funny and open to new ideas.

"What can we, South and North, do together in sports?" the North Korean ruler asked Kim-the-Tae-Kwon-Do-leader.

"The Sydney Olympics is soon," Kim Un-yong replied, "and the IOC is proposing that South and North enter together for the opening ceremony."

"Yes, I am well aware of that," the North Korean leader said. "What sports can we do together to top the world?"

"Ping-Pong," Kim answered. China always topped the world in Ping-Pong, and South and North Korea were usually number two and three. Together, the Koreas could take gold, Kim explained. You could call it "Ping-Pong diplomacy," similar to the kind practised by the Americans when they sent a Ping-Pong team to China ahead of President Richard Nixon's historic visit in 1972.

The North Korean leader replied that he would get back to him about Ping-Pong.

The two groups did agree that they should co-operate in Tae Kwon Do, however. Driven by a deep desire to end a fifty-year trauma — a desire shared by Koreans in both North and South — the men who ran Tae Kwon Do proved that they were not megalomaniacs and that kicks and punches could play a positive role during political talks. Choi was not in the room, but his organization would agree to Tae Kwon Do demonstrations as part of the Sunshine Policy. Along with family reunions and a railway link between the two countries, cross-border martial arts visits became as important as Tae Kwon Do side kicks.[414]

What few people knew at the time was that the South Korean president had shovelled $500 million to the North Korean leader as an incentive for the North Koreans to participate in the 2000 peace summit in the first place.[415] Alongside these illegal political payments — no one used the word "bribes" — Kim Un-yong helped to "promote inter-Korean sports exchanges," as he put it, by delivering $1.1 million to a North Korean Olympic official, Chang Ung, who happened to be a leader in Choi's International Taekwon-Do Federation.

While the money flowed to North Korea and its Tae Kwon Do leader, North and South Korea agreed to walk into the stadium together during the opening ceremony at the 2000 Sydney games. They completed the deal at the last minute, but the whole thing would not work without proper uniforms. Both teams had to wear the same outfit, but the opening-ceremony deal had taken so long to finalize that Korean Olympic officials did not have enough uniforms. They ran from manufacturer to manufacturer during a Thanksgiving holiday to collect three hundred uniforms and delivered them at the last minute. "I believe that heaven helped us," Kim concluded.[416]

✗ ✗ ✗

A couple of months later, in September, with 120,000 spectators watching the opening ceremonies of the 2000 Sydney games, Kim Un-yong and Chang Ung, heads of the Olympic Committees and of the Tae Kwon Do organizations in their Koreas, entered the stadium holding hands.[417] Kim was overcome with emotion as he walked near a specially designed Korean flag that merged North and South Korean symbols. He had planned this moment for more than three months. Two days before the opening games, after someone had obtained two donated bottles of whiskey — "unification booze" — from the Uzbekistan team, Kim and South Korea's athletes and officials met North Korean counterparts for a party in the Athletes Village. "It was no longer than five minutes," Kim later wrote, "but this historical moment was made possible after many arduous complications and subsurface contact for negotiation." Officials agreed to exchange Tae Kwon Do teams in the future to show the world that sports could help with politics.

They should have helped in the ring more. An uncanny part of Olympic Tae Kwon Do is that the host country does well: in Seoul in 1988, the South Koreans took most of the golds; in Barcelona in 1992, the Spanish were the best after the Koreans; and at the 2000 games in Sydney, the Australians won gold in the first Tae Kwon Do match, creating a buzz and "boosting the sport's popularity in an instant," according to Olympic officials.[418] The silver and bronze medal winners at the 2000 Olympics thought that the cheering crowd had swayed the judges.[419] In fact, the alleged cheating was more concrete. A Korean journalist later reported that a Tae Kwon Do official, Lee Chong-woo, had swayed judging in key bouts before the medal matches.

At two Olympics, Tae Kwon Do had been a demonstration sport; it had not been part of the medal standings and had not generated enough world interest, partly because Koreans dominated. To ensure that South Korea would not win the majority of medals at the 2000 Olympics, Tae Kwon Do's leaders had developed a quota system.[420] In 2000, there were four weight categories for men and four for women, and all nations could enter only two men and two women. Australia, however, was allowed to enter double that number — eight athletes — which immediately increased its chances of winning Tae Kwon Do medals. Kim Un-yong had agreed to this arrangement, and Australia won the first gold. He later wrote that Korea did not do as well as expected but that Tae Kwon Do did well.[421]

Lee Chong-woo, who was a World Taekwondo Federation official, revealed a different side of Kim to a Korean journalist in 2002: "When Korean athletes captured a small number of medals, Un Yong Kim was so distressed that he just looked at me and didn't say anything . . . At that time, all the Korean athletes in the other sports had been beaten, and the last hope was for Tae Kwon Do. Kim said that 'even though we won three gold medals in the four weight divisions, because of the quota system we did not even enter four divisions, so we actually had to give away four gold medals.' During these hectic times, the hosting country Australia took whatever they could take, and Un Yong Kim went into a rage."

"At that time, as the Vice-President of the World Taekwondo

Federation, I was responsible for all technical matters for the Tae Kwon Do competition," Lee continued. "When we assigned referees prior to the competition, I was the one who decided most of all who was to be assigned or not assigned [for each match]. I could not openly ask judges to take care of Korea, could I? So when I hit the judges' backs, some were sensitive enough to understand what it meant, while the insensitive ones did not understand at all." Lee told a surprised journalist that the process was called "branch trimming." He explained how it worked and the underlying political motives for it:

Lee: . . . When they were told, "Be fair," they read my intention and sensed it. I was in charge of this kind of manipulation and I carried it out. Without it, we could not have taken any more than one or two gold medals. That sort of thing was accepted and worked out because we were Korean, not from other countries.

Reporter: I watched all three final matches where Korean players fought, and based on what I observed, I believe that all three Korean athletes won.

Lee: Only watching the final match would not be enough. In order to understand it as a whole, you have to pay very careful attention beginning with the first match. In this sense, it is not that simple. There are so-called tactics. That is, you kill the strong opponent beforehand. We are not the ones who kill. The judges do. When you tell judges to do their job fairly, they know what to do and they do it. From the beginning of the preliminary games, you have to perform *gagee-chigee* [branch trimming]. If not, at the end you will be in trouble . . .

Reporter: Do you mean that "branch trimming" is inevitable in order for Korea to retain its reputation as the strong Tae Kwon Do country?

Lee: Yes, I do. If a formidable person goes out as a judge, it is difficult to do it the way we want. It is also difficult to kill the Korean athlete's opponent at the final match. Therefore, from the beginning, you should have a good grasp as to which country is strong. Assigning judges is a skill. That is, so and so country will be in the competition. So and so country should not get into the finals. Therefore, so and so should be killed this way.

Reporter: From the point of view that Tae Kwon Do is a sport which puts its emphasis on courtesy, isn't that "tree trimming" unjust behavior, contrary to good sportsmanship?

Lee: When judges play tricks, the outcome of a match is reversed. If a judge says he did not see [a point], that is the end of it, and he can make repeated deductions of points. For this reason, I did this (moves his hand horizontally across his throat) to one of the judges. He was the one who caused the defeat of a female Korean athlete, by giving her a deduction. I gathered the judges together and instructed them absolutely not to call deduction of points, but to give a *choui* [pre-warning] for the first and second time, and then a *kyungo* warning for the third one. In spite of my instructions, he made deductions. After the match, I shouted at him, "You cannot do that! Do you have a problem?" After this match, the attitudes of the judges changed completely.

Reporter: Critically speaking, it seems to me that *gagee-chigee* is a precise way to manipulate results.

Lee: If this was disclosed openly, it would be a disgrace for Korea. But this is a reality. For example, if there were a final match between two strong competitors representing Korea and Germany, we would not make Germany lose in the final. If we perceived that the Korean athlete would have the disadvantage in a match against the German, we would "kill" this German athlete before he reached the final.

Reporter: I don't think that's fair. Upon hearing these words of the Vice-President, I am worried that Korea might cause some mis - understandings about the way Korea is maintaining a good reputation as a strong power in Tae Kwon Do through the use of result manipulation.

Lee: This is related to the national interest. This is a sensitive issue. When Korean Tae Kwon Do is destroyed, there will be chaos and then athletes' spirit will fall to the ground. Foreign athletes' skills have improved drastically. This [result manipulation] has been possible, because Korea has dominated the leadership . . . There is no fair play.

Reporter: Do you mean that in almost all the international games . . . this sort of unwritten rule is applied?

Lee: Yes, a country that holds dominant leadership is always a strong country [in that sport's standings] . . .

Reporter: What is your estimate of how many gold medals our Tae Kwon Do would be awarded if we competed fairly without privilege?

Lee: We would reap half, at the most . . .[422]

After the article was published in April 2002, Lee denied the story and WTF officials said that his allegations were "groundless." (In July 2008, the WTF's public relations director, Mr. Seok-Jae Kang, told me that there had been no official investigation, as far as he knew.) The reporter, Sung-chul Yook, was threatened and refused to comment in the uproar that followed. Lee had clearly been unhappy with the way things were going in the WTF and had "exploded" in front of journalist Yook, as one grandmaster explained it to me. Later, Lee's denials and the reporter's silence helped the controversy to die down.

Many people were careful in their reactions to the article, but some went on record to say they were not surprised, especially because Lee had not run for re-election as WTF vice-president the autumn before.[423] Herb Perez, a 1992 Olympic gold medal winner in Tae Kwon Do and a U.S. Olympic official at the time, read the article and said, "This has been the way Taekwondo is."[424]

U.S. Tae Kwon Do gold medalist Steven Lopez, who fought in the 2000, 2004, and 2008 games, was more forthright when he told the *Houston Chronicle* in 2002 that he had heard that matches were fixed in favour of Koreans:

"It's pretty bad, but it's something you have to live with in our sport," he said. "We have to deal with it in our own way, and we're still dealing with it. You have to train two or three times harder and smarter and realize even then that things are stacked against you."

. . . Lopez said he hopes the allegations regarding taekwondo will help clean up his sport.

"Enough people have been double-crossed, and enough people are sick and tired of taking it," he said. "It's time for people to open their eyes and do something about it."[425]

I asked David Askinas, the new CEO of USA Tae Kwon Do, what he thought of the 2002 article. He had not heard about Lee's statements, but said, "It would not surprise me. The WTF has had to take a lot of steps to prevent abuses in judging, and, yeah, I've heard stories and read things about bribery — things like that. They've pretty much cleaned that up."[426]

His counterpart, WTF Canada's Secretary General Wayne Mitchell, added that cheating was such a common practice that there was a name for it: branch trimming. "It was an extremely sophisticated way of cheating." It was accepted behaviour among leaders and common knowledge among some grandmasters. "To them, you had to lobby to get into the inner circle, so that you were the one on the good side of getting trimmed." Some referees knew it existed, but not all of them knew there was a name for it. "I think there was a circle of referees, because all it takes is a couple of them, or one of them in a match to not show points for a certain fighter, then, all of sudden, the game is over for you." However, when the Korean reporter publicized Lee Chong-woo's explanations about how the whole thing worked, people were shocked. Lee had been a high-ranking WTF official. "He was mad at somebody, then he tried to deny it," Mitchell explained. That somebody was Kim Un-yong.[427]

Amid the controversy, one heart-warming story at the 2000 Olympics was that of Esther Kim. During the U.S. Olympic trials, her close friend and training partner, Kay Poe, won a semi-final match but dislocated her knee. Esther Kim won the other semi-final and was booked to face Poe in the final, but Kim forfeited the match and a spot on the Olympic team so that Poe could win. Poe had already defeated her in an earlier match and was ranked number one in the United States, but Kim refused to fight her, scared she would wreck Poe's knee and career. At the Sydney games, the Olympic audience gave Esther Kim a standing ovation.[428] It was a rare moment in Tae Kwon Do. As one newspaper put it, "Kim's gesture has come to be mostly lauded as an exceptional act of sportsmanship and selflessness while sports are plagued by scandal, commercialism and greed."[429]

After the International Olympic Committee once again chose Tae Kwon Do as an official sport, this time in the 2004 Athens Olympics, Kim Un-yong announced that he would run for IOC president and would clean the Olympics of overcommercialism. He would be the first non-white president in more than a hundred years of Olympic history. Hoping for votes from thirty-seven IOC members from Asia and Africa and a handful from Europe and North America, he thought he had a chance. His one big worry was that Samaranch, a former ambassador in Spain's fascist government before the Second World War, would betray him.[430] Kim told him: "If you support me or keep neutral, I will win, but if you oppose me, I will lose." Kim remembered Samaranch's reply: "You are the only friend out of five IOC candidates," and he hugged Kim.

Controversies about judging refused to die down, Tae Kwon Do hit a new low, and the seemingly invincible Kim became target number one. It did not help that millions of dollars were flowing from more than 170 countries to the WTF with little transparency. Around that time, a group of WTF executives decided to rebel against the corruption, demanding that the WTF lower black belt fees. The rebel leader was expelled, but he began a reform movement.[431]

In July 2001, Kim Un-yong lost his bid to become IOC president, and he blamed Samaranch.[432] The old Salt Lake City scandal had been dusted off and sent to the media, fuelled by claims that Kim had offered $50,000 bribes to IOC members.[433] Dick Pound, who had also run for the presidency, had a more frank explanation: "I think Samaranch realized that, by then, with the reputation that Kim had, it would be a disaster for the IOC. He was certainly actively campaigning against Kim, and also against me, in favour of [Jacques] Rogge."[434]

Kim was devastated at the loss; in his view, the IOC remained a stronghold of white people, and the election had been corrupt.[435] This must have been one of the lowest points in his life; he had once awarded an honorary tenth-degree black belt to Samaranch, which in the rank-obsessed world of the martial arts, meant that Samaranch was a god. Only one other WTF person in the world held such a rank: Kim himself. Chang Ung, Kim's North Korean IOC compatriot, was also disappointed that Kim lost. Kim had been sending money to Chang Ung.

The game was over, Kim thought. It was perhaps then that his world began falling at the rate of a Himalayan landslide. In October 2001, only three months after his IOC loss, he drove to a hotel, the Seoul Olympic Parktel, for an 11 a.m. Korean Tae Kwon Do Association meeting to resolved internal disputes. Dozens of angry Tae Kwon Do masters and students strutted through the hotel lobby, along with dozens of Kim's supporters.

Kim walked into the hotel and up to the conference hall upstairs, leaving behind a wake of swearing and yelling between the two groups. Inside the hall, he could not conduct the meeting.

"President Kim, do the right thing and make up your mind!" yelled reformers in the lobby.

"He created Tae Kwon Do from nothing and you dare ask him to retire!" shouted Kim's supporters.

The yelling turned into pushing and grabbing, which I imagine is a potentially dangerous thing among Tae Kwon Do masters.

Kim said nothing, got up, and walked back to the lobby through the swearing and pushing, maintaining his composure, keeping his mouth shut. Through the fighting, he made it to his car, but some of the Tae Kwon Do instructors jumped on top of the car, stopping it. Kim sat there. What did he think as they stood on, around, and in front of him? Amid the shouting and shoving outside, did he imagine that this was a bad omen, that his supporters should have hired more muscle, and that his reign as a Tae Kwon Do king, a modern *yangban*, was over? Protestors finally let the car pull away at 11:15, but the shouting and fighting continued, which surprised foreigners arriving for an innocent international conference in Seoul.

The hotel melee was an extremely undignified display and, for the first time, the problems of Korean Tae Kwon Do — the gangsters, stealing, desperation, unfair tournaments — had spilled onto the streets of Seoul. Three days after the hotel confrontation, Kim was supposed to open the 15th World Tae Kwon Do Championship, but the rebel instructors did not care, because the last championship, in April, had been a fiasco, in their view. "It is the fault of Tae Kwon Do leaders for not preparing, for ignoring the situation after the April national championship," the instructors told a Korean reporter.

Kim Un-yong also became entangled in the South Korean

president's scandal over the $500 million sent to North Korea for the 2000 peace summit. After President Kim Dae-jung won the Nobel Peace Prize for that summit, an investigation began. So much money had flowed through various networks, through different companies, government agencies, and sports organizations, including Tae Kwon Do, that it made the KCIA Plan of the 1970s — Koreagate — look amateurish.

Kim Un-yong faced serious trouble within Tae Kwon Do. Few people knew that he had been accepting bribes from two businessmen in return for helping them to join sports committees and that he had been embezzling millions from the World Taekwondo Federation.[436] No one knew the details then, but coaches and black belts were wondering why Kim's relatives were on staff in Tae Kwon Do organizations, why there was little transparency when it came to money, and why rumours of cheating continued.

The game was not over for Kim, but he was in sudden-death overtime. He resigned from the Korean Tae Kwon Do Association in November 2001, and Koo Cheon-Seo, another politician, took over amid streets fights outside Koo's election.

Kim Un-yong felt as if the last thirty years of his life were flitting around him like a running-horse lamp, the images spinning on a single wire, the lamp becoming hotter, the horse running faster and faster, round and round on that single wire.[437]

PART V

INTEGRITY

If you're drowning, blame yourself, not the water.

— Old Korean proverb

염

치

Chapter 16

LIKE A CULT

It was a beautiful spring day in March 2001, when I accompanied Grandmaster Jong-Soo Park to General Choi Hong-Hi's house in Toronto, Canada. Park and I were both nervous. He had claimed that there had never been a plan to kidnap Choi, but the two had never discussed Choi's accusation. In turn, Park was trying to forget that Choi and his son had discussed assigning a gangster to kill Park. The General and Park had grey hair and were planning a reunion of masters and grandmasters that month while the WTF spun in turmoil.

As we stepped out of Park's rusted Mercedes, I stared at Choi's huge home. There were no trees because Choi hated squirrels. The little rodents had nibbled the cucumbers and hot peppers that Choi had grown in the gardens of his previous homes, and he did not want them scrambling around here.

Park gently lifted the door knocker, straightened his hair, and smiled when Mrs. Choi opened the front door. She bowed and immediately went to get her husband. Inside, we waited in a large hallway leading to four immaculate rooms and a spiral staircase that soared to the second floor. General Choi had replaced the cheap Leon's furniture that he had bought when he had first moved to Canada with Polish antiques that Jung-Hwa had shipped from Eastern Europe in the 1980s. Beside us, on a low shelf in perfect rows were embroidered Asian slippers. I slipped on a pair just as Choi materialized next to a parchment of calligraphy hanging on a wall.

Choi greeted Park and me with a slight nod. We bowed. His thin limbs stuck out of a plaid shirt and pinstriped pants — he looked like a large puppet. No wonder so many men had felt they could crush him. He did not fear for his life as much as in the old days, when he had once built a house on a hill, making it difficult for people to attack him.[438] Recently, when Park and Choi were out for a meal, Park had been surprised to discover that Choi still considered him a bodyguard every second that they were together; Choi asked Park to accompany him to the washroom, in case someone attacked Choi there.

Park, Choi, and I settled into the antiques in the living room and talked about Tae Kwon Do. It was difficult to get personal, but I eventually asked him about how he became a Karate expert.

"Talk a bit louder," he said, waving his hand. "My hearing is not okay." He refused to use his hearing aid.

I loudly asked about when he had lost his mother's life savings in a poker match with a wrestler — the crazy old story from 1938, when Choi's Korea was more Confucian and less Axis of Evil.

"Sir, did you ever meet the wrestler?" I asked.

"No, my friend told him that I studied Karate and he would not have a chance with me, so he avoided me." Choi chuckled. "He was just a country boy."

"Did you ever apologize to him?" I asked. I knew that Choi travelled to North Korea a lot, and I assumed that my question would be an easy one. After all, the General constantly preached about courtesy, self-control, integrity, and the other tenets of Tae Kwon Do, but he did not reply.

"Sir?" I said.

He turned his head away ninety degrees and stared at the foyer.

Park, who sat beside me, interrupted: "Of course, the General went to the hospital to see if he was dead or alive. That was a *sorry*."

"It was a five-cent bottle made of thick glass," Choi said, looking at me again. He laughed.

In fact, he had met the wrestler, Haak-Soon Huh, in North Korea, in the late 1980s, fifty years after the conflict in which Choi had knocked him out with an ink bottle.[439] To be more accurate, he did not meet him so much as summon him. By that time, Choi was an important person in North Korea and the wrestler was a commoner. During the 1938 poker match, Huh, a local wrestling champion, had been Choi's superior. During the 1980s meeting, the roles were reversed: Huh and his wife did not look directly at Choi and, as with everyone else in North Korea, they did not use first names; they addressed Choi as the powerful man he was, a friend of North Korea's leader. Choi assumed they were honoured to meet him. There were no chuckles about poker cheats, bottles flying, stolen money, near-death experiences, and — ha, ha — fleeing like a country boy, and how all the fear and silliness led to Karate and Tae Kwon Do. How ironic that one of the world's most popular martial arts was partly due to this wrestler bowing before Choi.

With Park sitting in Choi's living room in 2001, and me, a nobody, inadvertently asking impertinent questions, the General was not amused. He sat facing me with his chin tilted, like someone holding court.

But Choi's eyes lit up when he spoke about Tae Kwon Do and his efforts to improve it. He was proud that Tae Kwon Do dominated Karate. He had been fighting Japanese Karate since the Second World War. "They antagonized me then for politics; now they do so because of Tae Kwon Do," he said. His entire life had been a long war against the humiliation that Japan had inflicted on him and his people and, in 1961, against the humiliation from a South Korean dictator. In many ways, he had been fighting the same ghosts for fifty years. He had great respect for North Korea, partly because its leaders would not let Japan and the United States push them around, and also because the North Koreans liked his Tae Kwon Do.

"North Korea has original Tae Kwon Do — pure, one hundred per cent," he told me. "That's why they are very good." By pure, he meant there was no Japanese and Olympic involvement.

At the time, Choi was on a mission to force masters to learn how to jump over a standing person with no running starts, just as the ancient *hwarang* warriors had jumped over walls and kicked ceilings. Choi wanted his men to take only one or two steps and leap over an opponent — he wanted masters to train so that they could pull it off — but they rebelled and said it was impossible. In the past, some masters, such as Han Cha-gyo, had jumped over a man, but the vast majority could not and would never be able to. Choi's organization had fist fights about the issue, with some saying they should try and others declaring it was mad. Choi's demand was such an unreasonable request that a group of North Korean masters, those practising so-called pure Tae Kwon Do, said it was impossible. Choi slapped one of them.[440] He insisted that people should try.

Soon after, I met General Choi in his house again, alone, and he led me to a study, where he pointed to his 1965 and 1972 Tae Kwon Do books. Jong-Soo Park jumped on the covers. "He was my prize student," Choi said. A phone rang, but no one answered. He crouched and touched volume one of his fifteen-volume encyclopedia set. "History is in this one," he said gently. "This volume contains the Theory of Power. This one, hand techniques." He spoke as if he were in a church. "This volume is sparring," he whispered, as the phone rang again. "Patterns, here." He had created a condensed version of the fifteen volumes in the 1980s, he said, because people could not carry around all fifteen, which were more than a foot thick when piled together. "Too heavy," he said matter-of-factly.

He flipped through another volume until he came to the pattern *Tong-Il*, which means "unification." He was proud of this one, the last pattern of the twenty-four, because it symbolized reunification of the two Koreas. "See? It's easy to learn," he said, turning the pages slowly. "You follow the photos." As the phone rang again, we looked at the techniques in *Tong-Il*, the middle punches with the twin fists, the horizontal strikes with the twin knife-hands. If only politics had been as easy as a knife-hand in his own life — and in the lives of Kim Un-yong and all the rest.

I thought of what he had told me in the living room earlier: "To die is pitiful . . . It is lamentable that one cannot live as long as time permits." Choi was eighty-two years old and still fighting. The phone rang for thirtieth time. It had been ringing almost continuously for an hour.

✘ ✘ ✘

Nine months later, in January 2002, I met Jung-Hwa Choi, the General's son and the supposed heir to all things Tae Kwon Do. Their ITF was in trouble, as was the WTF. While the older man reminded me of stone, his son seemed like water — adaptable, hard to pin down, and transparent. Jung-Hwa lived in the same Canadian city as his father. His home was smaller but just as opulent. I walked into the living room, where he sat in a large golden chair wearing a blue tie and an immaculate white shirt. His wife stood in the kitchen. His right-hand man, Joe Cariati, sat across the room.

In the 1990s, Jung-Hwa began rebelling after he was released from prison, partly for personal reasons, but mainly because he thought that the General was destroying the martial art with Cold War politics. Jung-Hwa had learned from his mistakes but it seemed his father had not; for decades, they had pushed against one another, against the pressures created by Tae Kwon Do, against madness, but both men were now pushing even more. "I think he had always worried that his son would undo what he had built," Jung-Hwa told me. "Sometimes, I laugh at this, because he had a monopoly in Tae Kwon Do in the 1970s; there were no other competitors, meaning we had tens of millions of members. I can tell you now, we are in the hundreds of thousands." Worldwide. "If this isn't bankruptcy, what is?"

The conflict between father and son was embedded in a Confucian view of family relationships. For example, Choi rarely spoke to his son about personal matters. One morning, however, Jung-Hwa asked his father if he still dreamed about his own father.

"What a silly question," the General replied. "Do you know how old I am? I'm past eighty years old! Do you think I have memories of my father?"

That was not the answer his son had expected. Surely, the love of one's parents remained inside one's heart, no matter what one's age, especially for someone like Choi, who expected his son to show unwavering love and obedience.

"Did you enjoy conversation with your father?" Jung-Hwa pressed. He knew his father had lived under Confucianism, and therefore the boundaries of father-son relationships had been strictly observed, but he wanted to know if his father and grandfather had even talked.

"He was very strict with me, and he was very disciplined, so I had to observe father-son respect, not like you, who are out of line in asking such questions," Choi replied. That was how Jung-Hwa learned that he was to never discuss his father's father.

Choi's latest mission was to merge the International Taekwon-Do Federation with the World Taekwondo Federation, as part of the talks to help the two countries reunify. Choi expected Jung-Hwa to build a strong relationship with North Korea, but Jung-Hwa did not want to, and wanted to exorcize politics from the martial art. "He was always trying to ingrain in my head that I must follow North Korea, because they were so helpful towards ITF, and I said,

'I don't see anything that they are helping us with. In fact, it's weird, sacrificing not only our teaching to them, but becoming outsiders to our own people by following them.'"

It was in July 2001, three months after a seminar with General Choi at the Novotel Hotel in Toronto, that Jung-Hwa had fully realized the consequences of defying his father. It was around the time that Kim Un-yong was aiming for the IOC presidency. Choi and his son were standing in a hotel hallway in Rimini, Italy. Masters from around the world had recently elected Jung-Hwa as the next president of the ITF, much to his father's surprise. The young man hoped that his father would finally take a rest, would retire perhaps. But, as Jung-Hwa stood there, his father, the *chadol*, the small stone, was immobile.

"What's wrong?" Jung-Hwa asked.

"Please get away from me!" Choi said, shooing him away like a servant. "You are not my son!"

For as long as Jung-Hwa could remember, his father had humiliated him with this comment. Sometimes, the older man would add that he had sons elsewhere. Jung-Hwa stepped out of hitting range. Clearly, General Choi was unhappy that Jung-Hwa had become ITF president.

Later, as they drove to the closing ceremony of the world championship, Choi warned, "I promise you, boy, that I will unite ITF and WTF within one year. When I do, I will give everything to Kim Un-yong. I will never see you become president."

Jung-Hwa said that he saw his father's real face then for the first time in his life, and it was not human. The elder Choi despised Kim Un-yong — or so everyone assumed. General Choi was not demented, Jung-Hwa believed, but was under the influence of something stronger than old age: North Korea. He realized that his father was going to defy what the elected masters had decided; he, Jung-Hwa, would be ousted somehow.

Jung-Hwa soon quit the ITF and set up his own organization, also called the ITF. He claimed that one-third of the world ITF membership joined him, and he said that his father was lying about an ITF-WTF merger.

Negotiations between the two have often been a joke. The two groups have been abusing each other and discussing mergers the way beatings are followed by promises in a dysfunctional marriage. Negotiations between Tae Kwon Do factions began long before

Kim Un-yong arrived on the scene; in the 1950s, heated arguments took place between the nine main martial arts gyms in Korea, and in the 1960s, between the ITF and the Korean Tae Kwon Do Association. Since their divorce in 1973, the ITF and WTF have discussed reunifying many times, but often, the announcements about merger attempts sound like fantasies created for hopeful black belts around the world — and hopeful Koreans — who want mama and dada to get along.

"Whenever there was unrest in the ITF, or inactivity in the ITF, we would come out with certain statements, such as 'we are going to merge,' or 'our instructors are being invited to South Korea,'" Jung-Hwa Choi later told me. "In fact, I'm one of those who is guilty. I was instructed by my father to write a letter, as Secretary General, to our members around the world that we may be sending a demonstration team to South Korea and that we were looking for people who would like to take part in it. The letter even went further to mention that we may even send ITF members to South Korea to open schools. Of course, there was nothing to back this up."

For its part, the behemoth WTF does not need the pipsqueak ITF. The leaders of both meet every year or so, elevating hope that the powerful WTF will accept the traditional ITF. "Those groups are talking at a fairly high level to do a merger," WTF Canada's Wayne Mitchell said, "but I don't think it's going to be a merger as much as an absorption . . . we don't have much to gain from merging." He added that the ITF does not have access to the dollars and resources available to the WTF — the relationship is eerily similar to the political history between poor, proud North Korea and rich, suave South Korea.

Jung-Hwa Choi did not want North Korea to swallow Tae Kwon Do. He felt as if his father were running the Tae Kwon Do organization like a cult, another reason Jung-Hwa split off to create his own ITF. When his father visited Reverend Sun-Myung Moon to ask for money, Jung-Hwa was not surprised. "General Choi, I think, would be very happy if he were in the place of Reverend Moon Sun-Myung. You know? Moonie?" Jung-Hwa said. "He used to just lambaste Moon. He used to talk badly about him, but now I know it was jealousy. He did go and meet Moon one day. After he returned, he said, 'Why is he bad after all?' Even before that, he told me how, at Moon's snapping fingers, people would just stop moving and come to his command, and how he used to move people around. General

Choi was impressed. I said, 'Careful, sir, you're trying to use him, but how can a shrimp swallow a whale?'"

"The ITF organization was an absolute autocracy — there were no questions asked," Jung-Hwa said. Many Tae Kwon Do instructors agreed with this assessment, usually adding in the same breath that the General was a genius.[441] "As a matter of fact, General Choi said, 'Buddha comes from India, yet India is mainly Hindu," Jung-Hwa said. "Jesus comes from Israel, but there's not much Christianity there. Ironically, Tae Kwon Do comes from South Korea, but there's no ITF Tae Kwon Do there.' Does that mean he wants to become the fourth saint?"

Worse than the saint was the sinner. Jung-Hwa suspected that the darkest part of his father was attracted to a despotic government in North Korea, where millions of people suffered oppression. Once, during a sumptuous meal in North Korea, Jung-Hwa told his father that the economy was backwards, and his father replied, "How can you say that? We eat like this all the time. How can you say this country is poor?"

"This is not an everyday dinner for the common people," Jung-Hwa explained to him. His father refused to listen. In fact, he made it a mission to tell anyone he met, every day, that North Korea was doing well. Jung-Hwa realized that his father, who dined with North Korean dignitaries, could not care less for the average North Korean and the gulags that awaited commoners if they complained. Choi's entire life was Tae Kwon Do and he needed the North Koreans.

"There are two Generals," Jung-Hwa said as sat in his living room. "One is the great man General Choi." That was the "founder" of Tae Kwon Do. "The other is a child who grew up in a broken home and who always desired love. When he could not find love from his family, he turned to his disciples." If they failed him, he would feel betrayed, and he would turn on them verbally or physically. As they fell, he rose. "It is what they call Small Man's Syndrome, in which one has to appear the best, one knows the best, and one has to constantly prove that one is great, even to family," Jung-Hwa added. "Every day, he gave us a sermon, every breakfast and dinner, about how great he was." And the family listened. "One Christmas, he actually told us, 'Why do you believe in God? If you want to believe in God, then believe in my fist."

In fighting brutal men all his life, the General had become brutal himself and had wrecked many people — and had also suffered in the process. It was no surprise that he wanted to be a god. He had a hard time being human.

Not even the North Korean instructors were spared. "I have seen him really butcher people in front of others," Jung-Hwa said. Once, in 2001 during a Tae Kwon Do seminar, North Korean instructors asked Jung-Hwa to tell his father that they had not prepared a sparring demonstration. Choi had asked them to research new sparring methods, but they came to the seminar with only research papers and they approached Jung-Hwa for help: "They said, 'We know General Choi, so, if you please, can you tell him not to ask us to do any physical demonstration, because we've done only academic research.' I said, 'I will try.' I explained to General Choi, 'Is that all right?' and he said, 'Yeah, okay.' Suddenly, he was in a different mood and, the next day, he called them up to demonstrate, knowing they had not prepared. Of course, their faces turned white . . . They were almost out of their minds, because they were in front of many delegates. General Choi was screaming at them, 'Show it in physical form! . . . Shut up! Stop reading! You do the demonstration!' But they weren't hearing General Choi anymore; they were like zombies, reading, and we all cried for them. Then General Choi left. He could not keep his temper and he started to smash his hand on the wall, screaming. Many people thought he was going to have a heart attack that day — many people wished that he would have a heart attack . . . That was a turning point for many members."

Jung-Hwa knew what he was up against. Splitting from his father and starting an ITF organization meant a vicious conflict. For his part, General Choi did not trust his own son and thought Jung-Hwa was trying to kill him.

Chapter 17

THE LITTLE GIANT DIES AND TRADITIONAL TAE KWON DO FALLS APART

Master Sun said:
There are Five Ways to
Attack by Fire.
The first is to burn men . . .

— *The Art of War*, Sun-Tzu, sixth century BCE[442]

A month later, priorities suddenly changed, because Choi Hong-Hi contracted cancer and doctors gave him little time to live. The war in the ITF calmed slightly, and the organization continued to splinter as fast as the cancer that was spreading through Choi. The subsequent developments were a stunning display of what happens when one person rules an organization too long and pits executive against executive, son against surrogate son, in a battle to replace him.

Jong-Soo Park and a handful of other loyal disciples helped the elder Choi day and night. Choi refused to eat much and cried if anyone talked about Jung-Hwa. "My only son betrayed me," he would repeat.

It was difficult to feel sorry for him, but I did — and for Jung-Hwa as well.

One day, his son visited him at a Toronto hospital and went into a mild state of shock, for his father's body had deteriorated into skin and skeleton.[443] General Choi looked at him and said, "I don't want to see you, I don't want to see you." Jung-Hwa kept his head down, at a ninety-degree angle, until his mother, who was in the room, suddenly screamed at him. Jung-Hwa could not stand that and left, but he returned to the hospital parking lot on the day when his father was discharged. His mother emerged from the hospital, not escorted by bodyguards or grandmasters, and as Jung-Hwa waited, she walked past him. The younger Choi walked into the hospital and helped the old man to the car. Jung-Hwa was happy that he could briefly hold his father, but it did not end well, as usual, because his mother yelled that he was killing the older man. Jung-Hwa left.

He was the only son, and his father's favourite, so this three-year conflict must have nearly killed both of them. Once, when Jung-Hwa was two years old, he was playing on a windowsill and fell off, cutting his head and chin. General Choi had just returned from work when he saw his son's blood. The family did not have time to find a doctor, so the General removed his military jacket, wrapped his son in it, and ran many miles to the nearest hospital, forgetting his shoes at home. People wondered at the barefoot madman sprinting past with a bleeding boy.[444]

Now, over the weeks, the disease spread to the General's liver and he looked yellow. Jung-Hwa did not accompany him to international seminars, such as the one in Denver, Colorado, where the General taught from a wheelchair.

On a day in May 2002, however, as the General sat in a wheelchair at Toronto's international airport, surrounded by disciples and bodyguards and waiting for a plane to North Korea, he did not expect his son to show up. He still suspected that Jung-Hwa would try to kill him. His son arrived at the airport with Joe Cariati and other martial artists, and they walked up to the General. Standing near the elder Choi was the obsequious Master Soon-Cheon Jeong (who took photos), Grandmaster Kang-Sung Hwang (who lived in the United States), Grandmaster Woojin Jung (publisher of *Tae Kwon Do Times*), Grandmaster Jong-Soo Park, and others, all there to say goodbye to the General — and perhaps there for other reasons, too.

Jung-Hwa did not want to hurt his father. Instead, he sat beside him and held his shoulders. He felt mainly bones. He desperately wanted his father to stay in Toronto but dared not ask. It had taken all he had just to get to the airport. He tried to think of good memories and the love he had for him. "It's not that scary to touch my father," he told himself, because he had always felt that it would be scary. He touched the General's head. He wished that they could have been closer when he had been a boy and his father a younger man. What thoughts to have ten minutes before departure! Jung-Hwa's friend, a few feet away, was crying. "You know, I never had a Choi family," Jung-Hwa quietly told him.

"Can you apologize to me on the internet?" the General asked Jung-Hwa, who was taken aback. Jung-Hwa's allies had criticized the General's men, the disciples who Jung-Hwa had called hypocrites and "Tae Kwon Do geishas." There was so much that the two men should have resolved before Choi boarded the plane: how a father could brag about sacrificing his son, why the young man had used the name of his father's martial art, why violence lived in them like desire. Instead, Choi talked about the internet.

"And can you apologize to my boys — to the North Koreans?" the General asked Jung-Hwa, who assumed that his father wanted to save face, that his father wanted to assure the North Koreans that Jung-Hwa was on their side. It was perhaps surreal, and not only because a U.S. president had recently made a speech including North Korea in an "Axis of Evil." Jung-Hwa's father could never admit to losing.

"Sir, let's not talk about this now," his son replied.

General Choi spoke about North Korea's Arirang festival, a two-month event of gymnastics, dance, and arts involving hundreds of thousands of performers. Arirang celebrated the birthday of the nation's founder, Kim Il Sung, and was open to tourists and journalists. "You will come to see me?" Choi asked him. The Arirang Festival was worth seeing, he explained.

The younger Choi did not answer; he would never go to North Korea, not like this.

One of the masters took a photo of Choi and his son at the airport. Their eyes revealed nothing. The stone remained unchanged. Water flowed around it. But Jung-Hwa later stared at his father's face, for he wanted it ingrained in his mind. Then he pushed the wheelchair to the departure gate, where someone else rolled it away. When saying goodbye, it is a Korean tradition to keep your eyes on visitors for as long as possible, and Jung-Hwa watched as long as he could, watched his father shrink into the distance.

About a month later, on June 15, 2002, as Choi lay near death in P'yŏngyang, North Korea, he dictated his last will, which Jong-Soo Park heard. Choi appointed his successor then: Chang Ung, the North Korean Olympic representative to whom Kim Un-yong had been sending money. Ung had been a basketball player and he towered over the Tae Kwon Do grandmasters.

As Choi lay there, he remembered the wrestler, the ink bottle, the flight to Japan, the hardcore Karate training in the late 1930s. "If only I had been as tall as Mr. Chang Ung I could have had less opponents," he said. "My body was so tiny. There were many opponents."

Later, Park heard him say, "I'm the happiest man in the world, the happiest man in the world."[445]

✗ ✗ ✗

General Choi Hong-Hi received a state funeral in North Korea, which deeply worried his son because few people received state funerals in that nation, and he wondered if his father had been a spy or double spy. However, Jung-Hwa knew what to do: he would save his father's name and tell the world that General Choi had not been a communist. "We are ready to resurrect him once again," he told me.

The ITF split into three groups: one led by the North Korean, Chang Ung, according to the General's last wishes; a second, run by Jung-Hwa; and a third led by black belts who refused to join the other two.

Afterwards, court battles raged over who owned trademarks as the three groups eroded into smaller factions. A lawyer involved in one of the trademark lawsuits told me that everything seemed to be about money: "Everybody wants to know what they're getting. 'What's my cut?' they ask." Money was only a part of it however. Individual power, national politics, and historical legacies overshadowed the money, because the techniques would thrive far longer than the men, only some of whom would become immortal.

Choi would be an immortal. He was more sad than saint in the end, but he was a founding member of Tae Kwon Do nevertheless. His legacy is shadowed by a Confucian father, Japanese torture, Korean dictators, Kim Un-yong, and Choi's own demons.

Chapter 18

WTF Leaders Go to Prison and Olympic Tae Kwon Do Faces Oblivion

We've moved into a business age. It's far smarter to run those organizations like businesses rather than like criminal organizations or an extension of that sort of thing.

– Wayne Mitchell, Canada's WTF Secretary
General, referring to the WTF worldwide

In 2003, Kim Un-yong became vice-president of the International Olympic Committee, which meant that he was the second most powerful person in the Olympics and, given the controversies that he had survived, showed that he was perhaps as powerful as a wealthy *yangban* aristocrat of the Chosŏn dynasty. "He had the power to do anything," a Korean sports journalist told *Time* magazine. "He was God."[446]

But this was the twenty-first century and not even a god could prevent media leaks. As Tae Kwon Do limped to the next Olympics, rumours grew about Kim using bribes to finance his run for the IOC vice-presidency, and a worse one began that, in exchange for votes to become vice-president, he had undermined a bid by the South Korean city of P'yŏngch'ang to host the 2010 winter Olympics. The bid accusation was difficult to believe; if there were one thing that had been consistent in Kim's career, it had been his loyalty to his country. But Vancouver had defeated P'yŏngch'ang by fifty-six votes to fifty-three to host the 2010 games, and Kim became a scapegoat for South Korea's loss. The irony must have hurt; Kim and his Operation Thunderbird had brought the Olympics to South Korea in 1988 and his 007 operation had made Tae Kwon Do an official sport at the 2000 games. He had helped to place his tiny country at the top of the international sports scene — not only in Tae Kwon Do but in many sports — and here he was being accused of betraying his country.

In 2003, Kim met General Choi's successor, the North Korean Chang Ung, at a sports event called the Summer Universiade. They agreed to organize a joint march during the opening ceremony at the 2004 Athens Olympics, replicating the tear-jerker at the opening ceremony of the 2000 Sydney Olympics, but Kim did not make it to the 2004 opening. [447]

South Korean officials raided his home and office and found $1.6 million in foreign currencies in a safe. Bad timing, you could say. Reporters mobbed a white-masked Kim as police led him away. In total, prosecutors discovered $5 million in gold, diamonds, gems, and foreign currency.

Under attack from all sides, Kim resigned from South Korea's National Assembly and from the World Taekwondo Federation, from where he had embezzled $676,000 that had been donated by the Samsung Corporation, the company that had donated funds for the WTF's home, the Kukkiwon, in 1971.[448] He said that the charges were politically motivated, but he did not explain how.[449] "These suspicions are currently under investigation by legal authorities and the truth will soon come out, but, regardless of the facts, I bow my head in deep apology for distressing the nation with my misconduct," Kim said.[450] The Olympic Committee suspended him.

Internationally, Olympic Tae Kwon Do faced its worst crisis in history, and, country by country, Kim's network began crumbling as national associations closed and his Tae Kwon Do friends began quitting or defending themselves.

In South Korea, prosecutors exposed the overlap between organized crime and Tae Kwon Do. After Kim's resignation from the Korean Tae Kwon Do Association, the KTA had elected a new leader, Koo Cheon-Soo, who was a South Korean politician. In December 2003, police arrested Koo on charges of bribing officials and rigging his KTA election to replace Kim. Prosecutors later indicted Koo, accusing him of using 300 "gangsters and taekwondo experts" to stop rivals from attending the election and of paying over $20,000 to two association officials ahead of the vote. The seventeen delegates who got past the gangsters voted unanimously for Koo as leader of the KTA.

"The Korean Tae Kwon Do Association has been controlled by

politicians and criminal gangs," a prosecutor said. "Bosses have influenced the association since the 1990s," he added. "As pressure grew for them to stop doing so, the gangs pooled efforts to make Mr. Koo the association's chairman."[451]

Also arrested was an adviser to the KTA, Lee Seng-wan, the Tae Kwon Do master who had served time in prison for hiring fifty gangsters to disrupt a pro-democracy political party in 1987. Here he stood again, seventeen years later, sentenced to four years in prison for colluding with Koo and two others in preventing KTA members from attending the Tae Kwon Do election.[452]

Big bosses of organized crime rings had been attracted to the money-generating capacity of Tae Kwon Do. One godfather had received bribes from a company making electronic protective gear for the WTF, gear that was supposed to decrease cheating and mistakes in Olympic Tae Kwon Do sparring. Police also arrested eleven others in the 2003 round-up: three other godfathers, one politician, and seven criminals involved in a Tae Kwon Do bribery scandal in Taegu city.

The year before, in 2002, a Korean journalist asked Lee Chong-woo, a WTF vice-president, about all the gang members in the martial art.[453] Lee replied that gangsters gave Tae Kwon Do a bad name and that he, Lee, was a "sinner" for having allowed them in the organization.

> **Reporter:** You mean, hiring people [gang members] for occasions such as General Assembly Meetings or Board of Director Meetings . . .
>
> **Lee:** It is not just for that. There were numerous occasions [sic] disrupted by insignificant issues. In order to ease such a situation, sometimes making these people visible made for better circumstances.
>
> **Reporter:** You mean, they entered [the organization] because of the age-old factions in Tae Kwon Do?
>
> **Lee:** That's right.

Choi Hong-hi and his men no doubt led one of those "age-old factions." Lee ended the interview by lamenting, "For the second stage of Tae Kwon Do, a successor for Un Yong Kim should have come along a day earlier."

A year after this pitiable statement, a North Korean official sent a fax to Kim's office in Seoul, reminding him that he was behind in his payments to North Korea Olympic official Chang Ung, the head of Choi's International Taekwon-Do Federation. Kim told prosecutors about the fax.[454]

In the United States, in the same year, the U.S. Olympic Committee side-kicked the U.S. Taekwondo Union out of the Olympics, citing a lengthy list of problems with competitions, governance, and finances. Since 1984, the USTU had been head of the WTF in the U.S., a pillar of global Tae Kwon Do from the beginning. The USTU's president, Sang-Chul Lee, a friend of Kim Un-yong's, stepped down during the turmoil, and, soon, the entire USTU was abolished, along with all fifty state organizations. Around U.S.$1.2 million was missing, and the lawsuits began.

Non-Korean Tae Kwon Do experts in the United States took the opportunity to talk about their disenfranchisement, about the times they were ignored for WTF positions because they were not Korean, and about the ethnocentrism in a martial art that unfairly favoured Koreans.[455] When the battlefield cleared in 2006, the old dysfunctional Tae Kwon Do was gone and a new organization, USA Taekwondo (USAT), had replaced Sang's organization. USAT paid the $1.2 million back to the Olympic Committee and established a commission to improve things, especially to bring back the hundreds of pioneers and instructors who had not been corrupt.[456] "Only a handful of people messed up the organization," said Joon-Pyo Choi, co-chairman of the commission, "but they eliminated all the Korean-American masters and grandmasters who were pioneers in Tae Kwon Do in the USA since the 1950s. That was a big mistake." The in-fighting and resignations spread to other countries.

In Canada, Wayne Mitchell, Secretary General of the WTF, became heavily involved with the organization during the difficult time. "For Canada, it changed," he said, "and for the WTF it did when Kim Un-yong got caught with his hand in the till, which led to an emergency situation and the IOC saying, 'Clean up your act.' I think a lot of people stood up to the plate and said, 'Enough is enough.'" He added: "Sport Canada was going to stop our funding; we changed our constitution to a democratic one. The new push with the new president is openness and accountability. For the first time ever, you see budgets and books and audits."[457]

This is after fifty years of Tae Kwon Do.

I asked him why there was so much corruption. "I'm wondering if it's the time period they come from," Mitchell replied, "because Kim Un-yong was from the secret service . . . and, you know, South Korea was far from democratic, even though they called it that for a long time." In the early 1960s, Kim had begun his career in a haze of corruption embedded in a South Korean dictatorship. Forty years later, he ended his career in the same way but in a democracy.

In June 2004, two months before the summer Olympics, a South Korean court found Kim guilty of embezzling more than $3 million from sports organisations and accepting more than $700,000 in bribes.[458] Prosecutors accused him of turning his Tae Kwon Do and Olympic organizations into private enterprises and sentenced him to two and a half years in prison — and ordered him to pay a fine of more than $600,000.[459] His appeal to Korea's Supreme Court shortened the sentence to two years. His supporters said that the investigation and the jail term were part of a political vendetta, and that Kim was a scapegoat for South Korea's failed bid to win the 2010 winter Olympics, but no one provided details.[460] Kim kept those secrets to himself.

✗ ✗ ✗

After such trials in the WTF, how could its new president, Choue Chung-won, step into the job with his chin up, even with his martial arts training? Choue had been an executive council member of the Korea Taekwondo Association since 1999, president of a university from 1996 to 2003, and an architect of a Tae Kwon Do Department in that school.[461] After winning 106 out of 149 votes from WTF member countries, Choue told the media during his presidential acceptance speech that "now is the time for us to be reborn as a multi-national sports organization." He also announced that each member country would receive $20,000 and each continental Tae Kwon Do union $50,000 as a "reform fund" from the IOC. Two months later, he met North Korean ITF head Chang Ung at the 2004 Athens Olympic Games, where South and North Korea joined hands, just as Kim Un-yong had planned.

The immediate challenge for Choue was how to keep Tae Kwon

Do in the Olympics, because the IOC was considering dropping the sport after the 2004 summer games. The main controversies within the WTF were not only financial corruption and unfair judging; another worry was that Olympic sparring matches were often boring to watch and resulted in low television ratings.

"Tae Kwon Do is very very unpopular as a spectator sport in the Olympics," Tae Kwon Do pioneer Jhoon Rhee told me. "I've been crying out, 'Make the tournaments a little more interesting.' They use only feet, no punches to the face, so, naturally, they rely on kicking." Rhee had been extremely frustrated with Kim Un-yong, Uhm Woon-kyu, and other WTF leaders. "They had their minds set; they were not going to listen to me," Rhee said.[462]

Tae Kwon Do Times ran a frank article about the sparring problems in 2005. In "Saving Olympic Tae Kwon Do," journalist Chuck Stepan wrote that the 2004 Olympic sparring had been boring: "Even the referees were getting adamant, banging their fists together trying to get the competitors to mix it up. Other than the Korean team members, it is kind of a worldwide malaise where the competitors seem anxious to survive rather than to win . . . Hopping around then finally a step and a skip and a roundhouse to the vest — backing off and starting again or holding on, is the expected competitor routine. Any point fighter or barroom brawler watching an Olympic Tae Kwon Do match knows that a good punch in the nose would stop all the skipping around. Yet, Olympic Tae Kwon Do allows no face punching." He lamented that sparring no longer contained the older, artistic techniques: jumping back-kicks, aerial front kicks, jumping reverse kicks of all kinds. "Bring back the head punch and save the sport," he begged, adding that the corruption in U.S. Tae Kwon Do did not help and, worse, he disliked the attitude of a great number of competitors, "who would sit on the sidelines wearing caps weighed down with pins while they screamed out such phrases as, "Kill him, knock his block off" or other such niceties while participating in an activity I always believed to be a humbling and courteous undertaking."[463]

At the end of 2004, the WTF's new president, Choue, released a 188-page Strategic Plan that would make Tae Kwon Do more transparent and less boring.[464] He became the first president of the Korea Fair Play Committee in 2005, countering a WTF official's claim three years earlier that fair play in Tae Kwon Do did not exist. "Fair play is a really important thing," Choue told a reporter. "So what I am going to do as the [KFPC] president is to spread the fair play spirit to the sport."

In June 2005, after Kim Un-yong had served about a year of his thirty-month sentence, he was released on parole. He was seventy-four years old. In a written statement, he said, "While I look forward to rejoining my family and ending this long ordeal, I would like to take this opportunity to maintain my innocence of all allegations against me."[465] He then underwent prostate surgery.

✗ ✗ ✗

Korea is known for its astounding economic growth of the last forty years. The development of Tae Kwon Do is its second most incredible feat; the power and athleticism of the martial art put Korea on the world map, and its Olympic status gives Korea a stage on which to promote itself. Whatever happens, Tae Kwon Do's leaders do not want to lose Olympic recognition. A WTF Reform Committee told the media they wanted to make the martial art more action-packed in the ring and more professional in the office. The WTF was considering a rule to add points for attempting difficult kicks during sparring.[466] Marketing was also a priority. The WTF told a Korean publication that "the WTF would draw more attention from sponsors. The marketing proceeds would support the 177-member National Associations by providing uniforms and equipment, along with technical assistance, such as more training programs for coaches and athletes."[467]

A majority of the 116 members on the International Olympic Committee voted for Tae Kwon Do to remain in the Olympics for 2008 and 2012, thanks to recent WTF reforms.[468] Choue was relieved: "I felt some credit was recovered from the world's taekwondo people after Kim Un-yong's embezzlement and jail term," he told a newspaper.[469]

The WTF announced that it would adopt electronic protective gear during sparring, so that a kick would register points automatically. This means that a computer instead of a referee would score a sparring match. The WTF used the electronic pads at a 2007 national event, where 70 per cent of practitioners thought it was good. "It was kind of exciting, but it took the referee's function away," said Joon-Pyo Choi, who coached the U.S. Olympic team in 1988 and is helping USA Taekwondo. "The electronic scoring system will minimize human error and mismanagement."[470] WTF men such as Choi and Choue have high hopes for their martial art, but the electronic equipment will not be ready for the 2008 Olympics. Referees need training to use it and computer experts need to refine the communication between pads and computers to prevent hackers from tampering with a sparring match.[471] Then there are the kickback scandals swirling around the purchase of the equipment.

The corruption and chaos is not surprising. Tae Kwon Do was born into controversy and thrived among dictators for most of its life. The two men at the centre of the conflicts, Choi Hong-Hi and Kim Un-yong, are from another era and are now gone, but their disciples and legacies continue, as do the struggles to stop corruption and cheating:

- In 2006, South Korean police convicted WTF officials involved in selling fake Tae Kwon Do referee licenses to more than thirty people. The WTF dismissed the officials.[472]

- In 2007, the Australian Olympic Committee back fisted the Australian WTF organization out of the Olympics; the upheavals there seem similar to the ones in the United States and Canada a couple of years ago.[473]

- In 2008, a small global war began in the WTF after a vice-president complained about an international referee-selection course for the 2008 Olympics. The WTF formed a committee to look into the matter.[474]

Perhaps the most surreal development was in 2008, when Lee Seng-wan announced that he had become a director of the Kukkiwon, the world headquarters of Olympic Tae Kwon Do. Lee, who had been imprisoned for working with 300 gangsters and martial artists to disrupt a Tae Kwon Do election in 2002, said that it was time for the Kukkiwon "to reevaluate their personnel and get rid of those who are corrupted."[475] Coming from a long-time criminal, the irony was so blatant that it could mean only one thing: the turf wars in Tae Kwon Do were not yet over; the new leaders of the WTF are still fighting corruption and cheating.

Recently, Jhoon Rhee told me to contact Jin-Suk Yang, the WTF's new secretary general, because Yang represented a sophisticated, reformed WTF: "He speaks perfect English; he was mayor of a small city in California; he's very intelligent," Rhee said.[476] Yang was a Tae Kwon Do master who had once run his own gyms and held a high position in a Korean police force. Just before I called him, however, a news article reported that he had offered an envelope of cash to International Olympic Committee member Nat Indrapana, who was chairman of the WTF Reform Committee. Yang said that the money had not been a bribe, that he had offered the cash to replace Indrapana's lost luggage at an airport. An IOC Ethics Commission concluded it was not "acceptable behaviour, inasmuch as such conduct runs the obvious risk of being interpreted as a corruption attempt," and recommended the WTF take appropriate action. As of June 2008, the WTF was still deliberating about what to do.[477]

After the violence and megalomania of Tae Kwon Do's leaders, the next generation of organizers have more humble plans, like helping athletes to win medals. For decades, some of Tae Kwon Do's leaders have run the martial art like a cult or a crime syndicate — parts of the martial art headed by gods or godfathers. Perhaps the biggest accomplishment of Tae Kwon Do in the past four years is that no one has been caught stealing more than $1 million or planning to assassinate someone. The crimes are of a lower order and the threats still fly, but everyone seems in control. Children still attend Tae Kwon Do classes after school and athletes feel that there will be less cheating in the competitions.

In spite of the surreal problems, the WTF and the ITF groups are at least more transparent than in the past. "Ten years ago, the executive would just institute a change two days before an event and nothing was ever done about it," WTF Canada's Wayne Mitchell explained. "They could just do what they wanted. This year, they tried to make some changes before the Olympic world qualifier without asking the country members what they wanted, and the members rejected it. They told the WTF that if they tried to use those rules, then the event wouldn't run and everybody would pull out. So, I think they're understanding that they have to be fair to all the members. They can't be like they were in the past."[478]

Tae Kwon Do's dictators are retiring.

Chapter 19

Reprieve

The Bodhidharma once said that the farther away you are from the truth, the worse your life becomes and the better you feel. Lost, you feel more hate but also more pleasure. Self-deception (like good Scotch) helps to get through it all. The Bodhidharma apparently practised a martial art and taught it to his disciples, and some martial arts experts argue that Tae Kwon Do arose from those roots.[479] The men who started Tae Kwon Do, however, cut away all attachments to religion, even though they still adhered to the Bodhidharma's spirit of non-violence — at least in their tenets and moral teachings.

Tae Kwon Do is the art of self-defence, but it is also the art of killing and, after years of training, the art of empowerment. As such, it includes many responsibilities, summarized in the art's five tenets and five virtues — what Choi Hong-Hi called "moral culture." I walked into the backrooms of Tae Kwon Do to find out about this culture and discovered a group of generals, aristocrats, soldiers, country boys, and party animals preaching a mix of Confucian values and barroom slogans. Karate, T'aekkyŏn, and the old Korean arts provided Tae Kwon Do with a warrior's spirit, capitalism gave it a profit motive, and the Korean military and secret service added Cold War values, best illustrated by Mutual Assured Destruction. Choi was more concerned with justice than profit — and had his own MAD theory. Once, during a dinner with a group of black belts in the 1970s, he said that everyone in the world should learn Tae Kwon Do. That way, respectful and wary, people would not attack each other.

The General has passed away, but his son, Jung-Hwa Choi, runs an International Taekwon-Do Federation, and Chang Ung in North Korea oversees the bulk of the General's ITF and sits on the International Olympic Committee. Nam Tae-hi retired to California. Jong-Soo Park still teaches in his Toronto gym and has released a ten-DVD set, *Mastering Tae Kwon Do,* that sells for $450. Meanwhile, Jhoon Rhee told me Kim Un-yong is working underground to restore his position in the World Taekwondo Federation. "I'm publicly speaking out that he should never be allowed to come back," Rhee said.[480]

Many friends ask why I practise Tae Kwon Do. Why should anyone? With its flawed leaders, bizarre history, and aggressive techniques, why did I enrol my daughter in Tae Kwon Do lessons and why do I meet black belts to train every week? The answers lie in the training itself.

Last week, my ten-year-old daughter and I walked to our neighbourhood WTF gym for her class. Her *dojang* is similar to thousands of gyms around the world. You walk down concrete stairs to a huge basement with padded floors. On the walls, beside red and white chest gear, hang Choi Hong-Hi's five tenets in foot-high Korean calligraphy:

Indomitable Spirit
Perseverance
Self-control
Courtesy
Integrity

On a table near the office lies a Tae Kwon Do book by Kim Un-yong, and on another wall hang pages of martial arts patterns. On a bulletin board is a giddy article about the eternally positive Jhoon Rhee (perhaps the most widely quoted Tae Kwon Do expert in the world), in which he discusses training methods for older people and how they can live to be a hundred years old. To prove his point, the seventy-seven year old can still do one hundred push-ups without stopping. Also tacked to the bulletin board is a cranky article about "McDojos," the shoddy, money-making martial arts gyms similar to the one in the movie *The Foot Fist Way,* a parody of the worst aspects of a McDojo.

The gym in my neighbourhood is not a McDojo. The owner is a

humble man, a former national champion and, as with many black belts who have studied for more than thirty years, an expert in both traditional and Olympic Tae Kwon Do. He wrote words of advice on a whiteboard in the gym: "It's not the size of the dog, but the size of the fight in the dog." How right he is.

There are no animals in this gym — no Tae Kwon Do leaders; no soldiers, secret-service agents, or Korean geisha girls; no cheating and loud egos. The challenges are still here: the mild hysteria during sparring; the small injuries and complaints; the clashing personalities; minor disagreements over style and technique — normal, human conflicts that the owner handles with diplomacy. He is as dexterous in relationships as he is on his feet. For children and adults, he offers pep talks, explanations, and practical philosophy as a routine part of training.

As my friend Martin Crawford and I stretch at the back of the room, my daughter, Martin's sons, and two dozen children laugh during a special game of one-legged tag, a warm-up exercise that has them sweating and cheering. Afterwards, two teams play tug-of-war and a dozen children yank the rope until the other dozen falls in a heap. They groan and screech with joy. This is how Tae Kwon Do starts for children, with training that is fun. I watch my daughter's face as she stretches her hamstrings and, later, practises a front kick, a punch, a high block. Her face is serious. This is not ballet or gymnastics, not soccer or hockey. I can tell that she likes the striking and blocking, likes the space and the sport, likes the healthy competition and the raw athleticism, loves the large group of girls who encourage each other with "Go, go, go!" While I train with Martin, she works on her yellow belt, building to something that will eventually be an empowering art if she sticks with it. In this gym, it seems unbelievable that the "killing" part of this killing art once dominated the leadership of Tae Kwon Do — real threats, kidnappings, and murder attempts, and stealing, so that "Tae Kwon Do" once meant "Take My Dough."

When I train, I ignore the hidden history of Tae Kwon Do and the leaders who lied so much about so many things that they almost killed the art — and might still do so in the future. What counts is the grassroots history of the martial art and the instructors with integrity and the training itself. When I train, I do not doubt everything, do not think about the Rule of Opposites that I created from listening to various philosophers and instructors. The Rule of

Opposites, which embodies a cynical attitude that I developed over the years when talking to liars and sadists, states that you should consider the opposite of what someone tells you. It applies to past or present enemies, even gentle ones, and it sometimes applies to Tae Kwon Do's tenets.

Indomitable Spirit is supposed to mean courage, modesty, and wisdom when sticking to one's principals, even against overwhelming odds. But does it? Can it also mean the opposite? Can it mean hide your cowardice within bullying and your ignorance inside stubbornness?

Perseverance is continuing with patience and persistence, even when faced with opposition and internal weakness. It implies self-awareness, confidence, and humility. I sometimes wonder, however, if it means give up if the price is right. Let yourself be bought and sold? Cheat as much as possible?

Does Self-control mean become an animal, do anything to win a fight, release the beast? Can it mean rage itself?

Is Courtesy disrespect and a knife in the back?

Is Integrity a psychotic state?

In my dark moments, I thought that the Rule of Opposites applied to everybody (not only to enemies), but those moments have been few. Instead, I like to think about Choi Hong-Hi in his early years, when he was a brash, young general with a vision of how a martial art could empower himself and his soldiers, nation, and world. This vision seemed laughable back then. Empower the world? He sounded like a megalomaniac, especially when he talked about helping to reunite North and South Korea and bragged about standing up to South Korea's dictators. But someone had to, and he never gave up. He and Tae Kwon Do became as damaged as the men he had fought all his life, and he leaves a legacy that his followers must now live with.

And I think about Dr. Dong-Ja Yang, who was one of the first to rebel against corruption in the World Taekwondo Federation. In 1986, he was president of the WTF's Pan American Taekwondo Union and asked the WTF to consider lowering the exorbitant fees for black belt certification, especially for black belts in economically poor nations. Olympic leaders, including Dick Pound, heard his calls, but Dr. Yang lost that battle. However, he led a Taekwondo Reform Movement that still inspires martial artists today.

I think about men like Master Joe Cariati, who assisted Choi during many seminars of the International Taekwon-Do Federation between 1994 and 2002, and afterwards worked with Choi's son, Jung-Hwa Choi. Cariati has forty-seven affiliated ITF gyms, and instructors like him (instructors like the one who runs my daughter's WTF gym) are responsible for the explosive popularity of the martial art. Cariati witnessed vile conflicts between pioneers, organizations, and fathers and sons, and he heard so many lies that he almost lost his will to teach the martial art, which, for a full-time instructor like Cariati, is almost the same as losing the will to live. He finally quit the ITF and now focuses on running his gyms and an instructors association, the International Ch'ang-Hon Taekwon-Do Federation (ICTF).[481]

We cannot escape violent pasts. We can try, but the forgotten stories always sneak back like bad dreams and nail-biting, emerge as whispered gossip from instructors, as violent tidbits in martial arts articles and as disturbing scenes in hilarious films like *The Foot Fist Way*. Sometimes, in a gym, the violence takes over during a sparring match, when someone loses control. Violence is power gone wrong; most of us know that. The aggressive techniques themselves are both empowering and terrifying, and a diligent student with a smart teacher can become empowered enough to face fears, to name violence, to put terror in its corner.

Inside my daughter's gym, she kicks a target pad. The sound of her foot hitting the pad makes a "whack" that flies across the room. She and her classmates yell through patterns, the lower belts practise jumping front kicks, and the upper belts spar in the other half of the gym. Thick pads cover each sparring competitor's head, chest, forearms, hands, groin, shins, and feet; they look like chubby warriors from a science-fiction movie. The parents laugh as they watch. This WTF, sporty approach to sparring is extremely different from the ITF style that I practise on Saturdays, when, under Master Di Vecchia's and Master Gabbidon's charge, we spar bare knuckled, practise holds, locks and falls, and challenge each other with techniques that would be illegal in a ring. Thanks to these instructors, we have stuck with the traditional training.

Later, as my daughter and I walk home, she talks about Tae Kwon Do, which is not our usual topic. It is a beautiful winter evening, and not too cold, thanks to the light snow drifting between the street lights and maple trees.

"Does Tae Kwon Do make you stronger?" she asks.

"It will, if you practise a lot," I say. "Your body will get stronger and, one day, your mind, too." I could go on and on about it, but too many words at this point might ruin everything. I want to tell her that since its rough beginnings, Tae Kwon Do has empowered people to counter bullying, fight injustice, increase confidence, and strengthen nations. She is very smart and would understand in her own way — especially the bullying part, because her school runs an anti-bullying program.

I sometimes wish that all older children could study a martial art in school — take a regular class, as they do in math and music — because, unlike any other activity, a martial art offers a physical intelligence, a subtle awareness of how the body is put together, how it might move, what its limitations and strengths are, and how these things connect to mental and emotional states. I'll never forget watching one martial artist, a young woman in my Tae Kwon Do class, break a wooden board, and, the following year, break two boards, then three, then four — her awe, confidence, and power building with each board.

Another woman I know began traditional Tae Kwon Do because she had been assaulted and wanted to exorcize her fear and hatred of men while making herself physically stronger. Within two years, she developed into a confident green belt. One day, she was calling her boyfriend at a restaurant phone (he was late), when someone grabbed her from behind — a bear hug. She instantly dropped the phone, twisted within his grasp and punched him in the stomach with an uppercut. The man crumpled to the ground. To her horror, she saw that it was her boyfriend, who had been trying to surprise her.

After many years of training in Tae Kwon Do, physical intelligence and dexterity can grow into a keen mental ability to perceive people's motives and potentials. An obvious example is the nervous feeling you get when someone stands too close to you, invading your space. Training in a martial art can develop this sensation and provide a person with solutions to the invasion.

An instructor I know was once on a bus when he witnessed a man attack the driver, a woman who had insisted that the man pay a fare. The man refused and began punching her in the head, which ricocheted off a window. The attack happened so fast that no one on the bus moved. The instructor thought, Oh, no, isn't anyone going to do anything? Do I have to get involved? He just wanted to get home after a day at the office. Was the attacker crazy? He looked in rough shape but not so bad that he lived on the street. He could have been anybody. Then the man struck the driver's head with his elbow and prepared to elbow her again. That was nasty, thought the instructor. Something had to be done or the man would kill her.

The instructor quickly stood up, ran past the assailant and driver, stood on the street at the front door and called the man: "Hey, you!" he shouted.

The attacker looked at him.

"Yes, you," the instructor said. "Over here. Come out here. Just you and me!" The attacker did not move, but at least he had left the driver alone.

The bus was idling near a busy downtown intersection. The driver looked at the two men. She seemed dazed but okay. On the street, the instructor stared at the enraged attacker, who took one step away from the driver. Then another step. The instructor moved backwards on the road at the same pace as the man moving forwards in the bus, aware of the distance between them. He had no idea what would happen with the attacker. What would he do, exactly, if the man ran at him? There was a lot of distance between them — about ten paces. How should he take him down without killing him?

"Yes, that's it," called the instructor. "Come out! Just you and me! Here." He waved his hand at the guy, who stepped onto the road. "That's it," said the instructor. "It's just me. Nobody else." He maintained the distance between them as the enraged man stepped onto the road and walked towards him more quickly now. The instructor led him in a huge circle around a group of people. The man followed, trying to catch up. After they had almost circled the group, the instructor was now near the bus and the assailant further away but moving in for an attack. The instructor calmly walked onto the bus and the driver closed the door, hit the gas, and the bus lurched away, leaving the attacker on the street.

The driver was shaken and in a bit of shock, but she seemed okay. She thanked the instructor over and over. Later, perhaps, she would tell the police that he had saved her life. The instructor never saw her again, and no one knew that he was a Tae Kwon Do instructor. Had he used his martial art during the conflict? He had.

In the end, Tae Kwon Do is not the art of killing; it is the art of *not* killing, the art of understanding and diffusing conflict. The best martial artists are usually quiet about what they know and they specialize in avoiding fights. One of the common questions I get from people is "Have you used your martial art?" which is difficult to answer, because the answer is yes — but it is not a *yes* from a movie by Jet Li or Jackie Chan. One of the rare stories I tell involves *not* using it.

I was living overseas, travelling every week, and meeting many people, when one night, on the way home from a party, my friend and I were mugged by about a dozen men. I had no time to count them, because they fanned across the street and partly surrounded us. I sprinted backwards and sideways, so that none of them could get behind me, but two of them jumped on my friend. I thought they were going to rape her, because one was hanging over her as she screamed. In those days, I carried a knife with my travel gear, and I pulled it out. I realized that I had time to stick it in the back of the man over her. Kill him, I told myself. Stick it in his back! But a calm voice, a second voice in my head, told me not to, and in that second, the others in the gang saw the knife and attacked me.

Only later did I realize that the the calm voice had been right. In the moment, however, I sprinted around, terrified that they would kill me. I noticed that they had let my friend go. But now they were after me. I will never forget the look on one man's face, daring me to attack him; with his blood-shot eyes, he looked insane. I threw my small backpack on the street and one of them picked it up. No one got behind me; I kept moving, holding the knife in front. Then, suddenly they were gone, running up the street. They had wanted our backpacks, nothing more. Perhaps.

Had I used my martial art? I had avoided knifing a man. The calm voice in my head had assessed the situation before the killer voice had. The thugs had been drunken thieves, not rapists and murderers, most likely. I imagine that the situation would have gone badly for my friend and me if I had knifed a gang member from behind; there were all the other gang members. As it turned out, I escaped with only two months of nightmares.

✗ ✗ ✗

"How's the book?" my daughter asks. We are walking along the street, still hot from the punching, kicking, and jumping at the *dojang*.

"Fine," I say. "Almost done." She knows I'm writing about the men who started the martial art and that they did crazy things.

"Were those men bad, Dad?" she asks.

For a second, I don't say anything. I usually reserve "bad" or "evil" for murderers and people like them. Tae Kwon Do's leaders were bad only when they became beasts, which arose out of torment and frustration. After talking to them and reading about their lives, I could understand them — could guess at what made them do unthinkable things — but I could not excuse them.

"Not all of them were bad," I tell her. "Some tried their best. They came from a world that's completely different from ours."

"Where?" she asks.

"Korea — old Korea," I say.

"What was it like?" she asks. As we walk along, it is dark outside, but we feel good; it's the feeling after a workout, your feet solid on the ground, your muscles strong, your confidence peaking — "feeling jumpy," as my daughter puts it.

"Old Korea is hard to understand," I say. "It's on the other side of the world, near China. Tae Kwon Do started with a crazy poker game in 1938, when a young man lost all the money that his mother had given him for school."

"What was his name?" she asks.

"Hong-Hi was his first name," I say. "His family was very strict and they didn't have a lot of money. They were so strict you wouldn't believe it. He snuck out of his room, one day, to go play poker. He lost all the money for his education. His mother had actually warned him not to, but he did."

"Are you serious?" she says.

"Yeah, he was twenty years old, so he should have known better," I say. "After the game, he didn't know what to do. He sat there, looking at a wrestler who had won all the money. Hong-Hi was short — he was about as tall as you — and the wrestler was huge. That's where the bottle of ink came in. Hong-Hi grabbed the bottle, which was near him, and threw it at the wrestler. The bottle hit him in the forehead."

"Wow," she says. "That sounds bad."

"Yeah, it does," I say, "but it has a happy ending."

Notes

Introduction
1 Dukes (1994), p. 337.

Chapter 1: Men of the Sacred Bone
2 Lee (1964), p. 64. Po-Eun is a Tae Kwon Do pattern for black belts and is named after a Korean poet who lived from 1337 to 1392.
3 Cumings (2005), p. 61.
4 Choi (1999), p. 525.
5 Kim (2002), p. 5.
6 *Globe and Mail* (Sep. 19, 2001), p. A17.
7 Choi (c. 2000), v. 2, p. 90.
8 Interviews, Jong-Soo Park, from 2001 to 2008.
9 Choi (1999), p. 58.
10 Choi (c. 2002), v. 2, pp. 241, 360. Also, interviews with his children: Meeyun Colomvakos, Sunny Choi, and Jung-Hwa Choi.
11 *The Economist* (Nov. 12, 1994), p. 121.
12 Interviews, Jung-Hwa Choi (May and Apr. 2003).
13 Choi (1999), pp. 151, 542.
14 Many Tae Kwon Do grandmasters have acknowledged the Karate base, including Nam Tae-hi, Jhoon Rhee, and Duk-Sung Son.

Chapter 2: Though Ten Million Opponents Might Rise Against Him
15 Choi's *Moral Guide Book* (c. 2000), p. 11.
16 This scene is from interviews with Choi's family and details from his memoir (c. 2000), v. 1, pp. 34, 71–81, and v. 2, p. 469.
17 Cumings (2005) explains this virtue well. See pp. 57–61.
18 This is a translation of James Legge's, as quoted in Cumings (2005), p. 57. "Sim" encompasses both heart and mind.
19 Details in this chapter are from Choi (c. 2000), v. 1, pp. 19–55, 71–96, and from interviews with Choi's family. Quotation from p. 24.

20 Choi (c. 2000), v.1, pp. 26–28.
21 As Cumings (2005) puts it on pp. 21–22, "When they [Koreans] say, 'I think,' they point to their chest. Mind is mind-and-heart or *sim,* a visceral knowledge that joins thought with emotion . . ."
22 Cumings (2005), p. 147.
23 Young (1993), p. 53. Ouyang (1997), p.77.
24 Interview, Lim (Aug. 17, 2002). Choi never mentioned his first wife and daughter, not even in the first two volumes of his memoirs.
25 Interview with her (May 30, 2003).
26 The Japanese characters for his family name are "Nishiyama," a common name. Choi's Japanese name is found in a 1945 court document from the Second World War.
27 Funakoshi (1988), p. 26.
28 Draeger (1974), p. 12.
29 Choi (1999), p. 14.

CHAPTER 3: A Superpower on Every Border
30 Interviews, Lim (Aug. 2002 to May 2003).
31 Song (date unknown), pp. 376–79.
32 Details in this chapter are from Choi Hong-Hi (c. 2000), v. 1, pp. 123–94.
33 Oh (2001), pp. 3–19.
34 Choi (c.2001), v. 1, pp. 130–38. I obtained historical facts from Song (date unknown), p. 2, and interview with Palmer (Jan. 2005).
35 Cha (date unknown), p. 30.
36 P'yŏngyang Military Court (1945), p. 2.
37 Cumings (2005), pp. 178–79.
38 Levine (2000), pp. 144–45.
39 Interview, Lim (Aug. 17, 2002).
40 Cumings (2005), p. 187.
41 Cumings (2005), p. 198.
42 Interview, Lim (Aug. 17, 2002).
43 Cumings (2005), p. 207.
44 Choi (c. 2000), v. 1, pp. 218–24.
45 Funakoshi (1988), p. 24.
46 Dohrenwend (1997), p. 4.
47 Choi (c. 2000), v. 1, pp. 256–57.
48 Interviews, Meeyun Colomvakos and Sunny Choi (Aug. 22, 2002).
49 Interview, Lim (Aug. 17, 2002).
50 Choi (c. 2000), v. 1, p. 234.
51 Interview, Choi (Mar. 2001).
52 Interview, Colomvakos (Nov. 20, 2002).

CHAPTER 4: SuperNam
53 Minford (2002), p. 76.
54 Hessler (2001), p. 146.
55 As Cumings (2004) puts it "complete devastation between the Yalu

River and the capital" (p. 19).

56 Interview, Lim (Aug. 2002). Choi (c. 2000), v. 1, p. 345.

57 Interviews: Jhoon Rhee (Nov. 2007); Lim Sun-ha and Sandy Lim (Aug. 2002); and Song-Jook Choi (May 30, 2003).

58 Details about Nam in this chapter are from interviews with him (2001 to 2008). Many martial arts grandmasters, such as Nguyen Van Binh (Aug. 11, 2006) and Jong-Soo Park (Feb. 21, 2008), told me about Nam's battle.

59 Cumings (2005), p. 237, and Boettcher (1980), p. 11.

60 The battalion was in the Republic of Korea's Sixth Division. Nam was in the Twelfth Company of the Third Battalion.

61 This battle is so well known in South Korea that the Culture and Welfare Bureau promotes it for children's tours: see "Yongmun Mountain Battle" at the Demilitarized Zone website at http://kids.dmz.ne.kr/time/time21.asp. Other sources on the battle: Song (2004), Seo (2008), and the National Institute of Korean History, which is based in South Korea (http://kuksa.nhcc.go.kr).

62 In total, two battalions fought for three days on plateaus 353 and 427, according to interviews with Nam Tae-hi, and documents from Song (2004), Seo (2008), and other sources.

63 Guo and Kennedy (2004), p. 32.

64 Weiss (2000), pp. 82–84, and Dohrenwend (1997), p. 1.

65 He once announced that he was the founder of Tae Kwon Do, but the claim has been widely disputed.

66 Much of this paragraph is from Kang and Lee (1999), pp. 1–3, and Simpkins and Simpkins (2002), p. 6.

67 Talbott (1999), p. 1. The hand techniques don't add to ten, but Lee's point was that there were a small number of techniques.

68 Choi (1999), p. 94.

69 Interview with Jhoon Rhee. See also the Taekwondo Hall of Fame at www.lacancha.com/greatest.html.

70 Choi (c. 2000), v. 2, p. 96.

71 Interviews: C. K. Choi (Oct. 31, 2007) and Jhoon Rhee (Nov. 2007).

72 Kang and Lee (1999), p. 2 and throughout.

73 Burdick (1997), p. 39.

74 Cumings (2005), p. 97. The New York Herald called this battle "Little War with the Heathen."

75 Choi (1960), p. 20. Interviews with Nam Tae-hi.

76 Young (no date): www.blackbeltmag.com/archives/482.

77 Interviews with Nam Tae-hi (2001), Joe Cariati, and Parmar Rai (Jan. 2002), and Jong-Soo Park, among others.

78 Song (2004), p. 1.

79 Ouyang (1997), p.77–79.

80 Cumings (2005), pp. 302–303.

81 Kimm (2000), p. 49.

82 Young (1993), pp. 61–67. Ouyang (1997), p. 79.

83 Choi (c. 2000), v. 1, p. 423.

84 C. K. Choi (2007), p. 80, and interviews with Nam and Choi Hong-Hi.

85 Choi (c. 2000), v. 1, pp. 428–29, and Simpkins and Simpkins (2002), p. 5.

86 Kang and Lee (1999), p. 11.

87 Choi (1960), p. 21.

CHAPTER 5: Tae Kwon Do Is Named in a Korean Geisha House

88 Unless otherwise footnoted, details in this chapter are from Choi (c. 2000), v. 1, 435–37, and interviews with Nam Tae-hi. Choi (c. 2000) writes that the meeting took place in a *kisaeng* house, and Nam told me it was the Kugilgwan *kisaeng* house. Much has been written about the meeting but not the meeting place: Kimm (2000), p. 49; Kang and Lee (1999), p. 12; and C. K. Choi (2007), p. 81.

89 Many Korean-language sources provide details about the Kugilgwan and the personalities there: (1) the National Institute of Korean History (http://kuksa.nhcc.go.kr); (2) a five-volume culture and history collection from the South Korean government (http://seoul600.visitseoul.net); (3) an article by Yi Pom-jin in the March 20, 2005, issue of *Chugan Chosŏn* (http://magazine.chosun.com); (4) "Thirty-year-old tradition of kisaeng house," in *Minju sinmun* (May 9, 2006), a Seoul newspaper; and (5) an article called *Pak Maria* (who was Yi Ki-bung's wife) from the History Liberation Campaign Centre (http://bluecabin.com.ne.kr/split99/pmaria.htm).

90 See Cumings (2005), p. 356–57, for a caricature of *kisaeng*-loving politicians of this period.

91 Burdick (1997), p. 37–38, lists the meetings.

92 Hyun Jong-myung, who later became part of the World Taekwondo Federation.

93 Interview, Nam (Apr. 17, 2006).

94 Choi (c. 2000), v. 1, p. 436–38. Interview, Jung-Hwa Choi (Jan. 2002). Young (1993) outlines the myths that connect the two arts. Many martial arts leaders wrote these myths into reality. Chun (2006), pp. 6–10, for example. C. K. Choi (2007) comes closest to the truth.

95 Young (1993), pp. 51–59.

96 "Preface" of Choi (1960) and pp. 18–20 of Choi (1999).

97 In fact, T'aekkyŏn was linked to gang violence throughout its history. Ouyang (1997), p. 85.

98 Choi (c. 2000), v. 1, pp. 478–87.

99 "Preface" of Choi (1960).

100 Along with "front stance," "back stance," and "horse stance." Funakoshi (1988), pp. 53–61. Choi (1960).

101 Compare Choi (1960), pp. 73–75, to Funakoshi (1988), p. 53.

102 Choi (1960).

103 C. K. Choi (2007), p. 85, lists the men involved.

CHAPTER 6: One Coup, Two Presidents, and the Three Spheres of Power

104 Choi (c. 2000), v. 2, p. 51.

105 Choi's version of the widely reported coup is in Choi (c. 2000), v. 1, pp. 567–86.

106 Cumings (2005), p. 54.

107 Cumings (2005), pp. 355–56.

108 Park Chong-kyu, Kim Chŏng-p'il, and Kim Hyung-wook.

109 Cumings (2003).

110 Halloran (1973), p. 3.

111 KCIA director Kim Hyung-wook served from May 1963 to October 1969. See *KI-1*, p. 6.

112 Burdick (1997), p. 41. Kang and Lee (1999), p. 21.

113 Uhm Woon-kyu, Lee Chong-woo, and Hyun Jong-myung, for example.

114 C. K. Choi (2007), p. 86.

115 Choi (c. 2000), v. 2, p. 18.

116 Interviews, Nam and Chang (Dec. 2001).

117 Choi (c. 2000), v. 2, pp. 27 and 36. Details in this section are from Choi Hong-Hi's books and interviews with C. K. Choi, Nam Tae-hi, Jung-Hwa Choi, Meeyun Colomvakos, and Sunny Choi.

118 Choi had always surrounded himself with gifted athletes. In the 1950s, Nam Tae-hi had put together Tae Kwon Do's first two patterns, *Hwa-Rang* and *Choong-Moo*, both named after warriors (Choi [c. 2000], v. 1, p. 428). A couple of years later, Han Cha-gyo, had created *Ul-Ji*, named after a Korean guerrilla general from 1,400 years ago. In 1961, C. K. Choi, who would soon be Korea's first national sparring champion, had helped to create the fourth pattern, *Gae-Baek*, named after a strict general from 1,500 years ago (C. K. Choi [2007], p. 81). In Malaysia, Ambassador Choi imported Kim Bok-Man and Woo Jae-lim to help with sixteen of twenty-four patterns. The last four patterns would follow in 1966. For a reliable, concise list of pioneers who taught and developed Tae Kwon Do in the 1950s and 1960s, see the "Early History" chapter in C. K. Choi (2007), which is also available online.

119 Interview, C. K. Choi (Oct 31, 2007).

120 Choi (c. 2000), v. 2, p. 52.

121 Interviews, Park (2002) and Choi (2001).

122 Interview, C. K. Choi (Oct. 31, 2007).

123 Choi (c. 2000), v. 2, p. 255.

124 Choi (c. 2000), v. 2, p. 146.

125 Interviews, Nam (Sep. 5, 2006) and Nguyen Van Binh (Aug. 9, 2006).

126 For Karate: Draeger (1974), p. 127. For Tae Kwon Do: Choi (c. 2000), v. 1, p. 517.

127 Durand (2004), p. 3. Kang and Lee (1999), p. 8.

128 Cumings (2005), pp. 321–22. Last Korean troops left in 1973: *KI-App*, v.1, p.124.

129 Interview, Nguyen (Aug. 9, 2006).
130 "Other Guns," *Time* (Jul. 22, 1966).
131 "Letter to the Editor: Tiger Skins," *Time* (Aug. 12, 1966).
132 Durand (2004), plus other sources online: "Battle at Tra Binh Dong" at www.vietvet.co.kr and "Blue Dragon" in archives of www.talkingproud.us.
133 Details about this battle are from Durand (2004) and "A Savage Week," *Time* (Feb. 24, 1967).
134 Durand (2004).
135 Durand (2004).
136 Interview, Kong Young-il (Aug. 16, 2002).
137 Kimm (Jan. 2000), p. 54.

CHAPTER 7: The Ace Team and the Korean CIA
138 The friend was Choi Duk-shin, a powerful politician who in those days opened doors for Tae Kwon Do in Vietnam, Germany, Egypt, Italy, Turkey, Malaysia, and Singapore. Kimm (Jan. 2000), pp. 50 and 53.
139 Choi (c. 2000), v.2, pp. 86–105, describes the tour.
140 Interview, Cariati (Jan. 8, 2008).
141 Choi (c. 2000), v. 2, p. 73.
142 Interview, Kong (Aug. 16, 2002).
143 Interview, Kong (Aug. 16, 2002).
144 Interview, Choi (Apr. 2002).
145 Interview, Lu (May 17, 2003).
146 Interview, Cormack (May 2, 2003).
147 Choi (c. 2000), v. 2, p. 77.
148 Interview, C. K. Choi (Nov. 28, 2007).
149 C. K. Choi (2007), pp. 87, 90, 94.
150 Kang and Lee (1999).
151 Choi (c. 2000), v.2 , p. 107.
152 C. K. Choi (2007), pp. 93–94.
153 Choi (c. 2000), v. 2, p. 71. Burdick (1997), p. 42. Chun (1976), p. 11.
154 Larkin (2003).
155 According to Gregory Henderson in 1968, as quoted by Cumings (2005), p. 361.
156 Larkin (2003).
157 Choi (c. 2000), v. 2, p. 127. Choi (c. 2000), v. 2, pp. 129, 323, mentions the instructors involved in the East Berlin Incident. Interviews with grandmasters provided details.
158 Transcript of interview with Isang Yun on *Weekend*, a program on *NBC-TV* (May 1, 1976), reprinted in *KI-Acts II*, pp. 70–75.
159 "K's Situation," *Der Spiegel* (Aug. 28, 1967), p. 23–26.
160 Besides *Der Spiegel*, many sources extensively covered the incident. In the *New York Times* of 1967 for example: Jul. 5 (p. 8); Jul. 6 (p. 9); Jul. 8 (p. 6); Jul. 9 (p. 1); Jul. 14 (p. 4); Jul. 15 (p. 9); Jul. 23 (p. 5); Jul. 30 (p. 5); Dec. 7 (p. 10).

161 *KI-Acts I* (1976), pp. 7, 93.

162 *Der Spiegel* articles that quote historian Hannes Mosler and others (Aug. 28, 1967), p. 23–26.

163 Choe (2005), p. 1. Cumings (2005), p. 371

164 Choi (c. 2000), v. 2, pp. 129, 323.

165 Boettcher (1980), p. 354.

166 Isang Yun on *Weekend*, NBC-TV (May 1, 1976), reprinted in *KI-Acts II*, pp. 70–75.

167 Choi (c. 2000), v. 2, pp. 114, 117.

168 *Der Spiegel* (Aug. 28, 1967).

169 Kim Hyung-Wook explained how this worked. See *KI-1* (1977), p. 38.

170 *KI-Report*, p. 152.

171 Kim, *KI-1* (1977), p. 23.

172 Choi (c. 2000), v. 2, p. 217.

173 According to Gregory Henderson, as noted in Boettcher (1980), p. 354.

174 Choi (c. 2000), v. 2, pp. 143, 145, 149, 243–44, 277.

175 Interview, C. K. Choi (Oct. 31, 2007). Not until a 2006 Truth Commission would the South Korean government admit that the cases were mainly fabrications. Choi (c. 2000), v. 2, p. 135. A number of websites contain information about the meeting. A great photo is found at www.lacancha.com/oyama.html.

176 Isang Yun on *Weekend*, NBC-TV (May 1, 1976), reprinted in *KI-Acts II*, pp. 70–75.

177 "Song of a Wilted Flower," *Time* (Mar. 28, 1969).

178 Edwards (2002), p. A2. Interview, Cormack (May 2, 2003).

179 Kimm (Jan. 2000), p. 54.

CHAPTER 8: Enter the Cloud Dragon

180 Kim (2002), p. 219.

181 Kim (1990), p. 295. Details about Kim in this section are from his 2002 and 1990 books.

182 Kim (2002), p. 208.

183 Kim (2002), p. 227.

184 Kim (2002), p. 239.

185 Kim (2002), pp. 139–47, 257. Kim had been aide de camp and protocol secretary to General Song Yo-chan, who had become Prime Minister in the new regime.

186 Many sources have confirmed that Kim was in the KCIA: *KI-Report*, p. 76; "Testimony of Pak Bo Hi, Special Assistant to Rev. Sun Myung Moon and President of the Korean Cultural and Freedom Foundation . . ." in *KI-4*, pp. 176–178; Pak's KCFF lists Kim as being in the "Korean Secret Service," in *KI-4 Supp*, p. 672; a letter in *KI-4 Supp*, p. 11, lists Kim as a "KCIA official"; an article from 1975, in *KI-Acts II*, pp. 63–64, lists him as one of the "agents of the Korean CIA"; Jennings (2000), p. 187, and Simson and Jennings

(1992), pp. 139–140; Interview, Choi Hong-Hi (Apr. 13, 2001);
Interview, Jhoon Rhee (Jan. 16, 2008).

187 Kim (2002), pp. 151, 164.

188 Kim (1990), p. 295.

189 Kim (2002), p. 59.

190 Kim (2002), p. 171.

191 Interview, Rhee (Jan. 16, 2008).

192 Letter from the Vice President of the Foundation (Mar. 13, 1964), in
KI-4 Supp, p. 271. See also *KI-Report*, pp. 356–57.

193 Interview, Rhee (Jan. 16, 2008). Boettcher (1980), pp. 42–53, presents
a concise history of the Foundation, of two of its projects (the Little
Angles and Radio of Free Asia) and of Jhoon's Rhee involvement.

194 Kim (2002), p. 159.

195 *KI-Report* (1978), p. 357, and *KI-4 Supp* (1978), pp. 350 and 355.
The colleague was Mr. Pak Bo-Hi, who was Jhoon Rhee's cousin
and an intelligence official at the embassy (Boettcher [1980], p. 40).
Interview, Rhee (Jan. 16, 2008).

196 Interview, Rhee (Jan. 16, 2008). *KI-Acts II* (1976), p. 2.

197 Report from the American Embassy in Seoul to the U.S. Department
of State (Aug. 26, 1966) about Korean activities in the United
States, in *KI-4 Supp* (1978), p. 480.

198 "Statement of Donald L. Ranard, Former Director of Korean
Affairs, Department of State" (Mar. 25, 1978), in *KI-Acts I*, p. 69.
Rhee's involvement in Moon's church and Foundation is noted in
my interview with Rhee and in U.S. Congressional documents
about Koreagate, including: *KI-Report*, p. 317, 324, 357; *KI-
Append*, p. 397, 1463 1469; *KI-4*, pp. 397, 661, 718; and *KI-4
Supp*, p. 81, 104, 255, 301, 593, 607, 664.

199 For Kim's role with the radio station, see "Sworn Statement of Kim
Chong Hoon," the station's operations director from 1967 to 1972,
in *KI-Report*, p. 363. For his role in the Foundation, refer to a 1965
letter from Earl H. Voss to Arleigh Burke, the Foundation's
President, in *KI-4 Supp*, p. 364.

200 Interview, Rhee (Jan. 16, 2008).

201 The "Testimony of Pak Bo-Hi, Special Assistant to Rev. Sun Myung
Moon and President of the Korean Cultural and Freedom
Foundation, accompanied by John M. Bray, Counsel" refers to Kim
work for the Little Angels, in *KI-4*, pp. 176–78. For Kim's work
with the Freedom Centre, see *KI-Report*, p. 356.

202 According to Lee Jai-Hyon, a former South Korean embassy official
in Washington, the Foundation had a cable channel to the KCIA,
which also helped to staff the Foundation (*KI-Acts II*, pp. 8, 9). See
also a statement from a former ambassador to South Korea, in *KI-4*,
p. 52, and facts in the Koreagate report, *KI-Report*, p. 312.

203 Interview, Rhee (Nov. 12, 2007).

204 Interview, Rhee (Nov. 12, 2007).

205 *KI-4 Supp*, pp. 277–78.

206 Interview, Burleson (Jan. 24, 2008).

207 Although Tae Kwon Do's techniques did not arise from Korea's martial arts kicking game (T'aekkyŏn), Koreans knew that you had to kick to fight the Korean way. Ouyang (1997), p. 88.

208 Interview, Burleson (2007).

209 From the file of retired Admiral Arleigh Burke, Founding President of the Foundation, in *KI-4 Supp*, p. 216, and from a 1976 statement from Robert W. Roland, a former member of the Foundation, in *KI-Acts II*, p. 15.

210 Interview, Rhee (Nov. 19, 2007).

211 Elvis himself gained his black belt from a Korean Karate expert, Kang Rhee. See *Tae Kwon Do Times* (Sep. 2007).

212 Letter from Roland to the Foundation's president (Jul. 12, 1965), in *KI-4 Supp*, p. 405.

213 *KI-Report*, p. 362

214 Interview, Rhee (2007).

215 Choi (c. 2000), v. 2, pp. 126–27. At the time, a former KCIA director, Kim Chŏng-p'il, served as both the ITF's honorary president and the Moon foundation's honorary chairman.

216 Choi (c. 2000), v. 2, pp. 133–36, 165.

217 Interview, Rhee (Nov. 19, 2007). Choi (c. 2000), v. 2, pp. 196–97.

218 Interviews, Meeyun Colomvakos and Sunny Choi (2002).

219 Choi (c. 2000), v. 2, p. 219. Interview, Rhee (Nov. 19, 2007).

220 Cumings (2005), p. 53. Boettcher (1980), p. 78.

221 Kim (2002), pp. 166–72.

222 Kim (2002), pp. 58–59.

223 Also, Kim and a KCIA operative would soon be working with the South Korean president on a book about Korean history. See *KI-Append*, p. 1007, and *KI-Report*, pp. 307, 365.

224 Quoted in Jennings (1992), p. 139.

225 Kim (2002), p. 169. Yook (2002).

226 Kim (1990), pp. 295, 233–34.

227 Choi (c. 2000), v. 2, pp. 201–4.

228 Another dozen martial artists were on the KTA Executive Committee, men who were the pioneers of Olympic Tae Kwon Do. Kang and Lee (1999) has a complete list.

229 Kim (2002), p. 61.

230 Kang and Lee (1999).

231 Kang and Lee (1999).

232 Kang and Lee (1999).

233 From Pak Bo-Hi's testimony, in *KI-4*, pp. 491–92. Copies of the cheques are on p. 487.

234 Kang and Lee (1999).

235 *KI-Report*, p. 239.

236 In a December 13, 1971, interview with *Dong A Ilbo*. See Kang and Lee (1999).

CHAPTER 9: As if in a Bruce Lee Movie

237 Kang and Lee (1999).

238 Many have written about the Plan: Boettcher (1980), pp. 157–58, and Cumings (2005), p. 460. One of their primary sources was the "Statement of Dr. Lee Jai Hyon, Associate Professor of Journalism, Western Illinois University," in *KI-Acts II*, p. 10, and *KI-3*, pp. 1–2. Lee was a Korean embassy official who defected to the United States. See also *KI-Append*, p. 505, and *KI-Report*, pp. 105–06.

239 *KI-Report*, pp. 4, 121. Actually, the KCIA began the operation in 1966, but expanded it dramatically in 1970, when South Korean President Park Chung-hee became directly involved.

240 Such as Pak Bo-Hi (who was Kim Un-yong's colleague and Jhoon Rhee's cousin). See "Statement of Gen. Kim Hyung Wook, Former Director, Korean Central Intelligence Agency (KCIA)," in *KI-1*, pp. 29 and 64.

241 Jennings (1992), p. 140.

242 According to a former Korean embassy official who provided a copy of the 1976 Plan to American officials (*KI-3*, p. 2). The Plan is found in *KI-Append*, p. 519.

243 "South Korean CIA: Power Grows, Fear Spreads," by John Saar, John Goshgo, and Bill Richards, *Washington Post*, May 23, 1976. See also Cumings (2005), p. 371.

244 *KI-Append*, pp. 540–42.

245 *KI-3*, p. 137. Also, see "Statement of Gregory Henderson, Tufts University, Fletcher School of Law and Diplomacy," in *KI-Acts I*, p. 8.

246 *KI-Report*, pp. 93–97.

247 "FBI memorandum entitled 'Republic of Korea (ROK) Intelligence Activities in the United States,' dated September 9, 1973," in *KI-Append*, pp. 465–66.

248 *KI-Append*, p. 131.

249 Boettcher (1980), p. 206, and *KI-Report*, pp. 402–404.

250 Much of this section about Song is from his sworn testimony to a U.S. Congressional hearing, in *KI-5*, pp. 81–88, 204–13.

251 Limb Man-sung. His name is probably spelled "Lim" but U.S. Congressional documents use "Limb." More about him is available in *KI-Acts II*, p. 4.

252 "Signed Sworn Statement of Chung Tai Bong to Subcommittee Staff," in *KI-5*, pp. 214–17.

253 These details are from: *KI-Report*, p. 293 (for university facts); *KI-5*, pp. 13–31 and *KI-Report*, pp. 44, 150 (for Nidecker's testimony); and "Statement of Gen. Kim Hyung Wook, Former Director, Korean Central Intelligence Agency (KCIA)," in *KI-1*, pp. 23–27, 58–59 (for other details).

254 *KI-Report*, p. 76.

255 Details in this section are from *KI-Report*, pp. 104, 241, and *KI-Append*, pp. 716–18.

256 *KI-Report*, pp. 234, 242.

257 *KI-1*, p. 25.

258 *KI-Report*, p. 90.

259 Choi (c. 2000), v. 2, p. 300.

260 "Bruce Lee and I: Martial arts phenomenon Jhoon Rhee talks, Part two," in *Martial Arts Illustrated*. The correspondence between Rhee and Lee was particularly intense between 1967 and 1973.

261 Choi (c. 2000), v. 2, pp. 210–11.

CHAPTER 10: The Exiles

262 Son (1983), p. 6.

263 Choi (c. 2000), v. 2, p. 394.

264 Choi (1974), p. 453.

265 Young (1993), p. 62, 67.

266 Interview, Nam (Feb. 20, 2008).

267 *KI-Report*, p. 92.

268 Choi (c. 2000), v. 2, p. 286.

269 Choi hoped that Lee's murder had nothing to do with Tae Kwon Do (Choi [c. 2000] v. 2, p. 223–25). Lee was South Korean ambassador in France during the East Berlin Incident, which included Tae Kwon Do instructors (*New York Times*, Jul. 23, 1967, p. 5).

270 Boettcher (1980), p. 224.

271 Cumings (2005), p. 376.

272 Cumings (2005), pp. 396, 418.

273 Boettcher (1980), pp. 224–27. Also, see "Statement of Kim Sang Keun, Former Official, Korean Central Intelligence Agency, Accompanied by Mr. Hong Kyoon An, Interpreter," in *KI-5*, p. 61.

274 *KI-Appendix,* pp. 105, 109.

275 Details in this chapter are from seven sources:
(1) Interview, Rhee Min-Hi (Dec. 22, 2007);
(2) "FBI Memorandum entitled 'RHEE Min Hi,' dated November 13, 1974," in *KI-Append*, pp. 476–77;
(3) "Signed Sworn Statement of Rhee Min Hee (in Korean) to Subcommittee Staff . . ." in *KI-5*, pp. 218–21
(4) FBI memos from September 1973, about KCIA activities in the U.S. in *KI-Append*, pp. 457–66;
(5) Documents about KCIA links to the Korean-American Political Association, in *KI-Append*, pp. 1506–17 and *KI-5*, pp. 210–13;
(6) Articles and testimony from Song Sun Keun, former editor of the *Korea Journal* in San Francisco, in *KI-5*, pp. 79–95, 206–07; and
(7) Boettcher (1980), pp. 224–27.

276 Song called them "Karate students" (*KI-5*, p. 80) and Boettcher (1980) said they were "karate experts" (p. 225). More accurately, they were students of Korean Karate or Tae Kwon Do, which was popular in the United States in 1973.

277 Statement of Kim Sang Keun, former KCIA official, in *KI-5*, pp. 57–58.

278 Interview with Simon Rhee (Dec. 12, 2007).

279 The three sources that linked Rhee to the KCIA were: *Korea Journal* reporter Song Sun-keun, who had been in the hall; a sworn statement to U.S. Congress from Chung Tae-bong, who had been Song's friend and an advertiser in Song's paper; and Lee Keun-pal, who had been Kim Dae-jung's personal secretary in the United States.

280 *KI-5*, p. 1. Many publications reported on the incident and listed some of those involved, including "S. Korea Admits Kim Abduction Role," from the *Asahi Shimbun* (Oct. 25, 2007), by Yoshihiro Makino. The article is available at www.asahi.com/english/Herald-asahi/TKY200710240754.html. A full report from the NIS (formerly the KCIA) was available in Korean on the NIS website in November 2007.

281 See "Memorandum, Subject: ROK CIA Activities in the United States, Dated August 17, 1973," in *KI-5*, pp. 166–67.

282 A former head of the KCIA told U.S. investigators that Japan would be a better place than the United States for the kidnapping (*KI-5*, p. 62).

283 *KI-Append*, p. 466.

284 A number of sources listed the names of some of those involved in the incident:
(1) "Threat to Koreans in U.S. By Seoul Stirs Concern," by David Binder, *New York Times* (Aug. 17, 1973), p. 65;
(2) The *Washington Post* articles, "South Korean CIA: Power Grows, Fear Spreads," by John Saar, John Goshko, and Bill Richards (May 23, 1976), and "Koreans Here Seek Politician's Release," by Jaehoon Ahn (Aug. 20, 1973);
(3) Letter from Kim Sang Keun, a former KCIA official, in *KI-5*, p 172–77;
(4) "Statement of Gregory Henderson, Tufts University, Fletcher School of Law and Diplomacy," in *KI-Acts I*, p. 7;
(5) "Statement of Donald L. Ranard, Former Director of Korean Affairs, Department of State," in *KI-Acts I*, p. 13;
(6) *KI-Acts II*, pp. 81, 87;
(7) Kim Hyung Wook, former director of the KCIA in *KI-1*, pp. 11, 39–42.

285 "U.S. Knew Immediately of KCIA Role in Kim's Abduction," in *Kyodo News International* (Aug. 9, 1998), which quotes former CIA station chief Donald Gregg.

286 Klein (2007), p. 107.

287 *KI-Report*, pp. 147–48, 154. Boettcher (1980), p. 227.

288 Choi (c. 2000) v. 2, pp. 287–88.

289 Choi (c. 2000), v. 2, p. 246. Interview, Jong-Soo Park (Feb. 21, 2008). Interview, Cormack (May 2003). The U.S. CIA stationed Robert Walson in Ethiopia, where he introduced Tae Kwon Do.

CHAPTER 11: From Spooky *Kukki* to WTF

290 Chapter opening quote from Kang and Lee (1999). Kim (1975), p. 5. Kang and Lee (1999).

291 Kang and Lee (1999), pp. 30–40.

292 Kim (2002), p. 70.

293 Kim (2002), pp. 63, 67.

294 C. K. Choi (2007), p. 101.

295 Choi (c. 2000), v. 2, p. 351.

296 Kim (1975), p. 7.

297 Kim (2002), p. 63.

298 Kim (1975), p. 13.

299 Interviews, Jung-Hwa Choi (Jan. 25, 2002) and Sunny Choi (Aug. 21, 2002).

300 Interview, Rhee (Nov. 19, 2007).

301 Choi (c. 2000), v. 2, p. 241, 360. Interview, Sunny Choi, (Aug. 22, 2002).

302 Burdick (1997), p. 39.

303 Kim (1975), p. 38.

304 Interview, Tae E. Lee (Aug. 20, 2007).

305 Interview, Jae-Hun Kim (Jun. 22, 2002).

306 GAISF details are from Kim (2002), pp. 73–75, 93, and Kang and Lee (1999), p. 40–42.

307 Interview, Rhee (Nov. 2007).

308 Kim (1975), p. 20. Chun (1976), pp. 3, 12.

309 Anslow (2004), p. 50.

310 Kim (2002), p. 53.

311 Interview, C. K. Choi (Nov. 28, 2007).

312 "Conclusion" in *KI-Report*, pp. 153–57.

313 "South Korean Abuses Tolerated," by Don Oberdorfer, in the *Washington Post* (May 17, 1976), included in *KI-Acts I*, pp. 89–90. The Kissinger exchange is also from the article.

314 Choi (c. 2000), v. 2, pp. 277–78.

315 "Korean Consulate General: Condemned," by Yung-gil Kook, in *The New Korea* (Nov. 6, 1975), in *KI-Acts I*, p. 29.

316 Boettcher (1980), p. 7.

317 Choi (c. 2000), v. 2, p. 266.

318 Choi (c. 2000), v. 2, pp. 271–76.

CHAPTER 12: Whaaa!

319 Interview, Cormack (May 2, 2003).

320 *KI-Report*, p. 424. Most of *KI-1* is Kim Hyung-wook's testimony to a U.S. Congressional committee (see pp. 10, 31).

321 Boettcher (1980), pp. 260, 378.

322 Choi (c. 2000), v. 2, pp. 317–23.

323 Cumings' JPRI Working Paper No. 20 (2003).

324 Interview, Choi (Mar. 27, 2001).

325 Interviews, Meeyun Colomvakos and Sunny Choi (Aug. 22, 2002).

326 Cumings (2005), pp. 140–41.

327 The abductions took place throughout the late 1970s and early
1980s and were widely reported in 2002, when North Korea admitted to the mission. "Kidnappings latest bizarre tale from N. Korea,"
by Geoffrey York, *Globe and Mail* (Sep. 19, 2002), p. A19.

328 Burdick (1997), p. 37.

329 Cumings (2005), p. 472, ranks the incident with the 1968 USS
Pueblo crisis in which North Korea seized a U.S. spy ship. Many
websites contain details about the Tree Cutting Incident.

330 "Statement of Gari Ledyard, Professor of Korean Language and
History, Columbia University," in *KI-4*, p. 18.

331 Interview, Kong (Aug. 16, 2002). Anslow (2004), p. 48.

332 Interview, Nam (Apr. 2006).

333 "South Korean CIA: Power Grows, Fear Spreads," by John Saar,
John Goshgo and Bill Richards, *Washington Post*, May 23, 1976.

334 Choi (1980), p. 7.

335 Interview, C. K. Choi (Oct. 31, 2007). Kimm (2000), p. 56.

336 Interview, Cariati (Jan. 8, 2008). Choi (c. 2000), v. 2, p. 313.

337 Many details in this chapter are from Choi (c. 2000), v. 2, pp.
342–52, and Choi (1980), which is a long brochure that Choi printed about the trip.

338 Interview, Cormack (May 2, 2003).

339 Interview, Jung-Hwa Choi (Jan. 25, 2002).

340 Choi (c. 2000), v. 2, pp. 336–38.

341 Cumings (2005), p. 379.

342 Cumings (2005), pp. 343, 383.

343 Kang and Lee (1999), p. 46.

344 Cumings (2004), p. 76.

345 Cumings (2004), pp. 1, 2. Cumings (2005), p. 420.

346 Interview, Cormack (May 2, 2003).

347 Cumings (2005), p. 227–28.

348 Cumings (2004), p. 159.

349 Choi (1999), pp. 42, 148–49.

350 Interviews, Jung-Hwa Choi (May and Apr. 2003).

351 Interview, Jung-Hwa Choi (Jan. 25, 2002).

CHAPTER 13: Olympic Mania and North Korean Mayhem

352 Interview, Rhee (Jan. 17, 2008).

353 Dick Pound told me his nickname (Mar. 4, 2008).

354 Details about Operation Thunderbird are from Kim (2002), pp. 6,
78, 101–19, 230, and Seoul Olympic Organizing Committee (1989),
pp. 29–36.

355 Cumings (2005), pp. 383–84.

356 The KCIA was now renamed the Agency for National Security
Planning.

357 Their names are in Kim (2002), p. 113.

358 The U.S. House of Representatives, *The Olympics Site Selection*

Process (2000), p. 453, notes: "Peter Ueberroth's biography *Made in America*, describes the bidding process for the Seoul games that Ueberroth saw as tantamount to bribery." Ueberroth was the organizer of the 1984 Los Angeles Olympics and, later, chairman of the U.S. Olympic Committee.

359 "Olympics; Past Scandal Could Haunt I.O.C. Candidate," by Jere Longman, *New York Times* (Jul. 15, 2001).

360 Kim (1990), p. 60.

361 Jennings (1992), p. 138, argues, "The Seoul games were conceived [partly] from a desire by a military junta to obscure their brutal image . . ." See also Cumings, JPRI Working Paper No. 20 (2003).

362 Kim (1990), p. 61.

363 Interview, Cariati (Jan. 2008).

364 Choi (c. 2000), v. 2, pp. 349, 431.

365 And wealthy North Koreans financed his martial art; Chon Jin-shik in Japan gave $200,000 to Choi for a championship and became a vice-president of the International Taekwon-Do Federation. Chon's nephew, Phang Jin, later became head of the ITF in Japan. Interviews, Jong-Soo Park (Jan. 5, 2003 and Aug. 20, 2004).

366 Some of this section is from interviews with Jung-Hwa Choi (Jan. 2002 to Apr. 2003) and Michael Cormack (May 2003), and details are from Canadian newspapers, such as the *Globe and Mail* ["Plot on S. Korean President Foiled," (Feb. 25, 1982), p. 4; and other articles]; from the *Toronto Sun* ["Cops Plan More Plot Arrests" (Feb. 26, 1982); "Court Hears Plot to Kill Top Korean," (Feb. 17, 1984); "Cops Arrest Suspect in Murder Plot: Korean Prez Target," (Jan. 23, 1991), p. 34; and other articles]; and from the *Toronto Star* ["Man Jailed in Disco Bombing Planned Blast While in Prison," (Oct. 19, 1985); "Disco Bomb Trial Ends With Plea Bargain Bang," (Sep. 13, 1986); "Mississauga Man, 36, Pleads Guilty In North Korean Assassination Plot," (Jan. 24, 1991); and other articles].

367 Choi (c. 2000), v. 2, pp. 355, 369–74, 397. Interview, Cormack (May 2003).

368 Interview, Jung-Hwa Choi (May and Apr. 2003).

369 Choi (c. 2000), v. 2, p. 401.

370 Interview, Choi Hong-Hi (Mar. 2001). Choi (1999), p. 299.

371 Interview, Cormack (May 2, 2003).

372 Interview, Lu (May 17, 2003). "Phap Lu: A Survivor," *Tae Kwon Do Times* (Jul. 1997), p. 96–105.

CHAPTER 14: The Olympic Summer of Love

373 Seoul Olympic Organizing Committee (1989), p. 42.

374 Details in these first two paragraphs are from Kim (1990), pp. 133, 138, 142, and Kim (2002), pp. 119, 157, 274.

375 Choi (c. 2000), v. 2, p. 417.

376 Choi (c. 2000), v. 2, p. 414, 453. Jennings (1992), pp. 232–33.

377 Kang and Lee (1999), p. 40.

378 Choi was not the only martial arts leader challenging Kim. Many WTF leaders rebelled against what they saw as corruption in the WTF. In 1986, for example, Dr. Dong-Ja Yang, president of the WTF's Pan American Taekwondo Union, asked Kim Un-yong to consider lowering the exorbitant fees for black belt certification. Kim refused and the WTF ousted Dr. Yang, who went on to start a Taekwondo Reform Movement. See http://www.tkdreform.com/about.html.

379 Kim (1990), p. 60.

380 The Yongpal Incident was widely covered by the Korean media. See BBC News for coverage in English: "S Korea Tae Kwon Do chief held" (Dec. 5, 2003).

381 Cumings (2005), pp. 392–93.

382 Jennings (1992), p. 147–48.

383 Cumings (2005), p. 332.

384 Kim (1990), p. 237, 261.

385 Seoul Olympic Organizing Committee (1989), p. 394.

386 Seoul Olympic Organizing Committee (1989), p. 145, 271.

387 Jennings (2000), p. 188.

388 Interviews with Joon-Pyo Choi (Nov. 28, 2007) and Young Su Choung (Oct. 2005).

389 Yook (2002), p. 8.

390 Details in this chapter are from Kim (2002), pp. 80, 82, 87–88.

391 Barcelona Olympic Organizing Committee (1992), v. 4, p. 301.

392 Choi (c. 2000), v. 2, pp. 440–41.

393 Choi (c. 2000), v. 2, p. 496–99.

394 A Korean-language article in *Sports Hankook* (Dec. 12, 2005), which is affiliated with the *Korea Times Daily*. See Hankooki.com.

395 Kim (2002), p. 6.

396 Simson and Jennings (1992), back cover.

397 Jennings (2000), p. 184. In 1999, the *New York Times* reported on the story.

398 Media around the world covered this story. For example: "IOC on road to credibility: Pound, Samaranch wins vote of confidence as six members booted out," *Toronto Star* (Mar. 18, 1999), p. 1; "Who Will Clean Up After This Man?" *Asiaweek* (Feb. 23, 2001); "Fugitive in games scandal arrested," *Deseret News* (May 21, 2003), p. A01; "Sports Briefing: Olympic Games; Testimony: I.O.C. Member's Son Hired to Help Bid," *New York Times* (Nov. 18, 2003).

399 Jennings (2000), pp. 98, 193. U.S. House of Representatives, *The Olympics Site Selection Process* (2000), p. 518.

400 Kim (2002), p. 26.

401 Yook (2002), p. 7.

402 Interview, Jung-Hwa Choi (Jan. 25, 2002).

403 Choi (c. 2000), v. 2, p. 531.

404 "Cops Arrest Suspect in Murder Plot: Korean Prez Target," *Toronto*

Sun (Jan. 23, 1991), p. 34.

405 Kim (2002), pp. 52–53.

406 "Olympics; Past Scandal Could Haunt I.O.C. Candidate," *New York Times* (Jul. 15, 2001).

CHAPTER 15: "Branch Trimming" at the 2000 Olympics and the Street Fight Soon After

407 Kim (2002), p. 52.

408 Kim (2002), p. 272.

409 Kim (2002), pp. 82–84, 272.

410 Cumings (2005), p. 442. Meanwhile, in the mid-1990s, Korea's ten largest companies — which means ten Korean families — controlled 60 per cent of the South Korean economy (Cumings [2005], p. 330).

411 "Taekwondo riot demeans new Olympic sport," *China Daily* (North America ed.) (Dec. 10, 1998). "Bangkok judging under the spotlight," *New Straits Times* (Nov. 26, 1998).

412 Kim (2002), p. 289.

413 Cumings (2005), p. 501.

414 "Koreas Agree to Family Reunions." Web site of the BBC World Service (Sep. 18, 2001).

415 "South Korean Leader Says Move Was Meant to Aid 'Sunshine' Policy: Payment to North Puts Seoul on Defense," *International Herald Tribune* (Jan. 31, 2003). Also, see Na (2004) and "Olympic Games: IOC Official In Bribery Row," *Guardian* (Jan. 10, 2004), p. 19.

416 Kim (2002), p. 47.

417 Kim (2002), pp. 7, 37, 39, 48.

418 Sydney Organizing Committee for the Olympic Games (2001), v. 1, p. 133.

419 Sydney Organizing Committee for the Olympic Games (2001), v. 2, p. 270.

420 "These restrictions ensured the traditional taekwondo nations did not dominate the tournament, an outcome that might have reduced world interest," according to the Sydney Organizing Committee for the Olympic Games (2001), v. 1, p. 134. "Had Korea been permitted to enter more categories the results of the tournament may have been different," from the same committee (2001), v. 2, p.271.

421 Kim (2002), p. 295.

422 Yook (2002), pp. 7–11.

423 "Motivation Questioned In Taekwondo Incident," *USA Today* (Aug. 5, 2002).

424 "Taekwondo Official Denies Judging Quotes," *USA Today* (Aug. 7, 2002).

425 Quoted in *Gazette* in "One Olympic Gold Gains In Value As Scandal Tarnishes Sport," (Aug. 24, 2002).

426 Interview, Askinas (Jan. 30, 2008).

427 Interview, Mitchell (Feb. 13, 2008).

428 Sydney Organizing Committee for the Olympic Games (2001), v. 2, p. 269.
429 "On the Olympics: Two Athletes, an Injury and a Sacrifice," *New York Times* (May 25, 2000).
430 Kim (2002), p. 19.
431 http://www.tkdreform.com/about.html.
432 Kim (2002), pp. 17, 21.
433 Kim said that he had been trying to be transparent and to decrease bribery by offering to pay $50,000 in expenses for IOC members (Kim [2002], p. 30).
434 Interview, Pound (Mar. 4, 2008).
435 Details about the vote and Kim's reactions are in Kim (2002), pp. 8, 30, 32, 95.
436 "IOC Official Jailed for Corruption," online site of the BBC World Service (Jun. 3, 2004). "Sports Briefing," *New York Times* (June 3, 2004).
437 Kim (2002), p. 5.

CHAPTER 16: Like a Cult
438 Interview, Meeyun Colomvakos (Nov. 20, 2002).
439 Interview, Jung-Hwa Choi (Jan. 25, 2002).
440 Interview, Cariati (Jan. 8, 2008).
441 Interview, Galarraga (Aug. 16, 2002).

CHAPTER 17: The Little Giant Dies and Traditional Tae Kwon Do
              Falls Apart
442 Minford (2002), p. 84.
443 Interview, Jung-Hwa Choi (May 28, 2002).
444 Interviews, Meeyun Colomvakos and Sunny Choi (Aug. 22, 2002).
445 Interview, Jong-Soo Park (2002).

CHAPTER 18: WTF Leaders Go to Prison and Olympic Tae Kwon Do
              Faces Oblivion
446 "Fighting Dirty," *Time* (Mar. 8, 2004).
447 Na (2004).
448 Kang and Lee (1999), p. 39.
449 "Official Quits and the I.O.C. Avoids Expulsion Vote," *New York Times* (May 21, 2005), p. D6.
450 "Olympic Games: IOC Official In Bribery Row," *Guardian* (Jan. 10, 2004), p. 19.
451 From *Korea Times*: "Taekwondo Head Koo Gets Suspended Jail Term" (Jan. 16, 2004) and "4 Detained in Taekwondo Probe" (Dec. 6, 2003).
452 "Godfather of Gangsters Controlled Taekwondo Association," *Hankyoreh* (Dec. 5, 2003), a newspaper in South Korea. See http://english.hani.co.kr or www.hani.co.kr.
453 Yook (2002), p. 27 of 29.

454 Na (2004).

455 Interview, Askinas (Jan. 30, 2008).

456 Interview, Joon-Pyo Choi (Nov. 28, 2007).

457 Interview, Mitchell (Oct. 2005).

458 IOC Ethics Commission, Decision regarding Mr. Un Yong Kim, IOC Vice-President (Feb. 4, 2005).

459 "IOC Official Jailed for Corruption," online site of the BBC World Service (Jun. 3, 2004).

460 "IOC's Kim sits in jail forgotten," *Deseret Morning News* (May 28, 2004).

461 Interview, Kwon (2008). "Choue Chung-won Elected as New Taekwondo Head," *Korea Times* (Jun. 12, 2004).

462 Interview, Rhee (Nov. 19, 2007).

463 "Saving Olympic Tae Kwon Do," *Tae Kwon Do Times* (Jul. 2005), pp. 46–47.

464 From *Korea Times:* "WTF Has Guarded Optimism on Taekwondo's Olympic Status" (Jun. 23, 2005) and "Taekwondo is Sport For Everyone" (Oct. 26, 2006).

465 "Ex-IOC Official Jailed in South Korea for Embezzlement Released on Parole," *Canadian Press* (Jun. 30, 2005).

466 Yang (2005).

467 "WTF Task Force Identifies Reform in 16 Key Fields," *Seoul Times* (Jan. 27, 2005).

468 Chun (2006), p. 19.

469 Yang (2005).

470 Interview, Joon-Pyo Choi (Nov. 28, 2007).

471 Interview, Mitchell (Feb. 13, 2008).

472 "37 charged in taekwondo crackdown," *Joong Ang Daily* (Apr. 11, 2006). Also, see WTF notices from www.wtf.org: "WTF Terminates Employment of Two Staff Members," (Mar. 7, 2008).

473 "AOC Ceases to Recognise Taekwondo Australia" (Nov. 2, 2007), found in the News section of www.olympics.com.au.

474 "Clarification of WTF Position," www.wtf.org (Mar. 6, 2008).

475 "Kukkiwon is slowly drowning," a question-and-answer article by Jun Chul Shin (Feb. 21, 2008), found at www.mookas.us/media_view.asp?news_no=1323.

476 The former secretary general, Moon Dong-hoo, had resigned after the WTF president announced that the organization would "transform the WTF in a drastic way and put more internationally minded and professional staff into the secretariat."

477 "Bribe? Envelope for IOC Bigwig an 'Innocent' Gesture," *Associated Press* (Jan. 11, 2008). "'WTF' No Foul Play!" from www.mookas.us/media_view.asp?news_no=1331. International Olympic Committee's Case No. 04/2007.

478 Interview, Mitchell (Feb. 13, 2008).

Chapter 19: Reprieve
479 Dukes (1994), for example.
480 Interview, Rhee (Nov. 19, 2007).
481 Interview, Cariati (Jan. 8, 2008).

SOURCES

Most of my sources are listed in the endnotes of the book, but below are important references I used and interviews I conducted. Documents that are available only in Korean are listed in English. An online bibliography by Kenneth R. Robinson was excellent for sources about Korean history (www.hawaii.edu/korea/bibliography/biblio.htm).

BIBLIOGRAPHY

Anslow, Stuart. "An Interview with Grandmaster Kong Young Il." *Tae Kwon Do and Korean Martial Arts*, vol. 9, iss. 10 (Nov. 2004): pp. 48–53.

Associated Press. "Attacks Alter Korean Peace Talks." *Globe and Mail* (Toronto, Sep. 17, 2001): p. A17.

Barcelona Olympic Organizing Committee. *Official Report of the Games of the XXV Olympiad Barcelona 1992*, Vol. 4. Barcelona: Barcelona Olympic Organizing Committee, 1992.

Boettcher, Robert B. *Gifts of Deceit: Sun Myung Moon, Tongsun Park, and the Korean Scandal*. New York: Holt, Rinehart and Winston, 1980. (Boettcher directed the U.S. Congressional investigations of Koreagate in the 1970s.)

Burdick, Dakin. "A History of Taekwondo." (This essay from 1990 has made the rounds on the internet, but Burdick published a more accurate version in 1997.)

_____. "People and Events of Taekwondo's Formative Years." *Journal of Asian Martial Arts*, vol. 6, no. 1 (1997): pp. 30–49. Pennsylvania: Via Media Publishing.

Cha, Mong-goo. "Escape From Japanese Hakhpyung." *The Church Under Japanese Occupation*. South Korea: date unknown.

Cho, Hee Il. *The Complete One & Three Step Sparring*. U.S.: self-published by Hee Il Cho, 1988.

_____. *The Complete Martial Artist, Volume 1.* U.S.: self-published by Hee Il Cho, 1981.

Choe, Sang-Hun. "Korea Opens Dark Chapter of History: Case of Missing Spy Under Investigation." *International Herald Tribune* (Apr. 5, 2005): p. 1.

Choi, C. K. (Chang Keun). *The Korean Martial Art of Tae Kwon Do & Early History.* Vancouver: self-published by C. K. Choi, 2007.

Choi, Hong-Hi. *Introductory Tutorial to Taekwon-Do* (or *Taekwon-Do Manual*). South Korea: Im Choonsik and Tunshwa Culture, 1960. (In Korean only. This is a reprint of his 1959 book.)

_____. *Moral Guide Book.* c. 2000. (Contains no publication information and was most likely published in North Korea.)

_____. "Road Map to Unification." *Baidal Times.* Canada: self-published by Choi Hong-Hi, 1980. (Choi printed this brochure after his 1980 trip to North Korea. Michael Cormack gave me a copy.)

_____. *Taekwon-Do and I, Volume 1, Motherland: The Land in Turmoil.* c. 2000. (Contains no publication information and was most likely published in North Korea.)

_____. *Taekwon-Do and I, Volume 2, The Vision of Exile: Any Place Under Heaven is Do-Jang.* c. 2000. (Contains no publication information and was most likely published in North Korea.)

_____. *Taekwon-Do: The Art of Self-Defence.* South Korea: Daeha, 1966. (This is a Korean version of his 1965 English text of the same title.)

_____. *Taekwon-Do (The Korean Art of Self-Defence): A Text Book for Beginning & Advanced Students.* Hong Kong: Everbest Printing Co and the International Taekwon-Do Federation, 1972.

_____. *Taekwon-Do: The Korean Art of Self-Defence.* Canada: International Taekwon-Do Federation, 1993. (This is his fifteen-volume encyclopedia.)

_____. *Taekwon-Do: The Korean Art of Self-Defence.* (1988). 5th ed. Canada: International Taekwon-Do Federation, 1999.

Chun, Richard. *Advancing in Tae Kwon Do.* (1983). Boston: YMAA Publication Center, 2006.

_____. *Moo Duk Kwan Tae Kwon Do: Korean Art of Self-Defense.* California: Ohara Publications, 1976.

Cumings, Bruce. *Korea's Place in the Sun: A Modern History.* New York: W. W. Norton, 2005. (This is an update of the 1997 book of the same name.)

_____. "JPRI Working Paper No. 20: Korean Scandal, or American Scandal?" *Japan Policy Research Institute* (2003). From www.jpri.org.

_____. "JPRI Occasional Paper No. 31: Some Thoughts on the Korean-American Relationship." *Japan Policy Research Institute* (May 2003). From www.jpri.org.

_____. *North Korea.* New York: The New Press, 2004.

Dohrenwend, R. E. "Informal History of Chung Do Kwan Tae Kwon Do." Cited and available widely on the internet, published c. 1997.

Draeger, Donn F. *Modern Bujutsu and Budo: The Martial Arts and Ways of Japan.* Vol 3. New York and Tokyo: Weatherhill, 1974.

Draeger, Donn F., and Robert W. Smith. *Comprehensive Asian Fighting Arts*. Tokyo, New York and London: Kodansha, 1980. (This is a reprint of their 1969 book, *Asian Fighting Arts*.)

Dukes, Terence (Shifu Nagaboshi Tomio). *The Bodhisattva Warriors: The Origin, Inner Philosophy, History and Symbolism of the Buddhist Martial Art within India and China*. U.S.: Samuel Weiser, 1994.

Durand, Lt. Col. James F. "The Battle of Tra Binh Dong and the Korean Origins of the U.S. Marine Corps Martial Arts Program: Lasting impressions of Korean Marines' martial arts skills led to the establishment of the MCMAP." *Marine Corps Gazette* (2004). (The *Gazette* is a professional journal of the U.S. Marines. The article is available online.)

The Economist. "New Kicks from Korea." *The Economist*, Vol. 333, Iss. 7889 (Nov. 12, 1994): p. 121.

Edwards, Peter. "He excelled at 'kicking, jumping, smashing.'" *Toronto Star* (Jun. 24, 2002), p. A2.

Funakoshi, Gichin. *Karate-Do Nyumon: The Master Introductory Text*. Trans. John Teramoto. Tokyo: Kodansha International, 1988.

Guo, Elizabeth, and Brian L. Kennedy. "Magic Martial Arts." *Classical Fighting Arts Magazine*. No. 5 (2004), pp. 31–37. California: Dragon Associates.

Halloran, Richard. "Seoul's Vast Intelligence Agency Stirs Wide Fears." *New York Times* (Aug. 20, 1973), p. 3.

Hessler, Peter. *River Town*. U.S.: HarperCollins, 2001.

International Olympic Committee Ethics Commission. "Case No. 04/2007; Decision with recommendation No. D/02/08." Lausanne: IOC, Feb. 15, 2008.

Jennings, Andrew, and Clare Sambrook. *The Great Olympic Swindle: When the World Wanted Its Games Back*. London: Simon & Schuster, 2000.

_____. *The New Lords of the Rings: Olympic Corruption and How to Buy Gold Medals*. London: Simon & Schuster, 1996.

Kang, Won-Sik, and Kyong-Myong Lee. *A Modern History of Taekwondo*. Korean book translated by "Glen U. and students," as noted on various websites, 1999. (This is the World Taekwondo Federation's unofficial history book, widely cited in English, even though it contains no references. Both authors practised Taekwondo and worked with the WTF.)

KI-Acts I: Activities of the Korean Central Intelligence Agency in the United States, Part I. Hearings before the Subcommittee on International Organizations of the Committee on International Relations, U.S. House of Representatives. Washington, DC: U.S. Government Printing Office, March 17 and 25, 1976.

KI-Acts II: Activities of the Korean Central Intelligence Agency in the United States, Part II. June 22, September 27 and 30, 1976.

KI-1: Investigation of Korean-American Relations, Part 1. Hearings before the Subcommittee on International Organizations, Committee on International Relations, U.S. House of Representatives. Washington, DC: U.S. Government Printing Office, June 22, 1977.

KI-2: Investigation of Korean-American Relations, Part 2. July 28 and August 3, 1977.

KI-3: Investigation of Korean-American Relations, Part 3. November 29 and 30, 1977.

KI-4: Investigation of Korean-American Relations, Part 4. March 15, 16, 21, 22, April 11, 20, and June 20, 1978.

KI-4 Supp: Investigation of Korean-American Relations, Supplement to Part 4. March 15, 16, 21, 22, 1978.

KI-5: Investigation of Korean-American Relations, Part 5. June 1, 6 and 7, 1978.

KI-Report: Investigation of Korean-American Relations. Report of the Subcommittee on International Organizations. Oct. 31, 1978, 447.

KI-Append: Investigation of Korean-American Relations, Volumes I and II of Appendixes to the Report of the Subcommittee on International Organizations. Oct. 31, 1978.

Kim, Bok-Man. *Practical Taekwon-Do Weapon Techniques: Art of Self-Defense: A Text Book for Advanced Students.* Hong Kong: Sun Light (P. T.) Publishing, 1979.

Kim, Hyung-wook. *Power and Conspiracy.* South Korea: *New Korea Times*, 1982. (Kim disappeared in Germany in 1978 and the *New Korea Times* published his controversial writings about South Korean President Park Chung-hee, Kim's relationship to him, their fallout, and Kim's exile to the United States. His book is in Korean.)

Kim, Un-yong. *Challenging the World.* Seoul: Yunsei University Publishing, 2002. (This is one of Kim's memoirs, available in Korean.)

_____. *The Greatest Olympics: From Baden-Baden to Seoul.* Seoul: Si-sa-yong-o-sa, 1990.

_____. *Taekwondo: Korea Background Series.* Seoul: Korean Overseas Information Service, 1975.

Kimm, He-Young. *The Hapkido Bible.* Louisiana: Andrew Jackson Press, 1991.

_____. "General Choi Hong Hi: A Tae Kwon-Do History Lesson." *Tae Kwon Do Times*, vol. 20, no. 1 (Jan. 2000), pp. 44–58. Iowa: Tri-Mount Publications.

Klein, Naomi. *The Shock Doctrine: The Rise of Disaster Capitalism.* Canada: Alfred A. Knopf, 2007.

Kuklinski-Rhee, Thomas. *Introduction and Transition of Taekwondo in Germany (1960–2000),* PhD thesis, Department of Physical Education, Graduate School of Korea National Sport University, 2009.

Larkin, John. "Cleaning House." *Time* (Jun. 9, 2003).

Lee, Peter H., translator. *Anthology of Korean Poetry: From the Earliest Era to the Present.* New York: John Day and UNESCO, 1964.

Lee, Tae Eun. *Mastering Taekwondo.* 2nd ed. Ottawa: Tae Eun Lee, 1995.

Levine, Alan J. *Captivity, Flight, and Survival in World War II.* U.S.: Praeger, 2000.

MacArthur, Douglas. *Reminiscences.* New York: McGraw-Hill, 1964.

Minford, John, editor and translator. *The Art of War: Sun-Tzu (Sunzi).*

U.S.: Penguin, 2002.

Na Jeong-ju. "Kim Un-yong Claims He Gave $1.1 Mil. to NK IOC Member." *Korea Times* (Jan. 6, 2004).

Oh, Bonnie B. C. "The Japanese Imperial System and the Korean 'Comfort Women' of World War II." *Legacies of the Comfort Women of World War II*, edited by Margaret D. Stetz and Bonnie B. C. Oh. New York: M. E. Sharpe, 2001.

Ouyang, Yung. "The Elevation of Taekkyon From Folk Game to Martial Art." *Journal of Asian Martial Arts*, vol. 6, no. 4 (1997), pp. 76–89. Pennsylvania: Via Media Publishing.

Pratt, John M., ed. *Revitalizing a Nation: A Statement of Beliefs, Opinions and Policies Embodied in the Public Pronouncements of General of the Army Douglas MacArthur*. U.S.: The Heritage Foundation, 1952.

P'yŏngyang Military Court. "P'yŏngyang Hakhpyung Incident Judgment Record." (This Japanese document from 1945 contains details of Choi Hong-Hi's court martial.)

Seo, J. B. Map from www.defence.co.kr. Seoul: Defence Korea, 2008. (Seo runs Defence Korea, a private online initiative.)

Seoul Olympic Organizing Committee. *Official Report, Volume 1, Games of the XXIVth Olympiad Seoul 1988: Organization and Planning.* South Korea: Korea Textbook Company, 1989.

Simpkins, C. Alexander, and Annellen Simpkins. *Chung Do Kwan: The Power of Tae Kwon Do*. U.S.: Tuttle Publishing, 2002.

Simson, Vyv, and Andrew Jennings. *The Lords of the Rings: Power, Money and Drugs in the Modern Olympics*. London: Simon & Schuster, 1992.

Son, Duk Sung, and Robert J. Clark, *Black Belt Korean Karate*. New York: Prentice-Hall, 1983. (This is an excellent review of black belt techniques, especially the mental aspects that should accompany physical training, by Duk-Sung Son, a founding member of the martial art who is based in New York City.)

Song, Hyŏn-suk. "53rd Anniversary of Yongmun Mountain Victory by Blue Star Unit." *The Korea Defense Daily* (May 29, 2004). Seoul: Defense Media Agency. (The article is in Korean. DEMA is a Korean government body. See www.dema.mil.kr/dema/portal.jsp.)

Song, Kun Ho. "P'yongyang Student-Soldiers' Rebellion Attempt." *Modern Korean History*, pp. 376–379. South Korea: Korean Theology Research Institute, date unknown. (Sun-Ha Lim provided this Korean-language document, which lists Choi Hong-Hi in the P'yŏngyang Incident.)

South Korea [Sŏul T'ukpyŏlsi Sa P'yŏnch'an Wiwŏnhoe]. *The History of Seoul Metropolitan [Sŏul yukpaengnyŏnsa]*. Seoul: Sŏul T'ukpyŏlsi, 1977. (This is a set of books about Korean people, culture and history. All five volumes, published by the South Korean government, are available at http://seoul600.visitseoul.net.)

Sydney Organizing Committee for the Olympic Games. *Official Report of the XXVII Olympiad, Volume 1: Preparing for the Games*. Australia: Paragon Printers Australasia, 2001.

_____. *Official Report of the XXVII Olympiad, Volume 2: Celebrating the*

Games. Australia: Paragon Printers Australasia, 2001.

Talbott, Jeremy M. "Won-kuk Lee: A 'Living National Treasure' of Korea." www.practical-martial-arts.co.uk. England: Practical Martial Arts, 1999.

U.S. House of Representatives. *The Olympics Site Selection Process.* Hearings Before the Subcommittee on Oversight and Investigations of the Committee on Commerce, Oct. 14, 1999 (The Need for Reform) and Dec. 15, 1999 (Review of the Reform Effort). Washington, DC: U.S. Government Printing Office, 2000.

Weiss, Earl. "Nam Tae Hi: Chung Do Kwan's Quiet Man." *Tae Kwon Do Times*, vol. 20, no. 1 (Jan. 2000), pp. 82–84. Iowa: Tri-Mount Publications.

World Taekwondo Federation. "WTF Reform Progress Updates," wtf.org. South Korea: WTF (June 2008).

Yang Te-sam. "Taekwondo Survives, but Faces Major Reforms." *Yonhap English News* (Jul. 8, 2005).

Yook, Sung-Chul (and translated by Soo Lee Han). "Chong Woo Lee, Kukkiwon Vice President, Involved in Choosing the Winners and Losers of the Sydney Olympic Games." *Shin Dong-A Monthly Magazine* (Apr. 2002). (The article is available in English at www.tkdreform.com/archives.html.)

Young, Robert W. "The History & Development of Tae Kyon." *Journal of Asian Martial Arts,* vol. 2, no. 2 (1993), pp. 44–69. Pennsylvania: Via Media Publishing.

_____. "Hee Il Cho: The Martial Arts Were Different Then." *Black Belt Magazine* archive at www.blackbeltmag.com/archives/482. U.S.: Cruz Bay Publishing and Active Interest Media, no date provided.

INTERVIEWS

Askinas, David, CEO of USA Taekwondo (USAT): January 30, 2008.

Burleson, Pat, Karate student who trained with Jhoon Rhee in the 1960s: January 24, 2008.

Cariati, Joe, former assistant to Choi Hong-Hi: Between January 23, 2002 (with Parmar Rai) and January 2008.

Choi, C. K. (Chang Keun), Tae Kwon Do pioneer and assistant to Choi Hong-Hi in the 1960s: October 31 and November 28, 2007.

Choi, Hee Jin, Secretary to Uhm Woon-kyu, who is Kukkiwon President, a Tae Kwon Do pioneer and a founder of the WTF: Apr. 7 to July, 2008.

Choi, Hong-Hi: March and April 2001, including a three-day Tae Kwon Do seminar in April 2001.

Choi, Joon-pyo, former coach of U.S. Olympic team and current USAT (WTF) commission co-chair: November 28, 2007.

Choi, Jung-Hwa, Choi Hong-Hi's son and a Tae Kwon Do master: January 2002 to April 2003.

Choi, Song-Jook, Choi Hong-Hi's first daughter: May 30, 2003.

Choi, Sunny, Choi Hong-Hi's third daughter: August 21, 2002.

Choung, Young Su, WTF grandmaster and former head coach of Canada's Olympic team: October 2005.

Colomvakos (née Choi), Meeyun (Mia), Choi Hong-Hi's second daughter: Between August 2002 and April 2003.

Cormack, Michael, former ITF executive: May 2003.

Chang, Gedo, Hapkido master: See Nam Tae-hi.

Cumings, Bruce, expert in modern Korean history: E-mail on January 19, 2005.

Di Vecchia, Lenny, my Tae Kwon Do instructor: 2000 to 2008.

Gabbidon, Alfonso, one of my instructors: 2001 to 2008.

Galarraga, Nestor, Tae Kwon Do master in Argentina: August 16, 2002.

Ha, Kee, president of Taekwondo Canada and head coach of Canada's 2004 Olympic team: June and July 2008.

Kang, Seok-Jae, the WTF's Public Relations Director, based in Seoul, South Korea: July 2008.

Kim Bok-Man, Tae Kwon Do pioneer and assistant to Choi Hong-Hi in the 1960s: August 13, 2002.

Kim, Jae-Hun, WTF master and former ITF instructor: June 22, 2002.

Koh, John, translator and interpreter: 2002–2008.

Kong, Young-il, Tae Kwon Do grandmaster: August 16, 2002.

Kwon, Soyoung, WTF President Choue Chung-Won's Special Assistant: February to July, 2008.

Lee, Tae Eun, WTF grandmaster and former auditor for WTF under Kim Un-yong: August 20, 2007.

Lim, Sun-Ha, and Sandy Lim, friends of Choi Hong-Hi in 1945: Between August 2002 and May 2003.

Lu, Phap, ITF official and Choi Hong-Hi's assistant in 1990s: May 17, 2003 and May 6, 2008.

Maidana, Jose, Tae Kwon Do expert in Argentina: August 16, 2002.

Mitchell, Wayne, Secretary General of the WTF in Canada: October 11, 2005 and February 13, 2008.

Nam Tae-hi, founding member of Tae Kwon Do: December 2001 (with Gedo Chang) to February 2008 (with Chris Nam).

Palmer, Brandon, Korean historian: E-mails in January 2005.

Park, Bu-Kwang, Tae Kwon Do grandmaster: August 16, 2002.

Park, Jong-Soo, my instructor from 1993 to 2006: 2001 to 2008.

Parris, Richard, ITF master: April 22, 2001 and April 29, 2008.

Pound, Richard (Dick), former member of the International Olympic Committee: February 12 and March 4, 2008.

Rai, Parmar, ITF black belt and assistant to Jung-Hwa Choi: See Joe Cariati.

Rhee, Jhoon, Tae Kwon Do pioneer: November 2007 to January 2008.

Rhee Min-Hi, Tae Kwon Do instructor: December 22, 2007.

Rhee, Phillip, Tae Kwon Do movie star and Rhee Min-Hi's son: December 22, 2007.

Rhee, Simon, Tae Kwon Do movie star and Rhee Min-Hi's son: December 12 and 21, 2007.

Son, Myung-Soo, Tae Kwon Do instructor: April 21, 2001.

Song, Sung-Keun, Vice President of the Kukkiwon: July 2008.

Sergerie, Karine, Canada's WTF world champion: May 2008.

Stanley, Craig, Tae Kwon Do master: 2001 to 2008.

Van Binh, Nguyen, Tae Kwon Do grandmaster from Vietnam: August to September 2005

Yang, Dong-Ja, former executive in the WTF and leader of the Taekwondo Reform Movement: July 2008.

Yook, Sung-Chul, journalist who wrote "Chang Woo Lee, Kukkiwon Vice President, Involved in Choosing the Winners and Losers of the Sydney Olympic Games," for *Shin Dong-A Monthly Magazine* (April 2002): July 7, 2008.

Young Su Choung, WTF Canadian and Ontario coach over the years: October 2005.

INDEX